D0711365

868
THE SHARECROPPER'S SON

The Story of A WWII American
POW's Life of Miracles

TINA FARRELL Ed.D.

XULON PRESS

Xulon Press
2301 Lucien Way #415
Maitland, FL 32751
407.339.4217
www.xulonpress.com

Unless otherwise indicated, Scripture quotations taken from
(Version(s) used)

Scripture quotations taken from the English Standard Version (ESV).
Copyright © 2001 by Crossway, a publishing ministry of Good News
Publishers. Used by permission. All rights reserved.

Scripture quotations taken from the King James Version
(KJV)–*public domain*.

Scripture quotations taken from the New American Standard Bible
(NASB). Copyright © 1960, 1962, 1963, 1968, 1971, 1972, 1973,
1975, 1977, 1995 by The Lockman Foundation. Used by permission.
All rights reserved.

Scripture quotations taken from the Holy Bible, New International
Version (NIV). Copyright © 1973, 1978, 1984, 2011 by Biblica, Inc.™.
Used by permission. All rights reserved.

Scripture quotations taken from the New King James Version (NKJV).
Copyright © 1982 by Thomas Nelson, Inc. Used by permission. All
rights reserved.

Scripture quotations taken from the Holy Bible, New Living Translation
(NLT). Copyright ©1996, 2004, 2007 by Tyndale House Foundation.
Used by permission of Tyndale House Publishers, Inc.

Scripture quotations taken from the New Revised Standard Version
(NRSV). Copyright © 1989 the Division of Christian Education of the
National Council of the Churches of Christ in the United States of
America.

Printed in the United States of America.

ISBN-13: 9781545630365

868

The Miraculous Story of a WWII American POW From Glen Rose, Texas, As He Returns from Forty Months of Captivity, Torture, and Slavery, into the Very Hands of God.

"Because he loves me", says the Lord,
"I will rescue him."
Psalm 9:14

Houston E. Lowe

Contents

Acknowledgements

It would be impossible to write this book without first acknowledging our Lord and Savior, Jesus Christ, for the great work He has done in the life of my father. It is simply beyond human comprehension how this man could have survived even one of the events he encountered in his almost one-hundred years of life. Men have traveled millions of miles, researched original documents, queried, argued, soul-searched, reenacted, and questioned the very core of God. They have doubted His ability to create, to change, to direct pathways, to heal, and to stop harm. It is inconceivable to me how anyone cannot see His mighty hand over this man. There is simply no other explanation for his survival, not just physical, but emotional, psychological, and most importantly, spiritual. He came away with no hatred in his heart. May we all be able to understand that there are things in this world greater than our own very finite human understanding. Although, we often cannot refrain for just a moment from dependence on our cherished, extremely limited intellect; which we unabashedly rely too heavily upon while interpreting the events of the world. Christ has made a way to surrender to the presence of Almighty God, the divine orchestra director of this symphony we call life.

This book is for my father, a humble hero who gave more than most as he crawled through the putrefying trenches of hell and came out on the other end washed clean in the blood of the Lamb. Daddy, I am forever grateful for your unselfish service to our country. You make me proud every day to be your daughter and an American.

This book is also for my daughter, Brandilyn Renee' and my granddaughters, Taylor, Kylenn, Addison, and Camdyn, who have been blessed to know and love their precious great-grandfather,"Poppie". By the grace of God, they have not, and hopefully, will never experience their country in a world war. Also, this book is for my sisters, Toni Lee Lowe, Serene, and Terri Lyn Lowe, Rodriguez, who know him as not just hero, but as Daddy.

Thank you to LTC. Fred L. Serene, USA, Retired, and Caryl Wilson, Ph.D., for your exhaustive editing of this manuscript. Thank you also to Al Spangler, volunteer, the Pacific WWII Museum, Fredericksburg, Texas, for your review of the book and the many historical photographs you located.

This story is for every veteran of war and their families.
When you go home,
Tell them of us and say:
"For your tomorrow, We gave our today"
— Inscription at Kohima Memorial, Burma, 1944

Preface

8 68 is an autobiographical, historical, narrative containing some fictional accounts based on the people and the times in life, as described by my father. It is, however, historically accurate and contains factual information during the years described; which I gleaned from the extensive bibliography at the conclusion of the book. Actual dates, facts, and locations discovered in the research confirmed my father's account of events. Credit is given to each source utilized and the interviewees. Because this is a narrative, in-text annotations and footnotes are not included. This provides for his story to be told as he told it, and without interruptions.

This narrative is written in my father's voice as if you were sitting at his knee as he retells his life story. Many of the stories contained within this book were gathered in this manner. His grammar, word usage, and vernacular have been replicated to tell his story, his way. Leaving school to work in the sixth grade gave him his unique, country language. Most of the stories are first-hand life accounts from my father, Houston E. Lowe, as well as his documented service records. Also, I have interviewed two WWII heroes, one a POW. I have used many first-hand accounts from WWII survivors' recorded stories archived by the Pacific WWII Museum in Fredericksburg, Texas, to frame the events. This museum has been dedicated for years to the telling of these stories and recently recorded my father's story.

The characters are all profiles of people my father described in his life. Only the family members' descriptions and actual names have been used. All other names are fictional and have been changed. Terms such as Jap, dame, looker, and doll-face have been included within this text as they were used within the timeframe in history in which this story occurs. The terms are offensive today and in no way reflect the beliefs of my father or myself. The biblical references are either scriptures he was taught in his early years or are used as examples of how incredibly profound the word of God is in the application of our daily lives.

This story must be told. Although this is his story, it is the unfortunate tale of thousands of men and women who fought so bravely for our country. He, like so many others of this generation, is a humble hero. He would never tell this story himself. He would not want to appear as if he did any more than anyone else. This story may be an account of his life journey, but it is recognition for the legions of others who walked his paths. This story is for the greatest generation this country has ever known, the hidden secrets of their wounded past, and the history they inscribed in their blood on ship holds, cells, bamboo prison walls, latrines, jungle floors, tarmacs, and battlefields. We have grown much too accustomed to our freedom-filled lives. We rush to claim freedoms that we never stop to recognize would not be possible without this story. May we never forget the depths of depravity inflicted upon these men and women and their sacrifices that have affected generations. The infernos of 'hot boxes' and rotting cattle train cars, the rusted, tetanus traps, feces-trenched holds of the hell ships, the anguish of severe starvation, the reek of decomposed bodies and death, the death call and rattle in their nights, the inhumane beatings and raging diseases, that robbed them of their health, strength, and finally their minds. We lost so many who succumbed to these atrocities. Generations of families were interrupted and lost, never afforded the opportunity to carve a new lineage. He survived some of the most desperate of human conditions to see freedom for us. My father personally attributes three things that kept him alive and pushing on: his faith in God and the blanket of prayers from his beloved mother, Nora Pace Lowe, his iron-clad, unabashed, resolute love of the United States of America, and his good ole country smarts learned in the cedar brakes on Squaw Creek, in Glen Rose, Texas. Somehow, he found the faith to survive so that we could live. This is his story.

*"The men and women who suffered through the atrocious
conditions of internment deserve our utmost gratitude and
respect. Their fortitude serves as an example of placing the
ideals of freedom and self-government above one's own interests.
Many thousands gave their lives as the ultimate sacrifice,
both on the battlefield and in the deadly prison camps
of the Pacific and Europe."*
— *U.S. President George W. Bush, 2001*

Chapter One

Country Grit and Gospel

Miracle One–My Birth

I only spect' that just about any country home birth was some sort of miracle. No real infection or pain control, no real medical training, justa' tough woman, some hot water, and God's fertile passageway to earth. 1919 was a slow year for babies. You see, the great war was just ending and our boys were coming home from Europe packing a deadly killer, influenza. In America, the flu took the lives of 675,000 men, women, and children. They dropped like moths on a hot light bulb. If you were doing your arithmetic right, that was ten times as many people killed in 'the Great War', (WWI). With all the peace this war brought us, 1918 was a year cloaked with painful death and suffering. Entire families were just wiped out. It was nothing short of a miracle that my parents survived so I could tell my story.

It was the coldest of blue winter days, the kind that seizes up your bones and makes your breath hang like icicle rainbows. Unusual for this part of Texas to get this cold, everybody was hunkered down. A woman deep in the wails of labor was heard throughout the cedar brakes along Squaw Creek, in Somervell, County, Texas, in a little town called Glen Rose. Her cries clung to the branches like ghostly caterwauls and whistled to the winds, telling the painful story of childbirth, chapter by chapter. All the womenfolk in the county were praying. Their prayers covered the skies like lightnin' bugs in June. They knew what her small 4'10" frame was going through. Daddy paced the floor like one of those caged circus lions we would see at the county fair once a year. The only country doctor was miles away, and I was coming fast, too fast. For the first time, my Mama was screaming at Jesus. " Lord, send your angels to guard this baby as my labor rolls each wave to delivery. Protect this baby from all harm and let this be quick."

My Mama talked to Jesus more that day than ever. I was a big boy, and my entry into this world tore her up pretty good. She was a fighter, and always told me she could do anythin' with Jesus by her side. She was in church every time the door flung open, and my Daddy was deeper in the brakes as far as he could get. People called them 'bible beating, tongue twisters' cuz they could shake the church down on Sunday. My Mama had visions. They came to her and woke her up in the night. Always told me she had some eyes of Jesus on her. I came into this world, nine pounds and three ounces, twenty-two inches long. I was born on top of the family dining table after seven long hours of labor. Mama had us there cuz it was easier to clean up and saved our sheets. She bled out pretty good, and the doctor had to stitch her back on up. I guess it was a miracle I didn't kill her that day. I 'spect it was a miracle most of us country babies lived and didn't kill our Mamas in the process. But she forgave me right away. I was her baby boy. She always called me Sonny Boy, and she loved me fiercely.

"A woman when she is in travail has sorrow, because her hour is come: but as soon as she is delivered of the child, she remembers no more the anguish, for joy that a man is born into the world." John:16:21

I got a double shot of ice blue eyes from her and Daddy. You cross my Mama's liquid crystal eyes with my Daddy's sky blue sapphires, and you got a set that can pierce through ya soul. I looked like an innocent fawn there with my button nose and little dimples. Mama said I was well-favored and goodly too. I had a del- icate shock of golden brown curls on my head. The day Mama took me to church to be dedicated, all the church ladies were cooing and fussing a storm over me. "You got you an angel boy for sure here Nora!" "How are you feeling?" I know you had a tough delivery over there." I always had a real good temperament. Mama thought I was gonna be one of her last babies, so I think she just cherished every moment with me. She carried me around like a little neatly wrapped package and never let me cry for anything. Babies, especially beautiful good-tempered babies, are like a jewel in a Mama's crown. My Mama was old for having babies, not like Sarah and Abraham; but for my time of birthing, old. She was thirty-five when I came, and I was one of her last sapphires, a gift from God's very hands. She said she was gonna make sure this reward to her was real special.

> *"Behold, children are a heritage from the Lord, the*
> *fruit of the womb a reward." Psalm, 127:3*

I started out life back then pretty much as I have lived it today, swaddled in prayer. I played outside in the dirt and followed my Daddy pretty much wherever he went. I may have both their sky-blue eyes, but I was still all Daddy. He was Houston Lee Lowe, and he named me Houston Edward Lowe. I was his fourth and final son.

> *"Yes, sons are a gift from the Lord, the fruit of the*
> *womb is a reward. Sons born during one's youth are*
> *like arrows in a warrior's hand. How blessed is the*
> *man who fills his quiver with them! They will not*
> *be put to shame when they confront enemies at the*
> *city gate." Philippians 4:8-9*

Daddy tolerated Mama's religion because she was like mountain elixir to him. She melted him like butter on hot cornbread. She was a petite little beauty, standing about four foot, almost nothing. Beautiful dark molasses hair all nicely pinned up under her bonnet. Little sapphire blue eyes and a button nose. Always kept herself neat as a pin with a little beet juice on her cheeks and lips. She always smelled like honeysuckle. Singing every hymn from the church hymnal, her voice was like a songbird. No one in the county could out cook her. She could make something out of nothing; and it would taste like a Sunday roast. Her biscuits stood four inches tall and just melt away in your mouth. Her people were from Lancashire, England and the beautiful Scandinavian country of Denmark. A hard-headed Dane she was! Her Mama's last name, Gaskill, was an old Norse word meanin goat *geit*–shelter *skáli*. My Daddy always called her 'Dutch'. She was a good Mama, always protecting her little flock. Daddy was smitten. His family was Irish and caring for the land was his heritage. They brought that good farming sense and love for the earth, immigrated on into Texas where the expansive land was their hope for a brighter future. Rumor has it; some Blackfoot Indian blood ran in him too. I'm guessing there was more than some land feuds going on around here! Daddy was a sharecropper. Never owned anything outright in his life 'cept an old truck he traded a year of crops for and a few beasts of burden. We was poor as polecats, tenants; and dirt was our master. No running water inside and an outhouse to do your business in. If you have no money or land, a person with land will let you work his acreage. In return, the owner would provide a house, well, really a shack, for the 'cropper' and his family to live in. The sharecropper would give the landowner usually half of their crop profits and enough food to survive on. These contract agreements were negotiated every year and upheld with a firm handshake and a look in the eye. It was rare for a sharecropper to stay working the same farm for more than three years. But even during the depression, Daddy didn't have trouble finding a place to farm as long as he wanted to stay. Irish blood ran deep in him, and farming was his birthright. His crops were bigger, stronger, and tastier than anyone's for miles around.

In spite of our meager wages, Daddy saw to it we had some farm animals he would trade or work extra for. Sometimes we had one old milk cow and one old 'shurance' beef cow when times were good. The shurance cow only would be slaughtered and eaten 'shuring' our next meals or would be sold paying our bills ifin we needed to. We sometimes traded for and raised a couple ole hogs. We also had one nanny goat named Ninny. She gave us milk to drink, and sometimes Mama would make a bit of cheese or goat milk butter. We had a rickety ole coop with a few laying hens. They were pretty good old gals and gave us a lot of eggs unless some old chicken snake got in. Squalled like they heads were chopped off! Scared em so bad they wouldn't lay for a week when that happened. Can't have cornbread with no eggs. I hated it when they quit laying. Messed up my gravy sopping! When they was on their right laying schedule, we usually had a few extra eggs to sell at the market. Mama always made Sunday dinner after church real special. She would go out in her yellow print apron and skirt towards the coop. You would have sworn those old gals knew what was coming cuz as soon as they saw her coming, they went from peeping they chicken gossip, to screaming bloody murder! She could wring a chicken neck faster than any man in the county! She used an old wooden broomstick. Throwed that chicken under that stick, put her feet on either side of the old gal's head while she was squalling up a storm. Yanked her head clean off her neck! Chicken running around the yard with no head at all. It was a sight! Just guessin', but I am pretty sure I got my stomach for blood and guts in that little arena. Mama wasn't scared of wielding an ax neither. She would strip those feathers off, burn off the quills, and before you spit in the dirt, she would have that hen dressed, battered, and all in pieces frying in her cast iron skillet. Cast iron skillets were heirlooms in country families passed down for generations. That's how they get their great seasoning flavor. Lots of years of country cooks will do that. Dutch ovens and cast iron skillets were perfect for cooking in fireplaces, open fires, or on stovetops. They can take the very high heat and are perfect for making stews or frying. A Dutch oven can sure make fine braised meat out of tough cuts, the standard for a farmer. You can bake in them too. Many cobblers and cornbread were baked in that skillet. They was also good for getting you a little bit of iron in your diet. Mama's skillet was over a hundred years old. It was passed to her from her great-grandmother in Denmark.

The Little Man Follows

I followed my Daddy around that ole dirt patch since I was in three-corner britches. Whatever he did, well, I did it too, he in his blue jean overalls and me padding behind like a little soldier. I'm in an itty bitty tattered pair with a patch on the knee and a broken catch that swung one strap like a clock pendulum behind my back. Ifin he did it; I did it too. We walked the farm him pointing out everthin' he knowed 'bout the land, the sky; and weather. "Houston, rain is coming soon. See them haystack shaped clouds moving out there? That's the pattern they take afore they get dark. Rain gonna come next. After the rain stops and soaks all up in the ground real good, we go up to Squaw Creek and dig us up some worms. They love the wet dirt where the leaves all fall and make a layered house. That's where you will find em." Dad had his worm patch up under the hen house; it was always wet and shady there. We would go 'worming' together after a good rain. You could find em all knotted up under river rocks. After our big catch, we'd take a big ole bucket of moss, leaves, mud, and problee, fifty big ole fat worms size of cord rope, and put them under them hens. They did the rest. Always had us some worms for fishin' in the creek. My Daddy was the best fisherman in the county too. He taught me how to throw back the babies and the young girls. Thatta way, they always be some fish for us. We would sit and put our cane poles between our knees and enjoy the great universe. Sometimes we pull up sweet grass, wild onions, or prairie grass. The little white stems near the roots are sweet, give you juice and vitamins. My Dad could be out in the woods for weeks and survive. He knew every plant you could eat or use for doctoring youself. I never had a belly ache he didn't get me some fruit tree leaves to chew on. Ifin I got a cut or sore; he would put them on those too. We would lay back awhile and be in our own thoughts. There was no place I would rather be than with my Daddy.

Larrapin' Good

We would pull up our crappy and catfish and hang em on a stringer in the water till we got home. Then Mama could fry them

6

up in her cast iron skillet. For dinner that night, we had fried catfish, hushpuppies (extra crispy), and string beans. Daddy loved providing for our little family, and Mama loved fixin' us good food. "This is larrapin' good catfish, Dutchie! Larrapin, now that is a word I heard most of my life. " Dutchie, you say that all the time from your folks and raising. Where did that word come from?" Mama said that her grandmother told her the word was used mostly by farm folks. They were using the Dutch word '*Larpen*.' It means to hit or thrash. Not sure how to thrash came to as the best and most delicious food description cept'n, maybe like you hit the nail squarely on the head. One thing in the country, with everything made from scratch and all; you always told a good cook something was larruping.

My Mama was my spiritual teacher while my Daddy was my manhood leader. I learned to respect the earth as a provider and how to survive from him; while I learned to rely on God from her. Mama always encouraged me to find Jesus for myself. She led me to accept Jesus in my heart when I was just a little toadstool. I was baptized in the Pauluxy River. Church was a half-day event in my life. We went to Sunday School in the early morning, mostly outside under the trees, and then we all gathered in the church for worship after that. Worship was a lively event with singing and dancing, and people speaking in tongues. Lots of healing went on in that little church, and they forged a bond as a body like no other. No matter what crisis came about, the church was there to help folks out. I learned the church is not a place, but an obedient people worshiping together and doing God's work. We helped feed hungry people together. Every first Sunday of the month, we had a big meal outside. Church members would bring what they could, and we would have a big ole potluck meal where we invited the community. Mostly the kids in the cedar brakes, barefoot and hungry would come along. They got a belly full and took some homemade pie to their families. We learned all the great stories and scriptures of the Bible, Noah, Abraham, Daniel, Solomon, David, Moses, and Adam and Eve. I memorized the order and name of all sixty-six books of the Bible to a little song. We got Sunday School points for memorizing scripture. Mama always told me everybody needed to have some scriptures memorized in their heart. "Someday you might need a scripture and a prayer Sonny Boy, and there might be no Bible for you to read." My favorite verse has always been John 3:16, *For God so loved the world, that he gave His only begotten Son, that whosoever believes in Him shall have everlasting life.* It has always been a comfort to me, especially knowing that Heaven is a real place where I will someday dwell with Jesus; even if I know He might have a few words with me first! My real challenge was to memorize Psalm 23. Mama told me there ain't a valley of death God would ever leave you in alone. He was always there shepherding us along; we just needed to call on Him. So, I memorized Psalm 23 and got a lot of extra stars on my chart in Sunday School cuz of it. I had to stand up and recite it in front of the other children. *"The LORD is my shepherd; I shall not want. He maketh me to lie down in green pastures: he leadeth me beside the still waters. He restoreth my soul: he leadeth me in the paths of righteousness for his name's sake. Yea, though I walk through the valley of the shadow of death, I will fear no evil: for thou art with me; thy rod and thy staff they comfort me. Thou preparest a table before me in the presence of mine enemies: thou anointest my head with oil; my cup runneth over. Surely goodness and mercy shall follow me all the days of my life: and I will dwell in the house of the LORD forever."* I was rightly proud of myself for that.

My learning from Daddy usually happened in the dirt or the woods. In the late afternoon, whilst Daddy and me was working in the fields, he never missed a time to point out birds, plants, or berries we could use. "Houston, you never go hungry in the woods, ya hear. It got all you need out here, food, shelter, medicine, protection. Someday you gonna be taking care of your own woman and family. You got to know how to get by. You swallow a worm if you got to. Crickets and locusts eat just fine. See up in that tree over there? Mama Mockingbird feeding them babies? She mashed up them worms real good like your Mama mash up sweet potatoes when you were a baby to feed you. She is taking care of weak little babies. They can't go out and feed they selves. Worms give em nutrients, keep em strong till they get big enough. All a circle, Houston, all a big circle. Just like the earth. You take care of the earth; she will take care of you. Everything circles back Houston.

What you put in, you will get back." He taught me how to live off the land and how to respect and care for what we had. I learned deep deference for the earth, and how the seasons and stars and moon, are a man's guidebook to life and well-being. We would go out deep in woods squirrel and rabbit huntin'. Daddy with his rifle and me armed with a y-shaped tree branch, slingshot. Thanks to him, I could shoot a black-eyed pea out of its shell at 100 yards.

Walking about, he would talk about all the native plants. "Some of these plants will kill you dead in your tracks, and some will save your life. Onlyist difference between plant medicine and the doctor's is how they give it to you. You just gotta know how much to use, it can treat you, or poison you...that's the amount you eat. See that plant look like Mama's church fan? That called a pal-metto, with some fruit juice and smashed leaves; you can help a cough and get rid of you head pounding. You ever eat something poison, you get that berry and leaves over there and crush em up and make a tea. Make you vomit it all up in no time." He pointed to a Holly bush. "This here plant, drop you dead in your tracks ifin you swallow it. First blow you throat up like a toad frog, then you gone." We walked for country miles me and Daddy. Just talking about life and pointing out nature. My Daddy liked being outside in nature more than life itself. There was nothing he didn't know about it either. Nature was Daddy's church and the only place he felt close to God.

> "But ask the animals, and they will teach you, or the birds in the sky, and they will tell you;
>
> [8] or speak to the earth, and it will teach you, or let the fish in the sea inform you. [9] Which of all these does not know that the hand of the LORD HAS DONE THIS? [10] In his hand is the life of every creature and the breath of all mankind." Job 12:7-10

We would go wild berry hunting in March. We could find us Maw paws, blackberries, or even Mustang grapes. Mama would be so happy to have those berries to make fried pies, jellies, and jams. We would take my little tin pail and pull four or five pounds of juicy blackberries; big as pecans. Gotta be careful with them things, woah! They thistles sting like ants! Hot, sweet, blackberry juice would be running down my throat. We stick our tongues out... look like spring plums! Along the fence line, in the wild blackberries, there are always bunches of healing weeds hiding. They are tall with sharply pointed leaves and grow a fluffy stalk like a squirrel tail. "Houston, those called Carelessweed. I ain't for sure, maybe because po'folks could care less about eating them! But they got plenty of vitamins for you. Mama cooks these for us, especially when we don't have no turnip greens. It will choke out our peanut and cotton crops ifin you let it. Remember when we pull them up when we are planting peanuts? Lazy folks won't do that...they peanut harvest never as good as your Daddy's. Animals drop dead if they eat it. They just know better. People call them dumb animals, ain't nothing dumb about em." We pulled us up a big bunch root and all. "Mama cook these up in a pot tonight." We pulled us up some chicory roots and put em in a sack. We would chew on the leaves. "Sonny, those leaves give you lots of vitamins. Keep you strong and able to provide. You eat em up now." You dry those roots out and grind them up to powder, got some mighty fine coffee too. We loved us some chicory coffee on an open fire. Put hair right on your chest! I was drinking chicory coffee and milk before I gave up the bottle.

The land was what he knew. He learned it from my grandpa, James H. Lowe, and he from his Daddy, Isaac Mason Lowe, and he from his Daddy, Isaac Augustus Lowe. There is a long line of farmers in the Lowe bunch. My family has been in Texas, South Carolina, or Georgia farming since the late 1700's. They knew all about nature too. How frogs live on flies, and flies live on rot. "You got rot; you got flies. You got flies; you got they babies–maggots." Anything with maggots got the rot. Crazy how those little white worms turn out to be flies...parta that circle Daddy talks about, I reckon. "Houston, maggots fit in that circle too. They gots a purpose. We all need each other. Birds eat maggots; maggots eat rot. You gotta bad sore on ya getting all green or black, snag you off some maggots to eat out the rot. They clean it out like a new shiny

10

penny." Wisdom was passed from generation to generation in a running dialog between fathers and sons. The home and the land were the places where my parent's influence seeped into my being.

> *"Hear ye children, the instruction of a father, and attend to know understanding. For I give you good doctrine, forsake ye not my law. For I was my Father's son, tender and only beloved in the sight of my mother." Proverbs 4:1- 3*

The Young Buck

When I got a little older, round six or seven, I got to help with the farming and crops. I spent most my days with my Daddy out in the fields. Ifin you weren't a scrawny little sickly kid, you was out in the fields too, girls included. Those ole books showing girls inside quilting weren't poor sharecropper kids, that's for sure! We didn't have no summer vacation. I guess nowadays it would be considered child abuse. Not for us. It was expected that you worked to help the family and if you wanted to eat anything but squirrel, when that rooster crows; you better pop outta that bed like a corn cake in hot grease!

> *"He that gather in summer is a wise son: but he that sleeps during the harvest is a son that causes a father shame." Proverbs 10:5*

Sometimes, after a long day of tilling, before planting time; me and Daddy would sit out at night before we went in for supper and burn chunks of limestone down to powder. He would cover the fire with a piece of tin roof that would create a mighty inferno there in that hole. The next day we would go and collect up the limestone powder in old tin cans. That was his crop magic. "Houston, get you a switch off that tree up there." Thought I was in for a whoopin. 'Stead, he shredded the end, spit on it, and dipped it in the charcoal ashes circling the fire that night. "Now scrub your teeth and gums real good now." Charcoal keep your teeth strong and your mouth healthy." That was just one of my lessons in country survival. I never went to a dentist, and I had a mouth of strong teeth cuz of that charcoal.

Daddy tilled the earth till his hands bled following behind Waitus, our mule, and Charlie, our horse. Yep, you heard me, Charlie horse! Dad had a sense of humor too. Charlie was a golden brown sorrel horse standing a massive 16 hands high. He was built like a Belgium Draft horse with mighty powerful hindquarters and shoulders; and a broad, deep muscled back. His enormous strength made him perfect for pulling heavy farm loads. Daddy used ole Charlie a lot to plow the rocky fields, pull wagons and move trees. He had a real calm and gentle nature about him. He was steady and reliable. Sweet ole boy, he was. His glorious flaxen mane and tail was the envy of all the girls. His coat shined in the sun like a new copper penny. He was just happy as a pig in mud to be next to his girl, Waitus. Charlie was quite the gentleman, just like Daddy. Being a man's horse, and he and Daddy had a bond forged in sweat like no other. Sometimes I think Daddy could talk horse. He would watch Charlie and know his thoughts. A little twitch or jerk of the neck could be a code for something. Daddy would make chompin' and snortin' sounds. Ole Charlie responded with a turn or stop. Charlie was a looker for sure, just like Daddy. They both were the envy of a lot of farmers.

> *"Know well the condition of your flocks, And pay
> attention to your herds." Proverbs 27:23*

My Father

Daddy would be bumping along in the owner's fields, the wood creaking and the dirt turning and spraying over in neat little hills. His muscled back and shoulders sweating through his cotton shirt was holding up the big leather straps aligning the blade against the strength of those two beasts. He was a mighty oak of a man. Standing six foot, two inches, weighing a whopping two hundred and twenty pounds of solid muscle. He was a strapping man with the back of mule and hands weathered and gnarled like cypress roots. His biceps were like Sunday hams, and his chest flexed out like a fifty-gallon whiskey barrel. I have seen him lift three hundred pounds of hay by himself. He had sharply carved high cheekbones shaping out his squared-off concrete jaw and his strong Irish nose. His twinkling, mountain stream blue-eyed stare, underneath that full crown black Stetson hat, was like a lightning strike when he caught your eye. He caught many a church ladies' eye too! It was not unusual for a few pies to make their way to the house unannounced. When he spoke, he commanded authority with his sonorous, masculine voice. Even his determined walk carried him like a warrior going to battle. I wanted to be just like him. We worked together with my brothers to make sure the family could eat. At night under the candy corn yellow moon, we would walk miles in those freshly dug trenches, dropping a small dusty stream of charred limestone in the soil. "Houston, look up there at that moon. She can tell you when it is right to plant or when it is time to woo. Her partner, cloud cover, is the eternal master of all secrets. That is why we is out here under the clouds with her." Because of his abundant crops, farm folks came for miles in the dark just to see what he must be doing during tillin' time. It was like being watched by some striped-suit movie picture detective, Boston Blackie. They was all but in our overalls! They never found out our little burnt-secret. Daddy said he had to protect his family. He hid that magic dust in his 'chaw' pouch. Reminded me of the 'Jack tales' we read in school. You know the magic beans in the pouch and the giant and all. Our little pouch carried real magic beans. If they did see something, they musta' thought he was dippin' mighty fiercely as he reached for that pouch a lot while tilling away in that moonlight. The earth just got richer, and the crops got more plentiful in our little patch behind the cabin.

Daddy's crops came up that Spring like earthworms poppin' out of a green apple. Heirloom and cherry tomatoes, green onion, cabbage, green beans (as long as a ruler), potatoes, corn, pinto beans, peppers, collard greens, and turnips. Acourse, we had a big ole crop of peanuts that we sold. The farmer daddy cropped for, Mr. Bog, provided us with a small cabin with two rooms. Mama cooked and cleaned and took care of me and my brothers and sisters, all seven of us. We got all the vitamins we needed from the earth. Mama said, "God will provide all our needs," and He shore did. No one questioned her direct line to Jesus. If she prayed about it, she was going to get an answer, one way or the other.

> *"And my God will supply all your needs according to His riches in glory in Christ Jesus." Philippians: 4:19*

Schoolhouse Days

I went to the local elementary school for a couple of years before I moved to the wooden schoolhouse in Hopewell, about two miles away. Early elementary grades were just for teaching manners, how to be good citizens, a little Bible, and some simple words. Most of my time was at the Hopewell school for grades four through eight. Some of the bigger schoolhouses in the counties around there had two doors. These were separate entrances for the boys and girls. Even though it was the law that black folks were free, the South was not friendly to them kids. There was still separate schools for the little black kids in the county. Most of those kids worked in the fields like me. My schoolhouse had only one door and two windows. It was for the poorer kids in our county. My teacher, Miss Loma Carvet, was single like all respectable women were who taught school. Ya couldn't be married and be a schoolmarm. Most teachers lived in the town's people's houses, and everyone paid a little bit to put them up for the school year. But Miss Carvet, well she had her own little house. Lots of men folks from the other towns came to court her. She was real smart, real sweet, and shore pretty! Some folks think she was a 'dirty leg', just cause she lived on her own. Seemed to me, she's just an independent woman not wanting a man to be in charge of her. Mama said Miss Carvet needed to go to church on Sunday and maybe God would bless her with a husband! We had four boys and six girls in my class. We did chores every morning. I started the fire in the stove, cuz me and Waitus always had some kindlin' wood. Schoolin' was pretty simple. We learned how to write our letters in cursive and how to read. We had to share our books cuz we didn't have enough for all of us. We started in the primers (baby books) and then if you were not dumb; you moved into small little readers. We helped each other too. Emma Sue helped me read, cuz I had a hard time, and she was a Cracker Jack. I wasn't too interested in those little books or reading. I loved the big ole paper maps of the world. I learned about geography, the presidents, laws; and some wars. Sometimes children would bring in old newspapers, and we learned about the 'war to end all wars, the Great War, WWI.' These guys just bound and determined to have their own empire. Just can't be satisfied with what they got. Mama says the Bible is real clear about that in the commandments.

> *"You shall not covet your neighbor's house. You shall not covet your neighbor's wife, or his male or female servant, his ox or donkey, or anything that belongs to your neighbor." Exodus 20:17*

Can't lead to nothing but trouble, but when it does happen; we gotta act. I learned how when men stand idly by and do nothing; evil will surely prevail. Miss Carvet always knew how to keep us interested. She would find something that each of us liked, and she would give us little assignments. She knew how much I loved my girl Waitus, so she gave me a book on George Washington. I read all about him. I guess we should all be thankful for our very first president. Ole George was a real American hero and a grand statesman before he was our president. I know why Miss Carvet wanted me to read up on him. Not very many people know he got the mules started in America. Country folk and farmers all over America gotta be grateful he came from humble roots. Having a big farm himself, he could see the need for a strong, independent, working animal like a mule. In 1765, the king of Spain, King Charles III; gave him a jack named Royal Gift. That jack sired a lot of the first mules in this country. Ole George wasn't just a great president and military man. He changed the whole farming business here with that one gift. This ole boy here is sure nuff grateful!

Most of the times, I was looking out the dusty windows wishin' I was fishin', but anything about history kept my interest. Always looked at the maps across the oceans to find the islands. Miss Carvet showed me a picture of Clara Bow from a movie poster. She was on a beach in a hula skirt. I told myself, "someday I am gonna see a hula girl and live on an island!" She taught us Arithmetic, or ciphering, which was one of the most important subjects. She taught us a poem we all memorized, called *A Test In Math*. This ole boy was trying to kiss this girl between her Mama's laundry lines of flapping, clean, white sheets. I can still recite it today. It goes like this......

He's teaching her Arithmetic
He said, "It was his mission"
He kissed her once
He kissed her twice
And said, "Now that's Addition"

And as he added smack by smack
In silent satisfaction,
She sweetly gave his kisses back,
And said, "Now that's Subtraction"

He kissed her and she kissed him
without an explanation
They both together smiled and said,
"Now that's Multiplication"

But dad appeared upon the scene
and made a quick decision
He kicked that lad three blocks away
And said, "Now son, that's long Division."

Author Unknown

A Boy's Gotta Have A Buddy

Me and Odell McTerlin was friends. His Mama and Daddy live up the road a piece. We met in Sunday school on the day we learned

16

about Moses parting the Great Sea. We always said when we got big, we was gonna get a big stick and try and part the Paluxy River just to see if God would do it again. Our Mamas, like most country wives, canned and made quilts together. Sometime when Mrs. McTerlin needed to go into town, she would bring Odell by and we would play a spell outside. We made our own checkers from flat river rocks from the Paluxy River. You could make some of them black using old burnt truck oil. We would draw a board in the dirt and play for hours. We didn't have a lot of time to play and there sure wasn't any spare change for any store bought toys. You were left to your own two hands and some genuine imagination. That's all me and Odell needed. We played leap frog, or sometimes we would build some tin can stilts to walk on. Toys and games were simple then. Kids didn't need much to keep them occupied. We cut some mesquite branches shaped like the letter "Y". We would whittle off a slingshot, and tie on old rubber strips sliced away from bad inner tubes. You could find those in town behind the shops, along with small scraps of leather thrown out behind the tanner's stall. We kept them in our overall pockets. Most folks thought slingshots were for vandals, but me and Odell; we was gonna be game hunters. Some of the rotten apples, the hooligans in town, would shoot out windows and hide in trees, and shoot girls in their pantaloons. Those knuckleheads gave all us big game, slingshot hunters a bad name. We would make up shooting games and set up small carnival stands with cans and bottles. No matter how hard Odell tried, he could never out shoot me. Kids are kids most everywhere I reckon, but country kids, they gotta be inventors of their own childhood magic.

We walked two miles to school together wagging our little tin pails. We would stop along the dirt road and pull off Mustang grapes. Sourest thing you ever ate! Make your face turn inside out! We would see how many we could hold in our mouths till someone yelled 'uncle'. It was usually Odell; he couldn't take me ever. I would pick a bunch on the way home to take to Mama. She made the best 'stang jelly in the county. Sometimes we could sit on rocks along Squaw Creek and shoot bottles and cans off the fence. Odell could never beat me at that either, and he was at least a foot taller than me. I could fire off pebbles and bust them bottles in a flat minute. "Houston, you think you could shoot a bottle out of that fork in the tree over there?" "Well sure, Odell, that ain't nothing!" "Not that tree Houston, the one with the fork in the middle behind it." "You mean shoot that bottle out of fork of the second tree through the branches in the first tree?" "Yep, shore do. Bet you can't!" "Bet what?" "Bet you two of my Mama's honey biscuits." "You are on!" So he ran about forty feet to the back tree. He climbed up and put the bottle up there in the fork, and ran back. Now you stand over here right in front of this tree and shoot. I scoped out that bottle, stretched out my left arm holding the y shaped branch, pulled that rubber band right next to my right eye; and let that rock rip. Shhhhwonk, tink, boom! That bottle blew up and sprayed glass everywhere. "Holy smokes Houston! You is a dead eye!" "Bring me them biscuits in the morning while they still warm, Odell! Hee, hee!" I slapped my knee, as I twirled around blowing on the 'barrel', before I shoved ole 'Mack', that's what I called my trusty slingshot, back in my pocket like a holster.

One day me and Odell snuck outta the schoolhouse when Miss Carvet wasn't looking and went cane pole fishing in Squaw crick. I loved to fish, and so did Odell. We caught us a good ole bunch of crappy fish on a stringer round lunch time. We sat and laughed, talked about Bobbie Mae, prettiest girl in the county. Her Daddy kept her pent up like a prize pig. He brought her to school himself on horseback and stayed around just for her to get reading and writing. He told her no girl needs math anyway, but he wasn't gonna have an illiterate daughter. She had crystal green eyes and hair like spun sunshine. Me and Odell was wondering what color her drawers were! Her hair smelled like honeysuckle jam. We was smitten. Me and Odell said ifin she got a little of the 'sweet ass' on either of us, we was gonna have to fight. We laughed a bit and chewed licorice sticks. We caught us a mess of crappy fish and then membered we couldn't take em back to the schoolhouse without Miss Carvet knowin' we was ditchin' school. So we tied our stringer to a tree and throwed them in the water let em swim around while we crawled in on our bellies like snakes. "Shhhh, you squeal on us, and I will whoop you good!" We slinked in pretty good into our desks. I think Miss Carvet knew all along; she just

18

let boys be boys once in a while. Miss Carvet rang the big bell around two o'clock, letting everyone know school is out. We run like scalded dogs to the crick before any other folks might find our catch. Just about that time, we see Stumpy Smith and Ace Rodgers running off on the other side of the crik swinging our stringer of fat crappy! We ran down the side of that creek yelling like Banshees at em. They jumped Joe Lee's fence and took off plundering our after-noon's catch. In country-code, them is fighting terms. You never take food from a hungry family or a day's catch from a couple of knuckleheads like us!

Me and Odell had to wait to set our place and time to sneak up on those boys and give em a piece of our fists. Daddy wasn't much on fighting, and Mama sho' wasn't. Mama said Jesus loves everyone and we should too. "You just give em the other cheek Sonny Boy. The good Lord will work out your feuds better than you can." Daddy, well, his people fought for so long to just keep what was theirs, their land and homes, and they dignity; he didn't want none of his boys fighting either.

> *"But I say, do not resist an evil person! If someone slaps you on the right cheek, offer the other cheek also." Matthew 5:39*

On Sunday after church, me and Odell planned our attack. We knowed that Stumpy and Ace would be working in the south field of Mr. Duel's corn patch. Corn is a great hidin' place for a sneak attack too. We snuck up on them boys and started swinging punches. Corn stalks was breaking, and corncobs was dropping off like bad peaches in July. We rolled around that cornfield scrap-ping and punching. We all got tore up pretty good. Me and Odell was no match for those two hen house snakes. They been scrap-ping their whole life. One last shot they took at us to make sure we knowed who was in charge around here, they picked us up by our britches and gave us a big kick in the pants. We was eating dirt, had corn husks all in our shirts, and corn milk all over our bruised up faces. A county scrap we started, and the victors not only got our spoil; they took our dignity right along with them on a stringer!

We busted up that section of the cornfield pretty good too. I knew my Daddy couldn't afford to lose any his crop profits and neither could Mr. Duel. I told Odell we better go on up to their house and offer some work for what we did or we was gonna be a lot worse off when we get home. We went on up and fessed up to Mr. Duel what we'd done and about how much damage. He put us to work cleaning up his coops. If you ain't never cleaned out a chicken coop or an outhouse, well then, you don't know stink! Make you gag on up in your throat. Chicken shit is plum messy and slimy like an ole bullfrog. He hands us hoes and rakes, and we get busy. His boys were no-good drunks who never lifted a hand to help him, so his pen was about ankle deep in chicken shit. Poor old gals, they bellies were covered in greasy crap. We washed those girls up too. They will lay better for him if they are happy. We cleaned it all up and put in clean shavings, hay, and fresh water. You know, girls like warm tub baths and fancy rugs to step on. We went on down the dusty road home. I had a big ole purple eye. Looked like a bad potato.... and Odell, well; he swallowed the only good tooth he had in that mule grinnin' smile of his! We started laughing how stupid we musta' looked running up on ole Stumpy and Ace. "We better practice some more ass whooopin' afore we go defending our territory next time! "We will be worse off tomorrow when we get to school, and everyone sees we got whooped in a fight we picked."

The 'Book of Nora'

I got home all bloodied and bruised up and the 'Book of Nora' was immediately opened! That's what we called it when Mama was giving you the holy what for. There may be sixty-six books in the Bible, but number sixty-seven was definitely Nora. She never wanted any fightin' from her kids. She always said to take care of it with words, like Jesus did.

> *"If your brother sins against you, go and tell him his fault, between you and him alone. If he listens to you, you have gained your brother." Matthew 18:15*

20

"Dutch, I'll take care of the boy, he ain't no baby anymore; almost a man. He got to learn about fighting from a man." My Daddy never laid a hand on me my whole life. I really wasn't sure how much trouble I was in. He marched me far away from the cabin down by the crick. He gave me my first rollie. He struck that match on his boot bottom, shoved that rollie in my mouth; and lit it up. "Now, Houston you getting bigger now and you gotta learn to be a man." So in one Sunday afternoon, I had my first fight, my first cigarette; and now a lesson in defense. "You gonna teach me to box? Stumpy got in a few shots at me afore I got one in on him." "You listen to your Daddy son. "People get killed for believing and doing what is right all the time." People can beat you, burn up your house, and take everything you own. It can well up some pretty fierce fire in your belly. You gotta keep your wits about you. You gotta know what is worth fighting for, or worth dying for. People been taking stuff that ain't theirs for hundreds of years. Everybody want the easy way. You take the hard way. Your Mama call it the straight and narrow way. Fighting don't fix everything. But don't you never forget this..... there is only one thing they cannot take from a man; you gotta hand it to them yourself. That is – your honor. What you do in the bad times is what defines your honor, son." Those were powerful words I never forgot.

> *"A man's pride will bring him low, But a humble*
> *spirit will obtain honor." Proverbs 29:23*

Daddy took me out behind the barn and showed me how to defend myself in a fight. We had to hide from Mama. "Heathens, just heathens," she would say if she heard about someone getting into a dirt fight. He would swing at my face and show me how to cover and move. He was so big and fists flying so fast, it was like fighting a windmill. He only had to put me on the ground once for me to learn how to protect myself, and to return a shot. That shot only made it to his hip, but it was a clean shot! "Let's get on outta here Houston for we get the Book of Nora throwed at us!" Don't ever let your Mama see you with a rollie in your mouth, you hear me? Especially, one I give you. She will never flap the sheets with me again!"

On our little dirt patch, along with our sorrel horse, Charlie, I had my Hinny, Waitus. Alongside Charlie, she was the other team-mate pulling Daddy's plow. A hinny is a mule, cept' the father is a horse stallion and the Mama is a donkey, jennet. These animals are built for hard work. She was not a pretty thing...ole gray and black scratchy looking coat, long ole lanky legs, and ears like a Texas jackrabbit; but I loved her just the same! She would stare right into your heart with her soulful, ink-black eyes. Her eyes held a thousand miles of dust-filled days. You could see her kindness shining right through from her heart. She would nuzzle her big nose up under my arm and put her head again my chest when I was trying to brush the dirt off her. When we had a little time, she would let me just lay on her back with my head on her big ole' country ass. I would be shaded under the trees with a twig in my mouth, just her and me, unaware of the whole universe around us. She knew when we both needed a little rest. One thing for sure, she was shore' smart! People think they are stupid and stubborn, but they just have their own opinions about things! You just gotta be kind and treat em nice, and they will do most anything you ask.

Waitus was a working girl, and as a boy growing up on a farm, not only my ride; but my best girl. We walked for miles together, her eating grass and chompin' on limestone, and me, just picking up kindling wood. I would ride her down to the mailbox on the country road and back. She was a funny thing, sensitive too. She didn't like any of my brothers, especially Leon. One day, she must have felt real charitable cuz my brother, Leon, was riding her down to the crick to go chop wood for the fireplace. For just no accounting, out of nowhere, she just stopped in the middle of the dirt road about a mile from the house; and wouldn't budge. He whipped her with a switch and yelled up a storm, but Waitus wasn't gonna haul wood on her back for him. So he left her there, just sittin' in the road. When they weren't back after a while, I went on up the road to see what was going on. I passed up Leon as he was just a cussing and spewing down the road. "Dammed stupid ole mule, ain't got a lick a sense." I went up to her and whispered in her ear "Now Waitus, you shoulda called me sooner!" She jumped up, I jumped on her back, and we took off. We walked on back along the road with the load of wood in my lap. We passed up Leon hunched over like an ogre and spitting out his nastiness. Her big tail just slapped him right on the back of the head as we rode on by. "This ole gal does more on this farm then the likes of you! Leon, you ever lay another switch on her, I will wring your neck."

> *"A righteous man has regard for the life of his beast,*
> *but the tender mercies of the wicked are cruel."*
> *Proverbs 12:10*

Mama could cook up a good pot of squirrel stew, and it was one of my favorite meals. One day when I was out gathering eggs, I took Mack, my slingshot, just in case I saw us a fat squirrel. After I talked all the gals outta their little perfect daily egg and put em in a bucket, I walked around the fence line where the trees were. I saw a big juicy red squirrel up at the top of the oak canopy. She was justa' screaming at me. She was hipping her tail like a wild stallion and running up and down the branch over a clump of leaves. She stopped for a second and held her tail curve up like a statue of a teapot, just long enough for me to get a little rock in Mack's worn leather sling pouch. I drawed that leather pouch up right next to my right temple making an invisible straight path right to her. Zingggshuck. I hit her square on. She fell to the ground like a rotten Fall apple. And so did that bunch of leaves and sticks she was Banshee screaming over. Out popped two little heads. It was two little baby squirrels, her little baby squirrels. No wonder she was kicking up such a fuss up there. Poor ole girl, she gonna be our dinner, I guess I owe it to her to take care of her younguns. I picked her up by the tail and flung her over my neck. Then I picked up the bucket and put the little nest with the two babies in there along with the eggs, and went on up to the house. "Mama, I got us a squirrel for supper." "What's in that bucket there Sonny Boy?" "Well, I hit a nest with these two babies in it." Right about that time, Mama swirled around spinning her apron around her waist. "I told you to be careful around those nests!" "Bring them on over here. We will keep them near the fire." She put them in a little wooden box and fed them warm milk and bread from a kerchief. She named them

Bunnie and Sissie. My Mama could get any animal to mind her, and she loved all God's creatures. Pretty soon, Bunnie and Sissie had the run of the cabin. They were funny too. Mama would sit and crack pecans, feeding Sissie and Bunnie a few. They would sit one on each shoulder excitedly doing a little dance waiting for their next little treat. She could get them to sit up and take a nut right out of her hand. My sister, Deanie, would put them in little feed sack doll dresses and baby diapers. It was pretty cute. I guess I got my love for critters from Mama. The animals all seemed to know we depended on each other to get along in this world. Lotta my lessons in life I learned from our little farm animals; especially Waitus. She taught me to be kind and patient, ...a little stubborn too; ifin you ask anybody!

> *"But now ask the beasts, and let them teach you;*
> *And the birds of the heavens, and let them tell*
> *you." Job 12:7*

Ruth

Mama named my older sister, Ruth, after a strong woman in the Bible. We learned all our bible stories in that little country church. I am guessing we learned to respect women in that little church too. That is where we learned about a woman's strengths, and how they complete a man. Ruth was so prominent; she had a whole book of the Bible written about her. Her and Esther were the only women of all sixty-six books. Ruth was a Moabite widow woman. She was kinda like us, moving where the crops were. After her husband died, she stayed devoted to her husband's mother, Naomi. They were all hungry cuz they didn't have no man to take care of them. So Ruth, said to Naomi, "Let me go to the fields and pick up the leftover grain behind anyone in whose eyes I find favor." That is where Boaz found her, working just like the men. He told her to stop, and he would take care of her. She asked him why he was paying favor to her. "I've been told all about what you have done for your mother-in-law since the death of your husband—how you

24

left your father and mother and your homeland and came to live with a people you did not know before.

> *"May the LORD repay you for what you have done.*
> *May you be richly rewarded by the Lord, the God*
> *of Israel, under whose wings you have come to take*
> *refuge." Ruth 12:12*

I always loved that story about Ruth. My Ruth, "Boog", as I called her; was just like that. She was loyal as a guard dog. She had the funniest laugh! Lose her breath, and all you could hear was the air in the back of her throat. She is a sweetheart. She accepted Jesus into her heart when she was a little girl. Carried a torch for Jesus all her life, just like Mama.

> *"Surely goodness and loving kindness will follow me*
> *all the days of my life, And I will dwell in the house*
> *of the LORD forever." Psalms 23:6*

Miracle Two–Bacterial Spinal Meningitis

I had a real sleepless night. Seemed my head was full up of crazy pictures and the cabin felt like the infernos of hell. Woke up not feeling myself. No eight-year-old boy should feel this bad. Mama thought I just didn't want to go to school. She knew I never really liked school much, just History and Geography. But I would go. My head hurt, and I was all wet and sweaty. I had taken a couple of draws off my dad's hand-rolled Chesterfield behind the shed before. That was what my head felt like, woozy and light headed. My neck hurt and was stiff like a new cane fishin' pole. Then I was just cold. I had the chills like it was the middle of a freezing winter, but this was March. Mama felt my head and knew right away I was in trouble. She throwed me up on the wooden dining table and put cold rags from the spring water on me. Boiled some yellow onions on the stove. I knew when they cooled down they were going on my chest. That's what Mama did for Daddy when he got the 'neumonia. She called my Daddy to take Charlie horse to

25

go get the country doctor miles away. "Houston Lee, he's in a real bad way." Your country concoctions won't help this time! "Hurry on now." It was not usual to call for the doctor. Country folk knew all kinds of medicine they selves. We didn't call for the doctor less something was really serious, baby coming out butt first, or the T.B. By that time, I was bowed up on that table like a cat stretching his back after a summer nap. I started to convulse. Not being able to control my body anymore, I lost my bowels right there on that table. I was covered in an awful purplish red rash, looking like some kinda wildcat. My neck was locked up like a rusted iron gate, and my teeth were clamped together like a sprung bear trap. I was soon knocking on death's door, and Mama knew it. A sound came outta her I have never heard before. It sounded like an ole scratchy bitch cat in heat in the summer. She was wailing in a language I only heard in church. "Omnla, sey tu sey, gashna, see, hulsa, te tu meh. Omnla, sey tu sey, gashna, see, hulsa, te tu meh." She was just chanting over and over. It was her feverish holy tongues. They took her over and only came out in really desperate times. They was powerful, charged conversations with God. When the Holy Spirit was intervening for her, anything could happen. You just had to stand back, you was on holy ground. Connected like an electrical line to the throne of God himself, Mama conducted her symphony of wailing requests. Omnla, sey tu sey, gashna, see, hulsa, te tu me. She came out of the Holy Ghost just long enough for me to recognize her cries for my healing. "Dear God of Mercy and Father of Comfort, I beg you to be with your servant, Sonny Boy in this illness. I am trusting You and Your word, Psalm 107:20 Send your healing to Sonny. In the name of Jesus, drive out all infirmity and sickness from his body. Amen." Then she fell to the floor in exhaustion. She mighta' used up all her conduit that time. I was helpless by then, convulsing, writhing on the table. Now I was real bowed up stiff like, my neck protruding out; and I couldn't control anything. The room went dark as I passed out from the fever. About an hour passed when the doctor toting his little black bag came in the room. "Nora, Nora, its 105 degrees. Your boy is in a bad way. Nora, wake up. He got the 'gitis. You gotta get up here and help me hold him down. Houston Lee, get over here and hold your boy down. He can't move a lick or this will kill him for sure." With my Mama holding down my feet and legs along with Jake and Leon, Joe was holding on to my hips and stomach; my Daddy pinned my chest down with me in a headlock. "Nora, I ain't gonna sugar coat this for you. I don't have much hope this is gonna work. Lots of full-grown adults die, go blind, or are paralyzed from this disease. It is a deadly killer. When I stick this needle up his spine, it can save him or kill him. One way or the other, we have to try." "Well, doc, let my Jesus take control." The doctor pulled out a metal syringe the size of a wooden school ruler. He stuck that nail of a syringe in my lower back trying to relieve the pressure of the fluids in my spine and my brain. The force of my spinal fluid was so great, it shot straight across the room and hit the opposite wall. My Mama dropped to her knees. She was still talking to Jesus. "Lord, heal this boy, heal my Sonny Boy." The doctor told her I would have died if she had not called on him. "He was walking the golden steps to Heaven, Nora. He is not out of the woods yet. You keep him covered up and give him this for pain. His brain is swollen up real bad, and he needs to rest. You keep him still. If he is gonna make it, it should be in a few days."

> " I share my good report as my God has done a mighty work in my life. I recognize your glory, Lord. I kneel here today, with my testimony that my Lord has once again revealed His mighty hand and proven Himself once again through His healing of my son." Nora Pace, 1928.

I was in bed for two weeks, and my Mama never left my side. "Sweet Sonny Boy...Mama told you Jesus had power over death and disease." She would stroke my head and put cool rags on me and feed me broth a spoon at a time. She would bring Sissie and Bunny on into my bed. We played hide and seek under the covers. They had to be my company now. My brothers and sisters weren't allowed to come near me. She knew it was lonely and I might need a pick me up. "Here is a fried blackberry pie Sonny." I just loved her fried pies! I got stronger each day, and pretty soon I got strong enough to get up a bit in the cabin. I had to learn how to walk all over again. It took a while before my legs worked right. Once I got over the 'gitis, things were not the same. My folks were more protective, kept a watch on me real good. I always had the 'busy feet'. I can't sit still real easy, gotta be fixin somethin' or moving about. Daddy would keep me interested and mostly still by bringing out the dominos or cards. I learned a lot of 'rithmitic that'a way. We would play a few games, me and Daddy and my brothers. Mama would sulk in the corner darning socks, rockin' so hard the pine floorboards would creak like a gusting wind tearing down an oak tree. Course, she was praying for our souls too! Mama didn't like cards and dominoes. Thought they was 'of the devil'. She always told Daddy they was a sin. "You know them cards are nothing more than the Devil's Bible; they make a mockery of our Lord! They named the Joker after Jesus. Just a sin I tell you, just a sin." We was a whooping and laughing having a good time playing ."Houston, you are leading our boys straight to the devil's own mouth! You keep playing those games, those boys gonna end up busting rocks I tell you!" "Dammit, Dutch! This just an innocent game of numbers between me and my boys. Why you always gotta make everything fun a sin? These boys ain't gonna be bustin' no rocks in prison!" Then he picked up the dominos and all the cards and dice and threw them right into the fireplace! Whoo, that's the maddest I ever saw my Daddy. He stomped out lighting up a rollie and slammed the door behind him. That was the last time we played cards, well, the last time in front of Mama!

Finding Tarzan

Every week Daddy would take us kids on in town to get supplies. He would trade some crops or sell what he could at Brub Young and Earl Earp Jr.'s Feed store. He sold eggs, peanuts, string beans, turnips, tomatoes; and okra there. Sometimes while he was doing his business in town, getting Charlie shoed at the O'Neal Blacksmith Shop or some sugar and cornmeal for Mama at Martin and Sons Grocery; he would slip us a silver dime from his profits. I know he felt like we all worked hard for him and he wanted to do what he could when he could. A dime was a lot of money in 1929. A dime could buy you a pound of navy beans, a pound of cornmeal, a pound of sugar, or a pound of flour. You could feed your family for a week with fifty cents. He would take my brothers and sisters on in for some penny candy at Don Hill's Five and Dime store. Once he got all us tucked in town, he would sit down and play some cards and dominos with the men in town. They would gather once a week at O' Neal's Blacksmith Shop. I would skedaddle on over to the movie picture theater in town. I would slide myself in those red leather movie seats and wait for the black and white picture show. There, surrounded by the fantasy and the sounds of the jungle, I would watch the greatest outdoorsman in the world, Tarzan! *Tarzan, the Mighty* with Frank Merrill, was showing and I couldn't get enough of him. Daddy would leave me be in there for hours while he took care of things in town. I also saw *Tarzan the Tiger* there. Picture shows have a way of taking you places, and I had never been west of the Paluxy River. When I would get home, me and Odell would hang some ropes in the oak trees and try to swing like Tarzan!

Rabbit Runs

Daddy often went on rabbit runs in the cedar brakes, just west of the farm. He taught my brothers to shoot a shotgun but neither of them had much of a shot, and ammunition is real expensive. Daddy couldn't afford to miss. I finally got to go along. Rabbit is one of the tastiest meats you can put in your mouth. It is a real treat cooked up in pan gravy with some biscuits. He never had a hound dog. We couldn't afford to feed another mouth, so he improvised his own method. "Boy, you got all the meat you need out here in these brakes. A man is in charge of feeding his family, and ifin you ain't got two dimes to your name, you can still feed them. Mama says "God will provide," and I say, God put me in charge of that." My Daddy had a Winchester 1893, twelve-gauge shotgun my grandfather gave him. He loved that old gun and kept it in real good shape. "Houston, a woman is a lot like a shotgun. She is sleek and beautiful. Needs a good cleaning and oiling up if you want her to perform. Just like a woman, if you don't treat her right, she can backfire and hurt ya good! You heard me call her by Miss Emma. This here is Miss Emma. I named her after a girl I met after the great war. Don't tell your Mama! She thinks I named her after my great aunt!" We went deep into the brakes looking for mounds of dirt or any tracks left behind. "We have to go where they can hide and live. They like it up in the dense brush and briars where the thorns keep the foxes and coyotes away. A hawk will swoop down and get them too, so they hide up in here." Sometimes there would be two or three hutches in a group in a small area under the cedar brush. "Houston, get on over there, pull them brushes back and stomp real hard on that little hill. That cottontail is gonna blaze outta there like his ass is on fire! I'll only get one shot afore he will be gone." So, I found the first fresh mound of dirt and Daddy set Miss Emma firmly against his right shoulder. I pulled back some brush kicking the mound and stomping my foot. Two little heads popped out. With dirt spraying everywhere, they both took out like scalded dogs. One went one way, and the other darted the other. They are as fast as greased lightning and can change their direction on a dime. I had no idea they were that fast, or for that matter, how on earth my Daddy ever brought any home. "Hang on Houston; I don't take my shot yet. Rabbits don't like to get too far from home. They will circle back here in a minute." Shore enough, they did just that. Scrambling as fast as they could to get to the hutch holes, they ran. Bam, Bam! Shots loudly rang out. From fifty yards away, one rabbit went down. "Rabbit, dang nabbit, go snag off that rabbit. Hee, hee!" Daddy didn't show a lot of humor, but that little jingle was a part of his hunting ritual. I took off after it and picked up a nice little cottontail. He showed me how to tie its back feet to my belt loop. He checked the sex of the rabbit and let him swing from my belt. "Thank you, buck, for giving up the ghost for my family." After he shot one more a little further out, he handed Miss Emma, the Winchester to me. "Houston, time to trade in your slingshot, boy." He showed me all the parts of the shotgun and how to load it. "When you are out here by yourself, it is even harder. You got to stomp and ready your gun faster. That's how I learned to wait till they circle on back. Gave me some time to get my aim and

30

footing". Off he went with a rollie in his mouth looking for more hutches. "You stay on behind me and remember, your Daddy is in the line of fire!" I was nervous as a possum on ice. I didn't want to disappoint my Daddy or waste any ammunition. "Get ready Houston. Look for the eye; they is black as coal. Aim about two inches away from the eye and you'll hit him dead on. Always look for the eye for your sighting." His big ole boots stomped on a pile. With his sheer mass and size thirteen work boot, he rattled a rabbit from one hole as two others sprung out from a hole about four feet away. "Wait, wait." Those cottontails just darted and circled until they all were headed back to the bushes they flew out of. Bam, bam, bam! I took three quick shots. I hit the far left one dead in the shoulder, the middle one dead in the belly; and the other one I missed. He was kicking up his back leg and rolling over as he ran back under the brush. "Shoot, bang, fire, Houston Edward!!! You is a shot, son. You is shore nuff a shot!" He went over and picked up a buck and a doe. "Thank this couple for feeding us, Houston. Could be some babies down in there. We will come back tomorrow and check on em." Right about that time, we heard a rattling in the bushes. Underneath a blood-stained branch, was the third rabbit! I had clipped him on the foot. "Pull him on outta there Houston, and put him out of his misery. We don't want no animal suffering cuz of us." I took a rock and smacked him good to make sure he didn't suffer no more. "Houston, you will be in charge of Miss Emma from here on! You can take her out hunting on your own now." From that time on, it was my responsibility to hunt rabbits. It gave Daddy more time to tend to the crops and me opportunity to sharpen my shot. We walked on back to the cabin talking all along the way. I had three rabbits stringing by me and he had two. We could eat good for a while on these. We will make rabbit jerky, rabbit stew, rabbit pie, and canned rabbit for the winter; out of this hunt. When we got home, Deannie, cried out in joy. "Daddy, you git us a rabbit!" "Your brother got you this rabbit little girl." He kissed her on the head and let her stroke the fur. "Now you thank this rabbit for giving up his life for us." Deannie said, "Thank you rabbit." We got a couple of hours of work ahead of us. We just dressed one for supper. "Son, one thing to know is, you shoot it, you dress it. You finish on up here and I will go help your Mama. I can depend on you Houston. You made your Daddy proud today." Hunting was in my blood. I was shore nuff glad it flowed through my Daddy first and I could make him proud.

> *"The father of the righteous will greatly rejoice;*
> *he who fathers a wise son will be glad in him."*
> *Proverbs 23:24*

Nora Pace Lowe, (Mama) Circa 1949 Courtesy Houston E. Lowe, personal collection

Houston Lee Lowe (Daddy) with "Dub" Cousin, and "Surance"
Cow (Only Known Photograph of Houston Lee Lowe) Circa 1923,
Courtesy Houston E. Lowe, personal collection

Houston E. Lowe (Eight Years of Age, Pre Spinal Meningitis)
and Sister Willadean, 'Deanie', Circa 1927, Courtesy Houston E.
Lowe, personal collection

Hopewell School House -Houston E. Lowe (right), with Odell (Middle)
and friend (Left), Teacher, Miss Loma Carvet, Circa 1930, Note: Scrawled
name of Houston on school house wall right. Courtesy Houston E. Lowe,
personal collection

Charlie Horse and Smart the dog, Deannie, Circa 1925,
Courtesy Houston E. Lowe, personal collection

Chapter Two

The Great Depression

When you are a sharecropper's kid, you is pretty used to gettin' by. We didn't have much, but we got along alright. Going to pee outside in the one-holer was just what we knowed. All my family's savings was in a coffee can hidden under the boards below the bed. When the banks went bust, we never had anything in there anyway, but it did get harder for us. Daddy got less and less for his crops. Mr. Bog was struggling to keep us on his property. We all had to work more. We stopped going to school for a full day cause the town folk couldn't afford to pay a full teacher's salary. That was just fine with me! The wild berries we loved to eat are now saved for canning and pies. We had to sell them for just a bit more than they cost us to get any money to live. Mama used wild honey instead of sugar; cause sugar got too expensive. She could make goat milk soap, so we sold that in town for three cents a bar. A lot of businesses closed down in town. The tailor shop and blacksmith shop both closed. Some of the farms around here were foreclosed on. Even with our life savings in a can, and the first time in my Daddy's life he could buy his own piece of land; he refused to go to the auctions. He just couldn't go take advantage of a man down on his luck. I know it just killed him that it was probably his only chance to be a landowner. The church had a few more potlucks, and we ate mostly off the land. We sold our old 'shurance' cow. We didn't get much, but it helped get us through a winter. She was slaughtered. I am sure she fed a lot of people. We had to kill most of our laying hens to help out. A man who uses his back and hands to make a living has to eat well. I noticed Mama not taking much of a serving. "Just don't have a taste for it today, Houston." I know she was saving it to keep Daddy stronger. Our clothes were worn and tattered, and the soles on our shoes were plumb wore out. I learned a lot of lessons during those tough times. We found out how resilient our family was as we depended upon each other more and more to survive. We all learned to barter. I could clean out a coop or pick vegetables for food. Daddy worked extra odd jobs for milk or sugar. You can make something out of nothing if you have to. We made soles for our shoes out of cardboard. It worked pretty good unless it was raining or cold. Mama saved every piece of string and rolled it in a ball for mending. We always wore hand me downs, but now Mama was making clothes out of pieces of bigger worn out clothes. The Depression was a really terrible time in our country. People were out of work and men had no way of taking care of their families. That led to a lot of depression and heavy drinking. People were in lines for hours to try and get some soup or bread. My Daddy's face began to look worn and tired. But our little family stuck together pitching in to get by. My Mama and Daddy made sure of that. President Hoover was working on getting the local communities to help out their 'neighbors' and provide relief to each other. Everything we learned about in Sunday School was being acted on here. Neighbors helped neighbors. We shared food, clothing, scrap iron, bedding, and furniture. We sold everything we could sell. Families moved in with families. When things just fell apart for folks, Mama and Daddy could always muster up a little bit more to help out a family.

> *"Do not forget your* friends or *your* father›s friends.
> If you are in trouble, do not ask a relative for *help*.
> *A nearby neighbor* can *help* you more than relatives
> who are far away." *Proverbs 27:10*

'Bogged' Out

Things got tough for the Bog family who we 'cropped for. The depression made him have to sell most of his land. He could no longer afford to pay us. With his sales dropping down real bad on his crops, Mr. Bog needed to cut some of his losses. Well, we was his losses! He came down the road and told Daddy we would have to get out of the cabin cuz he was moving in a family that actually could pay him a little bit for rent. His son had gotten big enough, so he had to take him out of school to work the fields my Daddy started. And just like that, we don't have a pot to piss in! Daddy told Mama, he heard about some cotton farming work we could do up in Wellington, Texas. It is located in southern Collingsworth County, right around the panhandle near Oklahoma. So, Daddy put on his signature black, full crown, Stetson hat, harnessed up Waitus and Charlie Horse to our old buckboard wagon loaded with Mama's quilts, kitchen skillets, Mason jars, and dry goods; and headed up the road. Any bits of furniture and belongings we had, we stored with Uncle Virgil and Aunt Gracie. Daddy had whatever money he had put away in the coffee can in his overall pocket. Mama was singing *'What a friend we have in Jesus'*, and me and Jake were playing cards under the quilt! We stopped along the road and Dad would offer to trade plowing or work if we could stay a night or two. Country folk are always ready to help a man willing to work. Sometimes people will pick us up along the way. They would keep Waitus or Charlie for a couple of days to work for payment and then give them a ride in their horse cart down the road a piece. Pretty soon we were all back together again.

> *"And do not forget to do good and to share with others, for with such sacrifices God is pleased."*
> *Hebrews 13:16*

Cotton Pickin' Wellington!

We moved up to Wellington and set up home in a little cabin attached to a cotton farm near the Prichard farm. Seems Bonnie and Clyde were flying through Texas on Highway 83 to get to Oklahoma, and missed a detour sign close by here. They spun that car right into a dry gully and tore it up pretty good. They was getting away from the law after a few of their famous hold-ups. Them two were no good! Mean as rattlesnakes on a hot rock, I tell ya. They killed a lot of innocent people just looking for money and hooch. Funny how you can get popular and in the newspapers for being rotten eggs!

We started off in the cotton fields the next day. Me and my brothers, Joe, Leon, and Jake; helped Daddy pick cotton. It was no 'high cotton', neither. Cotton takes lots of acreage and seems to go on for miles. I rode Waitus up the road. I had me a little potato, and a piece of bacon wrapped up in a cloth. If you ain't ever picked cotton, then you don't know and will never know hard work. It's hot when cotton comes out. Each of us had our own little blanket where we put our cotton clouds. Your hands and arms get all scratched up. You got to learn to 'snag off' those puffy cotton balls out the boll without touching it. All your fingers are swole up, calloused and stained. The thistles on the cotton bolls sting like wasps. If you was in high cotton, you only had to pick the top stuff; never bending over all day. We had burlap sacks strapped across our chests in an x, two at a time. We was looking like those Mexican gun fighters ready to take on a fight! With this get-up, you could use two hands, snaggin' off the little bastard white puffs! I hated cotton. Most of all, I hated how they looked at my Mama in town cuz of it. Might as well have one of those girly tattoos on our forehead. "We po'"! Everybody know you was po' and a 'cropper' kid. My Mama told me, "Sonny, ain't no sin in being poor, Jesus was poor. He saved the whole world." The really po' kids sold they pee. Yep, they did. Caught it in an old tin pot, and sold it to the hide tanners in town. My Daddy told me no matter how po' we got, we never gonna sell our pee. That's when you hear folks saying you is 'piss poor'. We ain't never gonna be piss poor long as Daddy is around. Mama said we can be po' as polecats, long as we rich in our faith.

> 'Hearken, my beloved brethren, Hath not God chosen the poor of this world rich in faith, and heirs of the kingdom which he hath promised to them that love him?" James 2:5

After a little lunch in the cotton fields, my Daddy and my brothers and me were resting under a tree. Leon was walking past Daddy to get Waitus some water. My dad stuck out his boot and 'accidently' tripped him. "Hey, whatcha doing!" I'm just walking here minding my own business." "Really boy, you didn't see my size thirteen boot sticking out there, did ya? When some ole guy my size does that to you, maybe you can learn to take care of yourself." Leon was a little cuss. He was short like Mama and a Mama's boy through and through. Truth be told, Leon would rather be on her apron string any day than out here with Daddy. Problee why he was always up for a scrap. He was always pushing the limits with Daddy. Mama would run to his defense cuz he was so small and all. Seemed like he always had gravel in his craw, and just couldn't wait to see if Mama was gonna win out for him. My Daddy knew it too, and we was a long ways from Mama's apron. He wanted his boys to be real men. "Get on up." Daddy said. "You really think you can take your Daddy, Leon?" Daddy was about to open the farmer's field guide to an ass-whoopin'! Leon cowardly said, "Well, nope, but I bet Joe, Jake and I can!" Just like Leon, pulling in recruits. My Daddy stood up like a two-hundred-year-old oak tree, casting his massive shadow over them. Well, most of them, Joe was about Daddy's size. Daddy said, "Alright, we gonna wrestle. You gotta learn how to put a man on the ground if you have to." So Joe and Jake, along with Leon; all came around dad. Joe and Jake knew what was gonna happen. They wanted Leon to get his full chapter in humility. Afore you knew it, Daddy had Leon and Jake in a headlock and took them all down when he pinned Joe. I just stood back and watched that mountain of a man pull down four hundred and ten pounds of country grit in two moves. He piled them up like a wad of dirty bed sheets. Then he sat on Leon's back as he was picking his teeth with his 'quittin' stick', an ivory toothpick his Daddy, James Lowe, gave him. Leon was squealing like a county fair piglet. Leon never thought about testing Daddy's strength again.

"A fool despises his father's instruction: but he that regards reproof is sensible." Proverbs 15:5

Miracle Three–The Twister

When you live out in the flats in the panhandle of Texas, sooner or later you gonna smack right into a twister. Me and Daddy and my brothers was out in the cotton fields, pickin'. The hot, crazy weather of Texas is legendary. People always say "Ifin you dont like the weather in Texas, you just wait awhile and itt'le change." We didn't have no early warning systems 'cept Waitus. Waitus always knew when something was amiss. She started slowing and stopping and sniffin'. Her lips curled up like leaves of iceberg lettuce, showing her big ole yellow buck teeth. Then she just sat down, square in the cotton and bowed up. Gray clouds are moving in twisted spirals across the horizon. The sky changed color right before our eyes. Just as it started to turn dark, it was beginning to rain. Daddy said, "Houston, get Waitus on up to the barn and go get your Mama and sisters in the cellar." He unhitched Charlie, jumped on his back, and took off. I led Waitus to tie her up to a metal hitching post in the rickety barn and went on up to the house to get everyone. Daddy was tying down and picking up anything that could fly off. The skies are blanketed in an eerie grey-green cast. Little veins of pink electricity starting violently snapping to the ground, licking the horizon line like demonic snakes. The winds began to blow, and sand and tumbleweed was blowing across the full cotton fields. Daddy tied his kerchief around his mouth and nose and kept tying down anything he could. I helped Deannie down the cellar steps. Mama, with help from Ruth, ushered the rest of the family down the steps. Daddy came in last with his hair all wind-blown, covered in dust and soot. His hat was all askew on his head. He moved the rusty switch locks in place, anchoring the tin metal door. He shoved a pine two by four board up between the stones on either side of the door. In good ole Texas fashion, she kicked up a powerful twister. Down in the cellar, we all sat on tree trunk seats clinging to the wet mossy, limestone walls. On the rickety shelves standing at attention, like soldiers in their blue uniforms, all the Mason jars of 'put-up' vegetables, fruits, and jellies; were saluting us. We had a barrel of spring water, some blankets, some ointments, and some animal feed. Mama began to sing loud enough to try to mask the roar of the locomotive that was careening by us. *"At the cross, at the cross where I first saw the light, And the burden of my heart rolled away, It was there by faith I received my sight, And now I am happy all the day!* "Sing along children", Mama said. "We gotta praise Him in His infinite strength He is showing us now." That twister rattled everything in sight. You could hear the house moaning and metal farm tools scraping and clanging together. Dust and dirt was raining in through the metal door, as it rattled away up top. Hinges are screaming, and bolts are wiggling and spinning like tops, right out of their holes. It roared over us like the earth was being sucked into a giant hole. The deafening sound was like a steam locomotive dragging mangled steel over iron railroad ties. Soon, it was just an awful wicked sound, like some depraved demon screaming in the depths of hell. Slowly it was whirling and whispering as it thundered, farther and farther away. Sand and dirt rained down, lining the cellar door like little lace curtains. After about ten minutes, an eerie quiet like a country cemetery at night set in. "Dutch, it is safe to take the kids on up. You follow me when I give you the call." "Joe, you follow me on out." He wanted to make sure we didn't see nothing that would scare us. We climbed out to see what we had left. Daddy ran to the fields first. Our just now ready to harvest, six-hundred acres of cotton, our full year's wages: were sucked right out of the fields. Nothing was left. The barn was gone, and the house is scattered like toothpicks all over the county. It was all gone. We literally had nothing to our name.

> *"The Lord is slow to anger and great in power, and the Lord will by no means clear the guilty. His way is in whirlwind and storm, and the clouds are the dust of his feet." Nahum 1:3*

I ran towards where the barn used to be, looking for Waitus and Charlie horse. There was debris, and rusty tin roof sections and wood scattered and piled. The barn is reduced to little bits of confetti, sawdust, and nails. Brush, tree limbs, and parts of people's houses and barns were piled up near the barn area on the fence line. I heard a faint bray as a few pieces of tin roof were shaking. There

she is! "Good God, ole gal! You musta been scared to death out
there!" That ole gal was still tied to the metal hitching posts that
were once inside the barn where I left her! I do not know how she
was not just blown into the next county. She was just standing there,
her big soulful black eyes, just a little wider. I grabbed her by the
neck and squeezed her tight. "If I coulda' brought you down in the
cellar, you know I would have, girl." She is rattled but standing tall.
Hinnies, like mules; tend not to panic as easily as horses do. That's
because they have a freeze reflex that kicks in any time they are
startled, or there is commotion. They just freeze up like a scared
rabbit. I was grateful she stayed calm and was spared. That crazy
ole gal just froze up and weathered it out! Now Charlie...he was a
different story. Horses have a flight reflex when they get spooked.
They can run for miles without stopping. I took out looking for
Charlie. With that strong back and neck of his, he had ripped that
leather harness clean off the metal hitching post; and ran off up
the road. It took us three days to get him back; he was so spooked.
It finally took me bringing Waitus on up there to calm his big ass
down! On my way back, I found a small little brown and white
dog, trembling in the grass. He was a real cute little mutt terrier
with a white head and body; covered in honey brown spots. When
I called him over, he sat up real pretty. He had little sad black eyes,
just shooting arrows in my soul. "Hey, little fella. Who do you
belong to?" There was no one around for miles. If he did belong to
someone, they could be long gone by now. He ain't got a chance in
hell out here in this torn up and destroyed place. I can't leave him
out here to die. He stood up on his hind legs and put out a paw to
me. "Well ain't you smart! I'm gonna call you Smartie." He fol-
lows behind me as I walk Charlie and Waitus on back. We had each
other, and our most prized possessions back. We could start over
anywhere with them. Our family was spared when many families
were not. Tornadoes take a lot of folks by surprise. They usually
get killed by flying debris. I knowed my parents were sure grateful,
cuz they never said a word about Smartie! He just joined on in like
he had always been there. It was nothing short of a miracle we all
survived. I guess it is our job to be worth being spared.

42

*"Though I walk in the midst of trouble, you preserve
my life." Psalm 138:7*

My Young Manhood

Neighbors gave us what they could to help us out. Country folk
do that. They may not have much, but they will give what they
can to help a family in need. They know how hard we all worked
in those fields. We got a broken up old wagon and some kitchen
goods and took Waitus and Charlie, and we were on the road back
home. Daddy had his fill of twisters and eatin' red dirt in the windy
fields. "We will take our chances back home. Least if something
happens, we got some family and folk who know us." Joe decided
to stay on with a family in Wellington where he could find more
work. We all said our goodbyes. "Dutchie, you get up on Charlie
with the girls, me and the boys will walk alongside." With the help
of a lot of folks along the three-hundred or so miles back home,
a few truck rides, and stops to barter for work; we made it back
to Somervell County. We stayed on with my grandparents awhile.
My grandpa, James Lowe, and my grandma, Sarah Antonia Hiner,
lived in a small little wood frame house outside of Glen Rose, right
before you get to Walnut Springs. I loved my grandparents. They
were good country folk. My grandpa raised honey bees. He had
Mason jars filled to the brim with beautiful fresh honeycomb and
thick, amber colored honey. It would clear up a sore throat, and
shore would cover a biscuit to happiness! He was a corn farmer by
trade and sold his dried corn for cornmeal. He kept it all in a cedar
house with a brick floor. "Grandpa James, how you keep from
being stung by all them honey bees?', I asked. "Sonny boy, I keep
me a little smoker going, and it calms them all down. They are just
protecting their queen." My Daddy loved his Daddy. They would
sit on the front porch at night and talk for hours. It is so good to
be out in the country with our family. The clean air and hard work
was just what my Daddy needed to recover from Wellington. My
Daddy worked his honey bees and helped him sell honey and cornmeal for a while. My grandparents were getting by alright, but they
couldn't keep up with a family of seven mouths to feed for long.

After a couple of weeks, we said our goodbyes and moved in with Uncle Virgil and his wife, Aunt Gracie, back in Glen Rose. He was my Mama's brother and a country Baptist preacher. He knew we had nothing. He told my Daddy that we could stay as long as we needed. My Aunt Gracie like most country wives could cook! She baked us up some sweet bread pudding and a pot roast. It was the best meal we have had in months. "May the Lord bless this food to the nourishment of our bodies and help us to spread the word of the gospel. In Jesus's name, Amen." "Amen!" "Thank you for having us here Uncle Virgil. We won't be too much trouble, and the kids can all help out here until we can get back on our feet. Houston is a dead shot. He will take my rifle out tomorrow and get some rabbits." "The Lord has been good to us Houston. We don't have much, but we are rich in faith. I know the Lord spared you all for a reason. He has work to finish here in this family. Stay as long as you need." Daddy worked Uncle Virgil's little vegetable gardens and worked on the church grounds to help out. We went to the schoolhouse, and Mama quilted and canned with Aunt Gracie. We learned to sleep on the screened-in porch or four to a bed. Nobody complained about our housing. We was all just glad to have a roof over our head. The best thing was, they had indoor plumbing! For the first time in my life, I didn't have to go out to the outhouse to do my business!! I went out into the woods and shot me a few rabbits and brought them home. My mama had to dress them. Aunt Gracie can sure cook, but she don't skin and gut animals; that's for sure!"

Praise the Dog

One Sunday we was all getting ready for church. We always had to leave real early cuz Uncle Virgil was preaching. My Aunt Gracie couldn't find one of her stockings. You know womens can't go into the church house without their stockings. She was in a real fret cuz the preacher is supposed to be there early to greet the congregation at the door. I think they just wanna know who ain't in church that day myself! We was all looking all over the place trying to find it so we could get on out. We tore through everything. All of a sudden, Smartie come flying around the corner with her

44

stocking in his mouth! "Praise Jesus!", my Mama said. "Well, you better praise the dog, he found her stocking!" That was my Daddy through and through! My Uncle Virgil laughed out loud. Today in church, he used it in his sermon...thanking Jesus for your lost stockings. He got a chuckle or two outta that story!

We helped around the house a lot. My job was to help keep the flower beds cleaned up and work in the garden out back. My Aunt Gracie had some pretty flower beds all around their house. Big river rocks were lined up in circle shapes with beautiful heirloom yellow roses in bloom. "Houston, I just love these flower beds. When we get on with another family, I would like to have me one." " I can get you a cuttin' to grow Nora," Aunt Gracie said. We was all just one happy family, 'cept my dad. He never wanted to be relying on someone else to take care of his family. He was always on the hunt for some work.

Logging Town

The Depression was taking its toll on my father. He yearned for a job farming, but there was just no work. With nothing available around Glen Rose, and with a family of seven to feed; he heard about some logging work in a big lumber mill in Crossett, Arkansas. Lots of men were leaving their families to go work in logging camps. It was the only way we were gonna survive. So, me, Leon, and Jake; went with Daddy on over to Arkansas for a while. To keep from being more of a burden on Uncle Virgil and Aunt Gracie, he let me take Smartie along with us. The work there was plentiful but hard. It was about a hundred and fifty men or so, and a few wives living in these small mill towns. Cuz we were single men, we stayed in makeshift houses or the train cars. There was Y.M.C.A. houses there too. We all worked in the mill helping saw and plane the wood into timbers. It was heavy, sweaty, work; but we was making some money during a time when a lot of the country was out of work. The days were real long, but in the evenings, they had some croquet and volleyball courts ifin we wanted to play. They was lit up too. Around noontime each day, a boarding train would pull in with a big ole table of hearty food to eat. It kept the men out of the bars in town at lunchtime and saved work time for the company. We could eat all we wanted long as we worked. The camp also had hot baths, free towels and soap; and a place to clean up. We felt like we was living in a hotel from where we came from! We stayed on there in Crossett for about four or five months while Mama and the girls lived with Uncle Virgil and Aunt Gracie. Daddy would write Mama letters and send her money to take care of things. He didn't mind hard work, but his hands were made for dirt, not sawdust. He missed the earth. I know he loves my Mama something fierce, and he is missing her sorely; you could see it in his eyes.

> *"And the Lord said, "It is not good for man to be alone, I will make him a helper suitable for him." Genesis 2:18*

Pretty soon things got a little better. My Daddy got hired on with another farm family for about half of what he normally made. We came on home to Glen Rose. We set up a cabin there and started all over again. You learn a lot about persevering in difficult conditions and being thankful for what you have. There were so many families in our same situation. People were sending their kids to live with relatives everywhere they could to help out. You needed their backs, but you couldn't afford to keep their stomachs full. There is no shame in being in need as long as you is willing to work. You can see what the preacher talked about in his sermons, about everyone being your neighbor and how we should all help each other. If you didn't have the kindness of people, a lot of folks would not have made it.

> *"For there will never cease to be poor in the land. Therefore I command you, 'You shall open wide your hand to your brother, to the needy and to the poor, in your land." Deuteronomy 15:11*

Me and Odell

Mostly my life was filled with work. Starting all over, setting up a farm is very toilsome work. Keeping everyone clean and fed, including the animals, took us from sun up to sun down every day. Because Joe stayed behind in Wellington, we were down a man in the fields. I met back up with Odell, and we took up where we left off. His Daddy ended up taking a job at the county courthouse, so we got to go in town a bit more often. We would still go down to the creek to fish, or skinny dip at Big Rock or Blue Hole. We loved catching frogs. Them big fat ones would hide in the creek grass and lay their eggs. Odell would take an old feed sack, and I would take a worn wood plank with a rusty nail stickin' out of it. We would sneak up in the grass and find one ole boy. Whack! I smacked him in the head and throwed him to Odell, who put them in our sack. We was frog hunters, big game men indeed! We would fill that sack about halfway afore we brought it home for some fried frog leg dinner. Odell ate with us those nights. His Mama couldn't stand the sight of those ole bullfrogs! She'd holler into the next county if he came home with one in his pocket.

Somedays Chicken, Somedays Feathers!

Odell and I are now getting a little grown. We have to start taking 'nitiative for things. We gotta help put food on the table for our families. I took Odell out rabbit hunting a few times. His Daddy trusted him with his gun, and he knowed that if he didn't bag one; I would for sure. We could run those hutches all day. It was hot, sweaty, work. Walking and looking for their hiding places was the only thing easy about it. Odell would jump real hard on the brush and all. It seems to me that it was either feast or famine with rabbit hunting. Not sure why. They was so skittish that I thought they would jump at the first rumble. Maybe if they had a hutch full of little ones, they just froze up under there. This day, after four hours, we got nothing. Not a single head or cottontail for miles. "Somedays chicken, some days feathers, huh, Houston?" Odell would laugh, and we would walk on home. I learned that anything

47

good in this world takes a heap of patience. You sure better get a big serving of patience if you want to get anywhere in this world.

> *"Patience* is better than power, and controlling one›s temper, than capturing a city." *Proverbs 16:32*

The Hooch Hornswoggle

One time me and Odell dragged a pile of scrap wood from behind an old barn. "Watch that rusted nail, Odell!" You step on that you get the lockjaw for sure. Your teeth clamp up so bad on you; you can't eat. You so skinny now, you look like a licorice stick!" We built us a simple country fort leaned against a tree by the creek. It had a little platform deck we could just hang out on. We climbed up there like two kings surveying their kingdom. Sitting up there like he was waiting on a train, Odell said, 'All Aboard,' as he pulled out a little Mason jar with some shine in it. "If you can't get aboard, grab a shingle!," I replied. Odell hands me the Mason jar. I thought it was some spring water. I took a big ole gulp and a couple of swallows. I shook my head back and forth. My nose felt like I snorted lye, and my throat felt like I swallowed molten steel. It hit my belly like ignited black powder in a coal mine! My eyes was watering, my ears were ringing, and my lips felt like two slivers of shredded raw liver. I was wheezing like a mule in heat, and I was about to shit myself! I started stomping and gasping. I was either gonna pass out or go running through the fields naked! You could remove paint off a barn with this stuff! I am gasping for my last breath, and Odell is just jack donkey laughing! He almost rolled off the fort deck. "Odell, you son of a gun!!! Why the hell anybody wanna drink this stuff?" I was coughing and snorting like a wild boar sow. "Where did you get this?" "At the 'gettin place'! "Where is that?" "Well, that's for me to know and for you to find out, huh!?" We laughed. We both took a swig..Lordy! Huwwwwhhh! That was my first taste of 'fire water'. "You just wait Houston, it make you happy like a calf in springtime!"

*"Wine is a mocker, and beer a brawler; whosoever
is led astray by them is not wise." Proverbs 20:1*

We would lay up there at night and look at the stars, knowing
that God was watching down. The night sky is sparkling. It looks
like it is filled with bits of shiny rock candy. I love looking at it. I
could stare at it all night. Mama always said God had a plan for
each and every one of us. Me and Odell would talk for hours about
what God would do with us. "He ain't got no use for an old buck
toothed guy like you, Houston!" We laughed....

*"For I know the plans I have for you, declares the
Lord, plans for welfare and not for evil, to give you
a future and a hope." Jeremiah 29:11*

Odell and I started getting whiskers. Pretty soon we was tall
and lanky and thought we was ten feet tall and bulletproof! We
still loved to fish, but now we liked looking at girls just as much!!!
One day, we decided to go down to the Paulxy River and do some
fishing. We got out there about daybreak and set us up a good ole
place to catch us some catfish. Nice big ole cedar trees leaning
over, shading the water, making it cooler. We fished all damn day
and didn't get a bite! If there is anything I hate, it's coming home
with an empty stringer! Wasting time is just second behind that. We
walked about a mile down the river and came upon this ole man
cleaning a full stringer of big ole channel cats. Lordy, they were
pretty too! He didn't even look up under his old straw hat. He just
kept cleaning those fish. There musta been twelve or fifteen there.
"Hey, those sure are some pretty cats you got there," I said. He
keeps cleaning his fish as he replies, "Ummm, huh." "You musta
been here since before daybreak." "Ummmm, huh." "Bet you know
where the best fishing holes are in these parts." "Ummmm, huh."
"Well that is great, cuz we been on this damn river all day, and only
got our hooks wet!" "Ummmm, huh." "Would you kindly tell us
where you caught these fish? We shore be thankful." "Ummmm
huh, sure thing. You know where that big old pecan tree is hanging
over the river at the bend?" "Why yes sir, we do!" "Well, you keep

on walking a piece till you see that old abandoned shine shack."
"Yes, yes, I know where that is!" "Then, you know where that fence
line cuts through, and you have to jump it to get to the other side?"
"Yes, yes!" "You wanna go about fifty yards or so till you find a
big ole grey rock, like the ones at Big Rock. You know the one?"
"Yes, sir I do. I know that rock." "Well, good, good. Cuz, once you
get there sonny; you ain't anywhere near where I caught these
fish!" Weren't we the fools!!! No respectable fisherman is gonna
give away his fishing hole! We both knew that. It is some kinda
fishing code. Me and Odell just laughed and walked on down the
river back home. The lesson for the day, if it sounds too good to
be true, it problee is!

> *"The vexation of a fool is known at once, but the pru-
> dent ignores an insult." Proverbs 12:16*

The Big Green Ford Truck

Sharecroppers didn't usually own a truck. But my Daddy was
a good businessman, and he could fix anything. He traded some
crops for a busted up ole green, Ford pickup. It hadn't run for two
years and was rusting out in the field of a local farmer. He couldn't
afford to get it running. Daddy had to pull it down the dirt road
behind Waitus and Charlie. Dad said it was a bucket of rusty bolts,
but he needed it so badly it was gonna have to do. Mama told him
he wasted his trade on that scrap heap. He worked on that truck for
two months. One afternoon after oiling and gassing her up, with a
blast of black smoke, she kicked on! It didn't last. The engine was
all locked up tight. Daddy kicked the tire and cussed a storm. "That
was a waste of our money, Houston." Mama was pecking at Daddy.
That's what he called it when she was fussing at him about something. "Well dammit, Dutchie, if you pray about everything else
around here, even for a gosh dang lost stocking, if you want me to
keep feeding this family, you better pray over this dang truck!" He
lit up a rollie, and went down the fence line and sat down under the
hundred-year-old oak tree; just puffing like a locomotive. That's
where he went to get his thoughts together 'specially when he and

Mama had a spat. The only thing that made Mama madder was if he had some shine in a jar too!

Well, she did pray over that old truck. She knew we depended on it, and it would give Daddy some rest. "Jesus, you was powerful enough even to thwart death and the grave. You raised Lazarus right up out of death walking out in burial clothes white as a ghost. I know it is possible for you to raise this bucket of bolts to help feed our family. In Jesus's name, Amen." That ole truck did fire up the next time, and it stayed fired up too. No matter how many times Daddy saw Mama's prayers come to happen, he was still skeptical.

> *"But he must ask in faith without any doubting, for the one who doubts is like the surf of the sea, driven and tossed by the wind." James 1:6*

Days got a little shorter for Daddy with that old truck. Now he could get crops to market easier and load more supplies. With him behind Waitus and Charlie, tilling little valleys of dirt, I would be over in the next field loading up the crops. That was pretty much my life for the next few years. Since I stopped going to the school-house around sixth grade, I had a big responsibility here with him. Besides, I knowed all I needed to take care of my family. I could read and write, and cipher. I knew how to change money, how to add up what we owed, and how to collect what was owed us. I sure knowed how to work, and my Daddy sorely needed me.

I was restless. I had worked all my life since I was in three-corner britches. I was ready to go see the world and find me a hula girl! Sometimes me and Odell would go to town on Saturday for the county dance. Girls had their hair all curly and flowing, and red lips like shiny, summer apples. They would be standing around the cement or on the vacant sandlot. Whew-wee! I loved a good dance, and I guess my swimming hole blue eyes got me a punch on a few extra dance cards for sure! We wanted some shine. Me and Odell could always sniff out some shine on Saturday. We stood on the fence line just acting cool. We wanted to look like Clark Gable or Cary Grant, so we let our t-shirts show over the neck of our shirts, and hung a cigarette out of our mouths. A little country band was playing the Gene Autry song, 'Black Bottom Blues'. I finally got the courage to ask this beauty to dance. I figure ifin I just hold her hand and keep moving, I will be alright. "You sure look purdy," I told her. What is your name?" "My name is Florine; I live in Cleburne." She was a beauty, and I sure hoped I would get to see her again. "You gonna come to the dance next month?" "Are you asking me out?" Wow! I got a girl asking me ifin I was asking her out! We danced all night. I stole a smooch and told her I would see her next dance. Me and Odell walked home under the big, cantaloupe moon. Our path home was lit up and is dotted with spots of light between the branches above us. I had to straighten up before I got back. Good Lord, I couldn't let Mama smell fire water on my breath when I got home! I used that ole charcoal trick Daddy taught me. Just grabbed a branch and some charcoal dust and just cleaned my teeth before I came in. "Ain't gonna find you a Godly woman out there in those devil dances Sonny Boy." Mama would just be rocking away piecing a quilt together. "Maybe I don't want a Godly woman Mama!" Woah....them was fightin' words with her! I 'spect that I am getting' too old for Mama to be scolding me. She just let me go on back to bed.

"Charm is deceitful, and beauty is vain, but a woman who fears the Lord is to be praised." Proverbs 31:30

Mineral Water Star

There was a big gathering in town right in front of the courthouse. The town officials were going to open the Star of Somervell County – a mineral water spring fed fountain in the shape of a five-pointed star. It is built close to a new bandstand. It is covered in petrified wood. The town square was gonna be a real gathering place now, and on a hot Texas day, you could get a cold drink for you and your horse. Daddy let me ride Waitus on up there just to hear the band for a while. I loved that fountain. It bubbled and gurgled, and you could get a cold drink of water right in the middle of town. We listened to the band for a bit before I gave Waitus a drink and rode on back home.

My teens are mostly a constant cycle of work and going to town with Odell. We stayed busy taking care of our families, going to dances, Goodman's Dry Goods, and church. We had both grown over six foot, so we stood out in a crowd. That alone will keep you from trying something stupid! We never shamed our family, and we made darn sure we finished our chores before we took out on a romp. Sometimes we would hitch rides on up to Sycamore Grove, where the speakeasies were. Lots of pretty girls up them ways. Daddy started giving me a little pocket change to rattle around. He knows a young man needs to stay out of trouble. Nothing gets a boy in trouble more than when he needs to wander a bit on his own and don't have two nickels to rub together in his pocket. I learned how to dance the Lindy Hop and the Jitterbug there. Now Florine has been to a dance or two; we would meet up there. The most popular songs and dances are found in the barn dances, where we learned to Western swing and slow dance to country music. That suited me better. I love the sweet sounds of the Bob Wills band. Soon, that music filled Sycamore Grove, and country music became king. Harmonicas, guitars, drums, and a sultry, deep voice, created a new sound that combined some mountain, folk, and old-time sounds. The music told the story of many of us. Broken hearts, lost wages, and unrequited love, were ringing clear the country experience that defined us. Once we was at a little county fair in town and all the pretty girls are walking with their pin-curled hair and shiny red fingernails. Odell had his eye on one pretty little redhead. She was a little 'sturdy', as my Daddy would say. Odell likes em a little plump. Odell always said, "That a way, when things get tight, I don't gotta worry about her starving to death!" We ain't never gonna get any girl's attention in these overalls, Houston! There was a booth at the fair with a long cloth banner that read, "Step Up Partner- Be A Cowboy!" It was a photo booth with all the props, including a painted back canvas, a fence, guns, chaps, and even a kerchief. For one dime, you could dress up like 'Tex' Allen, Bronco Billy, Buck Jones, or Bill Cody! It was a great way to look pretty cool, and show off for the girls. We both had our pictures made there. Holding that pistol, leaning on that fence looking all cowboy; well, it drawed some girls over like flies to honey! Odell did go off dancing with Miss Pudgy, and I stole a few kisses from sweet Florine.

53

September 22, 1937

It was an extra hot September for some reason, not sure why. Usually, by now, things are cooling off, and everyone is not so heat-cranky. The summer country fairs were a distant memory, and the Fall meant a new crop of peanuts had to be planted. Mama had found some wild pecan trees out near the fence line. Those sweet nuts became another source of income for us. Both Jake and Leon had joined the Army, so it was just Daddy and me out there now. He was still stronger than most twenty-year-olds. Before we set out to work, Mama called out. "Houston, Farmer's Almanac predicting it gonna continue to be extra hot out there today. You keep yourself this Mason jar of spring water and get you some shade today, you hear me?" " I will have you a big supper when you get home." It was hot too. It was already in the nineties early in the morning. It felt like I was in the fireplace all day. It was a still heat, like a constant heat from a campfire rock. I used a bucket of river water to keep cool. We dipped our hats and kerchiefs in it too. Dad was off plowing, and I was out cleaning the crop rows, spreading more burnt limestone. At dusk, Dad shewed me on back to the house to put up Waitus and Charlie. "Go tell Mama I will be home for supper before dark." I went on back and gave Waitus a quick well water bath. After all, she was a girl. I know from my sisters, Boog and Deanie; that girls like they baths. I tied her to the fence and went on in the house to wash myself up. Mama had my favorite meal almost done: hot cornbread, snap beans, white potatoes, okra, corn on the cob, and fresh sliced, heirloom tomatoes. We had a little bit of fat back in the beans for our meat. I washed up and helped Mama put the tin plates on our table. It was getting dark, and I didn't hear the rust bucket coming up the road. Mama said, "Houston, run out and see if you can help your father get finished up. He is probably out there with a rollie and some shine." I walked out to the field, but I didn't see the kerosene lamp he always had on the truck roof when he was running late. I didn't see anything, just the moon-light shining down on the perfect crates of peanuts lined up along the paths Daddy had just finished. I could smell the fresh earth. Smelled like hot rain was coming. Daddy always said that fresh dirt and rain was the smell of money to him. Up in the clearing near the fence line, I saw a big heap. The smell of oil and gas rushed over me. It was the truck. I saw a silhouette of my Daddy sprawled on the ground behind it. I ran like a skinned rabbit to get to him. It looked like he just fell off the back of the truck and hit his head on a rock. The truck bed was full of big river rocks. Looks like he went on down to Squaw Creek and collected a few after he finished up. He problee was gonna start Mama's flower bed for her yellow roses. He was sprawled out on the ground. Blood was on his face and in his eyes, and a huge puddle was coming from under his head. There was a huge rock beside him. He had thrown up all over his overalls, and his skin looked awful pale, like a flour sack. "Daddy, Daddy." I am desperately grasping at his collar, pulling him up to me. He wasn't breathing. I gently laid him back down and reached over to feel of his neck. He was hot as a greased griddle in hell. Mama taught me to feel your heart in your neck. She said if you could feel your heart in your neck, you should thank Jesus. His eyes were open wide staring at the moon, and no breath was in his mouth. He was gone. That fast, that mountain of a man was gone! I knew there was no way for me to get him back. His arm was lying flat out, palm up. His hand was still clutchin' a lit rollie. I just sat there crying beside him. My tears were hitting the dirt like water poppin' off hot grease. I took that rollie out of his hand and sucked on it hard. I wanted to pull the same smoke and fill my lungs with what he just did. I just laid on him, crying and gently hitting his chest with my clenched fist. "Not now Daddy, Mama needs you". Like a crazed man, I was yelling as I took the rocks and throwed them all on the roadside. I just couldn't let my Mama know he died with her rock garden dreams. I knew I had to walk that dark, lonely path to tell her.

Mountains Do Crumble

Daddy was brought to the house and laid out on our country table. The same table I was born on and almost died on was the final preparation spot for my Daddy. Mama had him dressed in the suit they married in, and gently placed silver, 'Walking Liberty'

55

half-dollar on each of his eyes. I will never forget how that looked. It burned a haunting, ghostly image in my head. I had never seen a dead person before. I ran out the house before anyone could catch me crying like a girl. I couldn't believe he was gone. I reckon I stayed out past midnight that night. Mama was worried sick, but she knowed she better give me some space that day.

Sometimes in the country, they would send out for an embalming man. He may or may not work for a funeral home. It took about eight hours to do the job. We couldn't afford to have that done, so Mama said we had to get Daddy to the cemetery in two days. Doc Smith came on out to the house as a courtesy to Mama. He told her, "By the looks of him, and how hot his skin was when Houston got to him; he suffered a heat stroke. When he fell backward, he hit his head on one of those rocks." "What rocks?" "There were a few scattered out there, Nora."

We had a burial to prepare for. But most importantly, we had a burial to pay for. The burial bill for the cemetery plot, a small rock headstone, and a pine box, was $80. It might as well have been $80,000. We don't have that kind of money lying around here. Jake, Joe, and Leon all came in when they heard about Daddy. We couldn't even take time to say hello, we had the business of a funeral to take care of. We didn't want to worry Mama with it. She had enough on her plate to say grace over. Jake went into town and asked Lewis Merrill if he could borrow the money so we could get this sewed up right. Lewis was a cousin of ours. They had a lot of property in and around Hopewell and were a real fine family. Mr. Merrill was not forthcoming with his answer. "Jake, I wish I could help ya right now, but I just can't. We are property rich. But, like a lot of families, we are cash poor. Your Daddy was a good man, Jake. He took care of you kids and your Mama real good. You are going to have to rely on your good wits and looks to get you out of this one Jake, I just can't help you." Jake rode Charlie horse home with empty pockets. We knew the clock was against us before my daddy would begin to rot. We had to do something. Cotton was bursting out, and everyone needed help making their cut. Just our luck that last year, 1936, was the last year of any help from Roosevelt. Cotton took a deep nosedive in pricing, almost as bad as it was in 1932. Before, cotton was going for about twelve cents a pound. 1937 saw an awful bottom-out price of around eight and a half cents per pound. That amount belonged to the grower. We would be lucky if we could get three cents a pound to work. We was running out of time and options. So Joe, me, Jake, and Leon went on down the road in Daddy's green truck. We was carrying a mess of burlap sacks as we stopped from farm to farm looking for cotton picking work. Most of the people in Somerville County knows us, and how hard we all work. They also knew we were in need in a bad way. We picked for two days straight. We worked by kerosene lamp light through the night too. Everyone else was tucked in their beds while we was out picking. We left bags along the farm fence rows with a rope tied round the top. We slept in the bed of that truck on top of some sacks of cotton for a couple of hours. We had to pick almost three thousand pounds of cotton to pay our debt. A couple ole boys in the field put their cotton in our bags to help us out. "Thank you, brother!" On September 24th, by dinner time; we finally made our cash in. " Let's go tell Mama."

Dust to Dust

The country funeral was a gathering. We put Daddy in that pine box and placed his signature Black, Full Crown, Stetson on his head. After he is covered in dirt, I thought how much he loved dirt, and now he is now covered in it. They placed a little rock grave marker at the head. It was a pauper's grave marker: just a flat stone with his name, birth, and death dates painted on it. I thought to myself it just didn't seem right that a man as great as my dad should have such a simple rock as his headstone. Someday, I'm gonna do something about it.

Everyone came to the church and brought food by the house. People came by and told Mama how sorry they were, and what a good man my Daddy was. That day, Mama became a church widow, and I became the man in charge of our little patch of dirt. I growed up that day. I had to become a man right about the time I just shaved off my first whiskers. I told Mama I would keep the crops going, and I would find a way to look after her and my sister. Ruth had married by now, so it was just her and Deannie at home.

Growing up on a farm gave me the experience to learn valuable lessons for life. I had to put it in my hands now. Catching my Mama crying with her hands wrapped in her yellow print apron pressed against her face was one of the hardest things I ever did. She was praying this verse: *And we know that for those who love God all things work together for good, for those who are called according to his purpose.* "Mama, Mama, it's gonna be alright. You told me to rely on God, and not my own understandings. I don't understand why Daddy died, but I know I can take care of you with His help."

> *"Trust in the Lord with all your heart, and do not lean on your own understanding. In all your ways acknowledge him, and he will make straight your paths." Proverbs 3:5-6*

I worked for a while, keeping the crops, and helping her put up the fruits and vegetables in Mason Jars. We sold some eggs and pecans to get along. Mama even sold some of her beautiful 'Jacob's Ladder' quilts. She only used the fabric scraps that neighbors brought to her, or from feed sacks. They was beautiful with vibrant blues and purples. I went to town and sold the Ford pickup. I got $50 bucks. One night, while Mama was sleeping, I took Odell, and we went back to Squaw Creek. We loaded up those river rocks in his pickup. We dug out two big flower beds, and I got the yellow rose bush starters from Aunt Gracie; and planted them. Even if she can't stay here much longer, Mama needs some beauty around all this death and loneliness. I could see we weren't going to be able to hold on much longer.

Houston E. Lowe, Circa 1935,
Courtesy Houston E. Lowe, personal collection

Houston E. Lowe, Somervell County Fair, Circa 1937,
Courtesy Houston E. Lowe, personal collection

Chapter Three

"Gird Up Your Loins"

The Civilian Conservation Corps

The best way to take care of her was to ensure her some monthly money. All of my brothers had married, joined the service, or moved on. It was up to me, and me alone. I kept that little patch of dirt and crops going through the winter of 1937. The farmer who we cropped for had to let us go, and we eventually had to go on relief. It killed my soul to have to sign those papers, but I couldn't let her starve. People were poor, and the country was still recovering from the Great Depression. The only enemy a man has during tough times is his own laziness. I might be a bit of a rebel, but one thing I have never been lazy. Daddy made sure of that.

> *"For even when we were with you, we used to give*
> *you this order: if anyone is not willing to work, then*
> *he is not to eat, either." Thessalonians 3:10*

Franklin Delano Roosevelt had won the presidency back in 1932. After being sworn into office, he began to push legislation called the 'New Deal.' He was real committed to helping get America out of this financial jam. He also wanted to instill pride back into people by giving them opportunities to make a living. A lot of folks, especially young hooligans, got in trouble during the Depression. Nothing to eat will push you to do things you ain't proud of. President Roosevelt wanted to address the problem by building a 'tree army'. He hoped it would serve a double purpose of saving our natural parks while redirecting boys in the midst of their misspent youth. It seems hard physical labor outside is just the recipe for reforming a few knuckleheads. The bible says a lot about nothing but time on your hands.

> *"Idle hands are the devil's workshop; idle lips are*
> *his mouthpiece." Proverbs 16:27-29*

This outdoor army was getting a lot of attention from guys like Odell and me, cuz it was gonna let us work and send some money home to help our families. I've always had a strong back, and I can work like a mule. It was a perfect match. The *Glen Rose Reporter* newspaper, like many newspapers across the country, were running ads like this...

Looking for unmarried, unemployed, men between the ages of 18 and 26. You must be physically fit and come from families on relief. Work projects include beautification, building roads, construction of facilities for visitors to national forests, and parks. Must be willing to send the majority of salary home. $30 per month will be paid. $25 goes directly to your family. Enlistment is for six months. Sign up at the post office.

Knowing it would assure food on the table, and some security for our Mamas, Me and Odell went down and signed up that day. I hoped I could keep Mama and Deanie alive with a few bucks to buy groceries. Uncle Virgil was getting up in his years. If things got worse, Mama told me she had kinfolks in Oklahoma that would take her in. She told me not to worry about her. "The Lord will always take care of me Sonny Boy. I have to be faithful and thank Him, even in times like these."

> *"So do not fear, for I am with you; do not be dis-*
> *mayed, for I am your God. I will strengthen you and*
> *help you; I will uphold you with my righteous right*
> *hand." Isaiah 41:10*

The CCC's are a peacetime army. The assignment is to better America through work and progress. The U.S. Army was assigned to run the CCC's. After all, they had taken care of plenty of men before. I was assigned to the Eighth Corps (Texas /Oklahoma), headquartered at Ft. Sam Houston, in San Antonio, Texas. Me and Odell had to get there by 'riding our thumbs'. I didn't own anything, and I sure didn't have a car or money for gas. Waitus and Charlie would be held back here in case she needed something to sell. I put on my only pair of denim overalls, a starched white cotton shirt, and my Daddy's worn, brown, size thirteen; leather work boots. I packed up a few belongings and went to kiss my Mama goodbye. I assured her I would send her money and take care of her. "Now Mama, you keep on keeping on here. You's a strong woman of God. You will hear from me soon as I get to San Antonio. You keep the savings from the truck and your quilts for an emergency. Here is seven dollars and thirty-eight cents. You can get you some staples with that. I love you, Mama." "I love you too, Sonny Boy. Let me pray on over you, you hear me?" I kneeled down by her, and she put her little, worn hands on my shoulders. " Lord, protect this boy as he ventures out in this world. Place your holy hedge of protection around him. May every night moon be the beacon light that connects us no matter how far apart we are. Keep him safe. In Jesus's name, Amen." "Amen Mama. Mama, I put the money from Daddy's truck in the coffee can. You hold on to Waitus and Charlie as long as you can, you hear me? Plenty of farmers around here need these beasts. Don't let them short you either. They both got plenty of work left in them." I turned to head towards the little rubble barn. Hardest thing I ever did was leave that little woman all alone on that rickety porch. She was snapping the last of our purple hulls and wiping her tears with her yellow cotton apron. I went on over to the stall in the back of the cabin and met up with my real girl, Waitus. She looked at me with those black, doe eyes, and put her muzzle on my shoulder. She kept pushing me away. I would come back and put my arms around her neck to say goodbye, as she continued to nuzzle me away. I guess that ole gal knew this was our last time together. I buried my face in her neck and bawled. I just fell in a slump at her feet. She sat down, and I pressed my back against her chest. She hung her ole nappy head over my shoulder. Her hot, hay breath was filling my shirt. "You be a good girl...you pull whatever they put behind you, you hear! You be nice too...no pickin' who you like and who you don't! You work for whoever puts a collar on you! You is a good ole gal, Waitus." I pulled her jackrabbit ears down and kissed her on her gray velvet nose. Her whiskers tickled my nose and her hot hay breath warmed my face. Then, I picked up my bag and walked away. I couldn't look back. I will miss that girl. She taught me a lot in this life and brought a lot of sunshine my way. Off in the distance, I could hear her braying away. Animals know things, and she knowed I wasn't ever coming back. The lump in my throat could have choked even her.

I met up with Odell and, we walked the dusty roads for miles till we got to Hwy 281. We was tired of eating dust. I sat down on my Daddy's old leather luggage, and we lit up a rollie. I was in my own thoughts, and Odell was laying back under a tree. We were just waiting for a car to come on by. My thoughts always turned to Mama. I worried about her all alone with just Deanie there. I know she is a strong woman, and Lord knows; He got a holy hedge around her like no other. I remember all she taught me about faith and God's love for me, even though I do test Him a lot!

> *"My son, keep your father's commandment, and for-*
> *sake not your mother's teaching." Proverbs 6:20*

We walked about twenty-five miles to a little town called Hico, with me hanging my thumb out in the wind the whole way. Hico is a small cattle and cotton town on Honey Creek, in Hamilton County, Texas. It seems Hico is best known for being a hide-out and home for the infamous, "Billy the Kid." He seemed to be one to want to do justice for people, even though he went about it the wrong way. He was made famous as a cattle rustler and for a big jailbreak. He even confessed to his wrongdoings and wanted to make things right with his maker. This little town was full of stories about him, and some believe he is still hiding out here.

Me and Odell was sitting out on the road outside of town. My eyes are watering from the dirt, and my mouth was dry as a well in August. Out of nowhere, here comes a big navy blue, 1925 Ford, Model T Runabout. As it was screeching to a stop, it was spitting gravel and leaving a rooster tail of smoke for a country mile. Some ole guy was just a laughing out loud like a circus monkey. "What kinda damn, country corncobs are walking out here?" Shouldn't you two be on a donkey or something?" He just guffawed at us. He was a tall drink of water with wavy black hair and a little pencil line mustache. He looked like Clark Gable. " Well, I just so happen to have an ole donkey you screwball, and I shore bet her rickety cart ass will be a better ride than sitting next to the likes of you!" "Probably so!" He grabbed his belly and laughed again! "I know one thing for sure; no woman is going to be seen next to you two in those denim farmer's britches! My name is Bob Grinsley; people call me Grins." "Why they call you Grins? Cuz you look like a hyena!" We both belly laughed. "Get in. What're your names, and where are you headed?" "I am Houston, Houston Lowe, and this here is Odell, my best friend." He just busted out again!!!! "Houston, Lord be! You sure you ain't Amarillo??? Hooooweeee!" He swings over a flask of whiskey. "Take you a swig; it will make the bugs taste better! "Odell, well that is cob name for sure!" Odell didn't say a word. Grins hyena laughed again as we were tearing off that gravel shoulder. In about ten miles, seems like me and Grins knowed each other forever. "Me and Odell are headed to San Antonio to join the CCC's." "Shoot, me too! I am going to sell this ole bucket of bolts when we get there. San Antonio got lots of pretty girls, ya know. Houston, I'm gonna call you 'Rillo." "Well hell, then I'm just gonna call you Grins." "Odell, you is Odie." And that was that. For as long as I knowed Bob, I called him Grins.

We make our way to the northeast area of San Antonio and come upon a massive stucco, and stone beauty, Fort Sam Houston. Grins sold the Ford to some ole guy on the road outside the camp for a hundred bucks. "This will get us a ticket for a front row seat in the canteen tonight!" Ft. Sam Houston is a beauty. It is surrounded by limestone rock fencing and iron gates. The breath of history just whistles through the ten-foot mesquite and oak trees that are lining the streets. This place is full of military history. You can feel the presence of greatness surrounding you. I can't imagine the military might that has been here before us. The incredible oak trees surround the colonial style buildings. Curved red terracotta clay rooftops are capping the neat stucco structures. Each one is dotted with arched windows with iron grids, looking like wise owls standing watch. There was a hospital, a training center, and some quarters. The whole compound is in a square, with buildings facing towards a courtyard they call the 'Quadrangle'. In the middle of the Quadrangle, is an eighty-seven-foot watchtower with a clock and two big water towers. It was around 7:00 a.m., and a light grey, misty fog is floating above the grass. Dozens of whitetail deer are stirring the fog as they gently lower their heads to eat the grass seed below. A strange cry, like a frightened woman screaming, is ricocheting off the buildings. Beautiful turquoise and blue-green peacocks and peahens are freely prancing around in a courting dance. It is beautiful. With all the business of a looming war, this place can make you stop for a moment and see the beauty in a few of God's little creatures.

> *"How countless are Your works, Lord! In wisdom You have made them all; the earth is full of Your creatures." Psalm 104:24*

Back about a hundred years ago, in 1845, Texas was a Republic and just cutting her teeth on becoming a state. The Army laid down roots near the Alamo, and this was her beginning. In 1886, the Apache Chief Geronimo was held up in this very Quadrangle before he was sent off to Florida. This post was selected to be named for the great General Sam Houston in 1890. My grandfather named my father after Sam Houston, and my father followed with me. There are hundreds of temporary buildings here all in preparation for the necessary training and deployment of thousands of troops for the looming war.

We walked up to the CCC office and signed in. "You boys from Dallas?" "No, I am from Glen Rose, and Grins here....shoot Grins, where your people from?" "I am from Amarillo!" We laughed again. "Step over here." A guy in white uniform pants and shirt directed us. "Strip down to your skivvies and step on that scale. Odell, along with Grins and me, went through a gauntlet of checks. They checked our eyes, ears, nose, throat, and even our teeth. Lord, we was like cattle before a stockyard auction. The medic says, "Ok, drop your drawers. Step over here and bend over." Well, now that is a place I didn't think would be checked! What they expect to find in there, the good china! He barked out, "Turn around, now, cough, cough." That medic had a finger pressed firmly between both of my family pouches. His final orders bounced off the rafters, "Now, turn your head to the left, cough. Now the right, cough." I pulled up my drawers and was herded to the next station. They checked my size twelve boat feet. The next medic proclaims, "No flat feet here! You have an arch like the Brooklyn bridge! We will walk that right off you, boy!" We all hit the last table where a clerk threw a form across the desk for us to sign. Me and Odell put our Mama's address down where we would be sending our twenty-five dollars. Just like that, we were in the CCC'!. For the first time in my life, I was gonna make some of my own money.

That night after supper, we was issued a leftover World War I uniform and assigned to an enrollee-built barracks. Reveille blew around 6:30 a.m. the next morning. Our routine began, and we followed it every day, 'cept Sunday. We went to conditioning and exercises before we had a big breakfast of hash, eggs, toast, and coffee. I was sure glad to get a belly full and to be around a bunch of menfolk like me. Me and Grins got the same squad assignment. Odell got assigned to a different squad. That was the first time I had been separated from him since we was knee-high to a grasshopper. We all started in conditioning camp for about two weeks. It was hot as hell out there, but nothing I was not used to. We did pushups and carried big rocks across the old football field. Working together, we learned to become a team while we were getting ourselves in good physical shape. They called it conditioning. Hell, it was just farming work without any crops at the end! Our camp had around two hundred men. Every day after breakfast, we walked on back to the barracks, cleaned up and straightened our bunks. We hit the local quarry by about 8:00 a.m., where we worked very hard.

Depending on the season, it could be in the sun or cold, but it was always eight hours a day. We are assigned to projects around the city building small walls, entrances and benches for a local park, and a new football stadium. I was never so glad to see the lunch truck delivery around 1:00 p.m. each day. We would sit under a shade tree, and some ole guy would pull out a homemade transistor radio. We would listen to the baseball games or the Andrews Sisters. Sometimes Roy Acuff would come on with the Wabash Cannonball. We all loved that song. We would eat our sandwiches and have some coffee. Cookie always sent some Honey Drops. Those sweet cookies just melt in your mouth. Give you all the energy you need to make it till quitting time. We finished up around 4 o'clock in the afternoon and got cleaned up. We took care of our uniforms and shoes and squared away our bunk till chow.

Chow was always filling and served around 5:30 p.m. One thing for sure, they know how to keep a man working. We had meatloaf, mashed potatoes and gravy, green beans, and chocolate cake. I was sure glad to have a hot meal, but it was awfully bland. The meatloaf tasted like a day old brick. "Grins, you taste anything in that meatloaf?" "Naaahhh, just a chunk of meat. It is all I need, ain't complaining. I can eat a leather shoe if it is covered in ketchup." "Well, instead of covering everything in ketchup, they should cook it right in it." "Look, you don't like how things taste around here, you can cook for these guys yourself! Don't get no appreciation round here, damn civis!" The 'cookie', who is standing right behind me, is a big ole fat, tow-headed guy from Germany. He has a stogie hanging out of his mouth, spraying ashes every time he talked. He just heard every word I said! One thing I know, you don't talk bad about the cook. He bellowed at me, "Civi, you think you can do a better job in this crappy inferno, you go right ahead!" I had cooked a few meals myself next to Mama; I knowed a thing or two about making food tasty. I was a cocky young buck, always up for a bet. I told Cookie, "Look, tomorrow night, we will both fix the same meal using just half the rations. Nobody will know who fixed what. Everyone just takes half servings of each, and we will let the boys decide." "You are on Civi! See you tomorrow!" He threw his white kitchen apron at me and spun around, fussing and cussing, as he lumbered towards the kitchen. He looked like a locomotive puffing down the tracks. His caboose was about as big too! "Hee, Hee!" I slapped my knee.

After dinner, we had some free time for leisure activities like baseball or football, cards or board games, or reading. Most of the guys read the newspaper telling about the goings on in Europe and the Pacific. I would usually write Mama a short letter.

November 6, 1937

My dearest mother,

Well, I did make it. I am officially enlisted in the CCCs! They are real good to us, feed us good too. We work hard outside, but I am used to it. How is my best girl, Waitus? Have you seen Florine when you are in town? I hope Deannie and Boog are helping you out. Have you had to move to Oklahoma yet? You stay strong and remember I love you. I will send $25 soon.

Sonny Boy

About 10:30 p.m., we had Lights Out. Sleeping in a room full of guys wasn't such a big change for me. I was used to the cabin with all my brothers and sisters. I have had so many arms and feet in my face all night, babies crying and nursing and Daddy flapping the sheets once in a while! A bunch of snoring and farting guys didn't bother me a bit! At this time in my life, I was sure glad to have "three hots and a cot!"

We started building the park in January of 1938. It was still pretty cold, but we bundled up okay, and the hard work kept us warm. We were all new at stone cutting and building. We started on our first assignment joining a park called Brackenridge Park, and the local art museum, the Witte. Seems this park area has been around since Jesus walked the earth. It was founded because of a good fella named George Washington Brackenridge. Seems men named George Washington do a lot of good in this country! Mr. Brackenridge was a real dapper and smart guy. He started one of the city's best newspapers, the *San Antonio Express and News.* With his earnings and wealth, he wanted to beautify his city and bring the local people together. So, he donated about two-hundred acres of land to the city he loved to create what is now known as Brackenridge Park. The Witte Museum got the project approved by the Works Progress Administration (WPA), with outlined drawings for stone wall park entrances, bus benches, and low walls. They needed a low limestone perimeter wall built to separate the walking paths from the green spaces people would be enjoying the park. It would also showcase the beauty of the natural stone buildings in the area while using the remnants of the abandoned limestone quarry. We took big truckloads of cut stones and unloaded them in big piles every twenty-feet or so. We used a yardstick to measure from the street edge, and twine was rolled out to follow the natural curves around the park area. We carried thousands of pounds of rocks laying them into place. The masons spread on the peanut butter concrete from the local cement company, Alamo Cement. A couple of English fellas started that company right out of the rich dust there. Even the Texas State Capitol was built using this cement.

The Great Meatloaf Show Down

I went on back to the barracks that day a little early. Cap let me off early cuz I think he knew I could out-cook Cookie. He had a personal motive to let me in that kitchen! I took the dirty white apron Cookie threw at me yesterday. Cookie grumbles, "Here, put this paper hat on ... regulation!" I asked, "What are we working with Cookie?" "We are going to make the same meal as yesterday Civi! Meatloaf, mash potatoes, green beans, and chocolate cake. There is your half of the evening rations. Now have at it!" I stepped over to the prep station and started chopping up some onions and garlic. I cut me up some bell peppers and took some day-old bread from yesterday's supper and poured buttermilk all over it, beating in some eggs. I watched Mama rehydrate old stale bread and make some great dumplings that way. It should work to keep this meat

69

brick juicy. Cookie walked past me a couple of times. He was rolling his stogie across his teeth from one side to the next, slamming it tight into his cheek. "Humphhh." I put the wet bread mixture with the ground meat and mixed in some ketchup. I shaped those big loaves across a cookie pan and put them in the oven to bake. I had the potatoes boiling on the stove. I mashed the taters with some butter, salt, pepper; and a little milk. You fry you up some bacon, and you can make any bean taste good! The bacon and onions were sizzling away as I cleaned the beans to put them in. I would have made some of Mama's cornbread, but that was not on the menu. I did put some buttermilk in my chocolate cake and some leftover cold coffee in my icing. I know that will keep the cake moist, it works for cornbread. After about thirty minutes, the aroma of the onions and bacon started circulating. Pretty soon, we had an audience outside the mess hall. We shut the doors to the mess lines and covered up our work, setting up the half portions side by side. That a way, guys would come in and take a half-portion from each steam tray. From the hallway outside we hear, "Hey, when are we getting this shindig on around here?" "We are hungry out here!!!" Guys were fussing and cussing outside the big wooden swinging doors. Cookie was stomping around clanging pans, and sharpening his knives. He has been telling these guys the government rations were the blame, so now, his bloated red neck was on the griddle! We opened the lines up and they rushed in like a herd of buffalo. Guys put one-half ration on each side of the plate. We had already cut up half portions of chocolate cake. "Woooo-weee! this here is some grub!" Guys were just cooing like doves in springtime over my ration. Cookie had even added a little salt and pepper to his halves. From the mess hall, we hear, "This tastes like grandma's Sunday dinner!" "I may never stop eating!" "Finally a meal worth paying the price of admission for!" Pretty soon, a bunch of guys bum rushed me in the mess hall. I thought they were gonna run me out of town for making Cookie look bad. They just hoisted me up on their shoulders and placed a make-shift crown made of table napkins on top of my head. My scepter was a giant soup ladle, and my cape was a white kitchen apron. "Hip, hip, hooray! Hip, hip, hooray!" They paraded me all over the mess hall and set me down right next to Cookie. "Hey you old cuss, this here is the new Cookie!" "You have been dodging those rocks out here in this kitchen for too long now!" "Looks like you got a date with Miss Roxy and all her girls tomorrow!" Cookie rolled his stogie over his tongue. I thought he was gonna put me in a headlock! "Guter koch, guter koch"! In his German language, he was telling me I was a good cook. And that was it; my interview was over! I became the senior head mess cook that very day. It was my choosing to decide who would be my part-time assistant, and I chose Cookie. Turns out, he was okay with that. He got assigned to the mess hall because they assumed he could cook, being German and all. We only had a part-time position in the kitchen, and I knew that Cookie wasn't up to carrying rocks. We worked it out that I set the menus, recipes, and ingredients; and he did all the meal preparation. I cooked breakfast and dinner, and Cookie took care of lunch. It was a box lunch anyway! That way I could go out with the boys to the rock pile, and he could stay home in the kitchen cutting and prepping for the night's most important meal.

We worked six days a week on that park. Those benches and walls took about two years to complete, overall. In 1938, sometime in the late Spring, I got called in one afternoon and told I was getting transferred to California to cook at a CCC camp there. Thank God, I was actually getting called in to be assigned as a 'Cookie', and not 'cuz of my rock skills! I guess my contest worked out pretty good! I was glad to get out of the quarry for a while!!! For about six months, I cooked and trained in CCC camps in California, Arizona, and New Mexico, before being sent back to San Antonio. I went right back to my old barracks and found Grins. "You ole son of gun...gone on to be a Cookie, have ya?!!" I was glad to do that work; I loved the kitchen. I took off to find Odell! "You ole buck-toothed mule!!!" "Houston! how are you?" "I loved being the head in the kitchen. They sure got some pretty girls out West!!!" "Yup, I heard." "You get the sweet ass on anyone?" "Nope, but I talked a few into starching my khakis for me!!!" "Woo hoo!" "You better tell me all about it!"

The Horseshoe

A new assignment was on the boards the next day. A bright white paper list of hand-selected guys, to finish up a new project code-named: 'The Horseshoe'. Me, Grins, and Odell all had our names on the Horseshoe squad list. We got on a different bus and were taken further up the road than the park area. Pretty soon we were in this giant rock bowl. It was intimidating as Hell. We are surrounded by limestone walls on all sides. "Men, this old hole has been mostly cleared. We will be shaping the surface walls, and building the infrastructure for seating and a playing field. Some of you will be using dynamite to break up the larger slabs, and the remaining guys will be using picks to cut and shape stones." Busting rocks, yep that's what I was gonna be doing! I had to laugh at myself for a minute. Mama was right all along! I was busting up some rocks, but it shore nuff wasn't in prison! We hauled and set rocks about ten hours a day. This will soon become a great football stadium. It should be around for thousands of years the way we was building it, just like the Coliseum in Rome. It was an incredible project to build. We dug deep into those hillsides and cut every piece of stone that was laid. The design was pretty much taken care of by mother nature. Filling in the abandoned quarry naturally took on the shape of the horseshoe. It is nicknamed 'the rock pile', cuz, it was mostly Texas limestone that came from a rock pile. It was grueling work as I went in between my time in the kitchen and the horseshoe. But, I got in the best shape of my life in that quarry. I was lifting about a thousand pounds of rock a day. It didn't take long for me to become a muscle head.

When she was finished, that stadium was a wonder; standing tall in the beautiful Monte Vista neighborhood in San Antonio. It is a big ole arena for soccer, football, track, and other contests. The horseshoe had seats for just over 18,000 or so visitors. She was a glorious beauty, a real show palace for high school athletics. Electricians came in and set up big ole loudspeakers, an electric scoreboard, and tower lighting. It was a spectacle! We finished that grand place up right before it was dedicated, Friday, September 20, 1940. The whole city celebrated, and the mayor declared it

"Alamo Stadium Day" in the city. I felt real proud to be a part of such a stunner. I hope she brings lots of pride to the kids who will be playing in her for years to come. She carried a good name too. Texans are right proud of our heritage.

CCC jobs in San Antonio and across the country began to slow down. There was less and less work, and guys were beginning to get sent home. I continued to work in the kitchen and set rocks on opposite shifts when they needed me. In the evenings I would write Mama a letter.

January 28, 1941

Dearest Mama,

I hope that you are doing well. How are Deannie and Boog? I sure miss you all. I hope your heart isn't too sad. I think about you all the time. They are still taking real good care of me. I am learning a lot in the kitchen. I sure am glad that you taught me how to cook. I love the kitchen and hope someday to make it my full-time work. I am putting in another $25 for you to help get along. Say hello to Waitus, my girl. If you see Florine in town, tell her hello from me.

Sonny Boy

Me, Grins, and Odell would get a hankering to go on out to a honky-tonk in town when we was off. With only five bucks for the month, we had to get creative. We would buy us a pint of Jim Beam whiskey for about a buck-fifty. Any decent highball in town was about fifty cents. So we would each guzzle down about a third of that pint, and get us a little buzz going before we stepped on out. We would head on down to the Lamp Post Inn where we would shoot some pool and win some more money from the local punks who thought they could beat us. Truth is, Grins was a dead shot on the felt. His uncle owned an ice house beer joint where he grew up setting up racks for tips. When the bar was empty, his Uncle Will showed him a few things. By the time he was ten years old, he could beat any man in the joint in any game, including snooker. We could act like some real backward hicks if we needed to set the trap. I set up Odell and Grins for the felt run. Odell said to Grins, "Hey Spewey, you wanna shoot this here ball around a bit?" He replies, "Willis, you get that there triangle and we will get to shooting." We set up the rack and messed around making a few shots. We would bet each other a buck a game. Some local yolks come around smelling the bait. "Hey, do you couple of 'boots' wanna play some pool with us?" "Five clams a game, you in?" Odell spits back, "Five clams, well Hell, I can buy a month of groceries for that!" Boots, they think we are in the military seeing our uniforms and all. Grins tells them, "Sure, we can play a game." "Willis, where we gonna come up with five bucks?" They set up the rack while Grins set up his trap. He stooged a few shots and lost two games in no time. "Willis, give the man his ten bucks and let's get outta here while we can still buy some smokes!" I hand him over our ten bucks we put together, and we start to head to the door. "Hey, ok, ok, don't go. You got a pretty good shot. Let's do one more, double or nothing." The hook is in the wide mouth bass now! I whisper over to Grins, "You know what the monkey said when he cut off his tail? Well, it won't be LONG now, hee, hee!" Grins tells him to set up the rack. "Give me the first shot, the break, right?" "Ok, Boot, fire away." Grins steps up and blasts that pool cue like a brick into a cement wall. You could hear the crack over the jukebox and all the drunken laughter. "We take stripes." Grins rolls his smoke over his teeth and clenches it tight on the right side. He commences taking that table by storm. He was cracking that cue ball, as he strategically fired each of the striped balls into their assigned pockets. The cue ball would roll right on back to the perfect position for his next shot. In four minutes and twenty-three seconds, he cleared the table and sent the eight ball on a two-rail hike to the left corner pocket. With a rollie clamped in his teeth, Grins tells them, "That'll be twenty clams, boys!" "Son of a bitch!" He slams a Jackson on the felt table and walks away.

We get a few odd jobs mostly finishing work on the limestone walls around the zoo area. We did extra work around the camp to pass our time. A few more guys are sent home, and we feel that we may be next. Me, Grins, and Odell was washing our socks outside in the water faucet. Our captain came up and wiggled in between us. He grabbed the garden hose and told us to listen up. He whispers, "Look, you three guys have been busting your ass here for quite some time. You are some of my best. Never had to worry about you shagging on the job like some of these shirkers. You earned every cent you got. But for what I hear out there, you guys better go off and find you some work. We got notice the CCC's are gonna close up shop, and there won't be no more work around here." "Thanks, Cap, thanks." We went off for a smoke and talked about the rumblings in the newspapers about Japan and Europe. We are right here on a military base. Thinking they would have plenty of jobs, we thought we might just enlist in the Army Air Corps. So, that is 'zactly what we did.

February 11, 1941–Enlisting in the Army Air Corps

Just like the three Musketeers, we packed up our stuff in our canvas duffle bags, got our last payment, and went over to the enlistment office. I figure we better get in while we can. I wanted to go to an island you know...and anywhere General MacArthur would be serving. I was gonna sign-up for the Philippines. Odell, well you know ole Odell, he wanted to sign up and stay stateside. Now Grins, he said, "Guess this is where we part, Rillo, I will go anywhere but the Philippines! Come on now, Houston... you stupid?!"

The Rectal-Cranial Inversion

Me, Odell and Grins, step up inside the canvas hut to report. They send us off to the Medical Unit to get our physical exams. "Head out to the Pecker Checker boys, hut 58." We make your way to the Hospital Corpsman's office, and once again, me and Odell are naked as jaybirds standing in front of the medics. Grins likes

75

taking his clothes off. He is quite proud of what the good Lord gave him, and he would use any opportunity to sling it around! We all go through the usual tests, and then we move on over to an eye test station. We didn't have to test our eyes or ears for the CCC's. A strong back and healthy heart were pretty much all they were looking for. The medic barks over, "Ok, Private, cover one eye and read that chart. What is the smallest letter you can read?" Sir, I see, "K-I-D-O- H-X-N-L-S-V..." "Ok Private, that's enough–"You got 20-15 vision boy! You should be able to shoot a plane out of the sky a half mile away!" "I hope so sir!" I move to hearing screening, when I overhear Odell through the white curtain wall, as he is stumbling over his chart taking to the examiner. "Uh, O or U, uh, could be a D, Sir, not for sure." "Son, what line are you reading from?" "Uh, I think the second one from the top, Sir." "Read it again son." "Ummm..I think it is an O or a D." "Which one son, which one?" "The top one Sir, the damn, top one!" "Good Lord man, you are blind as a bat! "Cover your right eye and read it again." "I can't see nothing out of my left eye, NOTHING!" "Well that's ok ain't it? I can see well enough to hold my own out there." "Pull your head outta your ass man! Uncle Sam ain't taking a blind man to battle!" Kapflunk ....the big metal stamping machine slammed down on the papers, leaving a two-inch REJECTED notice in big red letters on top of the eye exam. Odell failed his eye exam! It seems he is blind in one eye!!! "Well, no wonder you couldn't shoot a pea shooter worth a damn Odell!!! You is blind in that eye!!!!!" Odell was upset. He stomped back to get his stuff and was immediately going to be processed to be sent back home. He turned in his gear and blanket. "Write me a note once in a while ya punch bags!" "I will. Tell my Mama I said hello and that I will be shipping out soon!" Odell punched me in the chest and turned around and walked out. That was the first time since I was a baby in Mama's arms me and Odell were not together. They sent him off to the bus stop downtown to get his ride. And that was it. He was back on a bus back home with a Rejection Stamp from Uncle Sam himself. He will be alright. He always is. Now he was gonna go to Ft. Worth to see if he could get a job driving big rig trucks. Grins passed with flying colors. We were both processed in and moved to the barracks.

'Brows'

I am on my own now. Even with the likes of Grins around here, pretty soon, we will be split up, and he will be stateside while I am a world away. I am just gonna be here for a couple of weeks before they ship me off to the Philippines for my 'OJT'. With the need to get guys strategically placed quickly, my basic training will be in the Philippines! I have a job to do, and I am gonna do it to the best of my ability. Daddy taught me to love this country, and I am willing to die to keep it safe. My job now is to follow instructions. Within a few short weeks, we are all gonna change from lanky unrefined, greenhorn recruits, to real airmen. For my short stay here, I am assigned to one barracks within the 'Long Barracks,' and Grins was assigned to another one. All of the barracks were two-story buildings about a hundred and twenty feet long and thirty feet wide. One company of troops, about fifty enlisted men, were assigned to each barracks. Upstairs where we slept, there were two big bays lined with khaki green wooden bunks. Each bunk had a rolled-up mattress, a green wool blanket, two starched white sheets, and an issued footlocker where we stored our uniforms, skivvies, and personal items. Each bunk was like a little personal apartment. Pictures of girls were pinned to the wall or stuck in the mattress above. Some guys had their bibles or a cross on the bed. An old radio was playing Benny Goodman. It was real nice, like the CCC's. On the bottom floor, there was a real nice dining area and kitchen, with a dayroom where we could hang out. There was also a quarters for a cook and one for the first sergeant. Seems to me that the cook is a pretty good position to be in. I hope to get myself in that line of work full time.

From the barracks floor we hear, "Shh, shhh, shhh, Chest Candy coming on deck, Chest Candy, you hear! straighten up!" A few guys are scurrying around pulling on their canvas belts, buttoning their shirts, spitting on their hands as they stroke through their hair. "Awww crap, its Captain Brows!" He stands in front, commanding the room. "Listen up, boob squad! Line up in front of your bunks! You are in the Army Air Corps now, ladies!" In steps our Sergeant. He was a big ole fella with a chin like a steel lock, and piercing black eyes covered in bushy brown eyebrows. His cap was pulled down so low on his forehead, every time he said something; his eyebrows moved his hat up and down. He spoke with authority, and when he did, you better listen! "You will be neat; you will be clean! You will be the best trained military men on the planet! You will soon be sent by Uncle Sam to blow the enemy right out of the air. No room for pussies in this army! Training begins today. I don't care where else you will be finishing it up! I will be sending one of your whiney asses home to your Mama before sundown! Anyone wanna volunteer first? His voice is booming off and shaking the wooden rafters above us. "If you can't hack it here, you aren't fit to be out there with a man's life in your hands. We play for keeps around here, and there are no do-overs. You get it right the first time, or it could be your last time! That means all of the aces, all wool and a yard wide, all the time! That includes your shot, your bunk, your uniform, and your conduct! All you apron chasers, when you go out fishing for an ammunition wife, you better be wearing a hat; or you will be carrying home more than a broken heart! You better read up on the 'Off Limits' lists over there on that wall! Every flea-bit, clap-infested honky-tonk is listed there! Uncle Sam expects you to keep your whistle clean. Don't get caught with your trousers around your knees in one of those joints or the MPs are going to drag your ass straight back to me! When I come back here, I better be able to bounce a silver dollar off your sheets like it just ricocheted off the ass of a government mule! You hear me, boys?!" "YES, SIR!!!!" A resounding symphony of male voices yelled out a perfectly timed, corporate response. "At ease, ladies." His boots clicked on the wood floors and his brown khaki pants swished by in a perfect cadence. "Wow, they even care about our peckers, huh?" "You stooge, they only care if your pecker finds itself in some deviant and immoral sexual activity, in one of 'those' joints!" "Well, I'll be John Brown!" These 'Off-Limits' lists came from some legislation called the May Act. It gave military police the power to regulate the 'goings on' of enlistees. Ifin you are looking for some hotbeds to get in trouble, these lists would be your first stop. I only went to the sixth grade, and I could figure that out!

"My son, pay attention to my wisdom; listen carefully to my wise counsel. Then you will show discernment, and your lips will express what you've learned. For the lips of an immoral woman are as sweet as honey, and her mouth is smoother than oil. But in the end she is as bitter as poison, as dangerous as a double-edged sword. Her feet go down to death; her steps lead straight to the grave. For she cares nothing about the path to life. She staggers down a crooked trail and doesn't realize it. So now, my sons, listen to me. Never stray from what I am about to say. Stay away from her! Don't go near the door of her house. If you do, you will lose your honor and will lose to merciless people all you have achieved." Proverbs 5-7

Blow it Out Your Barracks Bag!

Chow 0600 hours, SOS, hash, and eggs on toast, black coffee. This is already my last day here. "Hey boob, pass me the axle grease." He is pointing his knife at the one pound stick of butter on the table. " That's the only thing that makes this 'bull in a can' taste any better." He was right. The chow was not first-rate. There must be a million names for the food we eat. Alligator bait, albatross, bully beef, camp strawberries, hand grenade, Irish grapes…. I never heard so many names for stuff to eat! If there is a word out there, I guarantee you, some old guy has named it something else around here. It is like a foreign language. We finished up our chow and moved out to artillery training. After our training drills for the day, I got called to the office of the clerk. He said, "Hey you and you, the other boob standing over there, get over here. We got a problem. You two look like you could be trusted to help out with some military intel. We have a new recruit we think is AWOL, you know, absent without leave, gone, astray, lost, adrift, kaput! His name is Private Al K. Hall. We need to find him right away. He is probably hiding on the base somewhere whining to his girlfriend cause he is gonna be shipped out soon! He didn't show up to roll

79

call. You two go to the quartermaster's desk and request a ID-Ten-T form. This is what you fill out when you find him. He wrote the form document number on a telephone message sheet ID-10-T. This is the form. Get back with me right away. Yes, sir! We saluted him and took off to get this underway. "What's your name?" "I am Rick Mason." "Okay, Rick, you go look in the canteen and the bathrooms for Al, and I will go get the form." So Rick took off calling Al's name, and I took off to the Quartermaster's office. "Sir, I am here to obtain a ID-10-T form, sir; we have a missing recruit." "We do?" "Yes, sir. Private Mason and I were sent by the clerk to find him, and to complete that form." "Is his name Al?" "Why yes, sir, how did you know?" "We have had trouble with this recruit for a while now. This is probably his last chance before he gets sent home. I do not have any of those forms here. Check in T Building, Office 3700." "Yes, sir, have a good day, sir. Oh, and sir, if Al is some kind of knucklehead that needs a lesson, me and Private Mason can take care of that for you. You can trust us, we will find him." "Dismissed!" I took off to T Building looking for office 3700. The clerk, a big ole burly guy, grumbled through his newspaper, "What do you want!" "Sir, I am here on intel from the Office of the Clerk to retrieve a ID-10-T form, sir." "Oh, so you are, are you? Well, those forms aren't stored here any longer, they moved to personnel. You need to head across the base to Building G, Office 23; and ask for the Administrative Assistant." "Yes, sir!" So off I am now running across the base again, not having a clue if Rick has located Private Hall or not. Breathing heavy, wiping the sweat from my forehead, I enter G Building looking for Office 23. It has a big sign on the door, Out of the office until 1600. I sit there in the hallway on an old wooden bench for an hour and a half. At 1600 hours on the dot, in walks the assistant. "Can I help you, Private?" " I am here to pick up an ID-10-T form sir." "Oh, okay. I have that form right here in this file." "Thank God, I thought I was gonna have to go to another office, and for sure I would be late getting Private Hall back." "No problem at all. You take this envelope with the form in it back to the clerk, and he will get it filled out for you." "Yes sir, thank you, sir." I run like a rabbit to the other side of the base to get to the clerk's office before it closes at 1700. Panting and huffing, I come to the office door to find Rick Mason. He is lined up in the hallway with about fifteen or twenty other guys. I hand the clerk the envelope. "I finally got the ID-10-T form, sir. I told you that you could count on me." "Well, you sure did son, you sure did!" He just guffaw laughs, and that just busts out every man in the hallway in a concert of laughter. Seems, it is at our expense. The clerk opens up the envelope and slides out the form inside. It read: Dear Private, YOU ARE THE ID-10-T we are looking for! AL K. Hall is a twelve-ounce, malt liquor!!!! "Well I'll be a striped-ass ape! They got us for sure huh, Rick!?" Rick blurts out, "Running my ass around this base all day like a damned fool, shit!" Awww, blow it out your barracks bag, Private! Welcome to the Army Air Corps, son!" Everyone in the hallway is in hysterical laughter. Seems Rick Mason was not amused being the butt of this old joke. "Since you are such a JAAFU, you can report to bubble duty this afternoon!!" The clerk laughs right at us. Rick stomped on out while the men in the hallway was slapping at his head on the way out. I'm guessing ifin I'm gonna be proved a fool in God's presence, it best be a part of my training in this man's army!

> *"The fear of the Lord is the beginning of knowledge;*
> *fools despise wisdom and instruction. Proverbs." 1:7*

A Floating Parade

The city is finishing up on the beautiful river project, creating a sweeping limestone encased river running through downtown. We get a little R and R time, so we pack up and head to 'the river' for a little carnival and night parade. There are a few nice stores in the downtown area, and I was itching for a pinky ring. I was poor growing up and didn't have much. I had just gotten my first bit of enlisting money, and after sending some to Mama; I wanted to get me one. It was my way of saying I made it out of the cedar brakes! "Come on Grins, let's go pick me out a cool ring! All the smooth guys in Hollywood are wearing them. Danny Kaye, William Powell, and even Cary Grant!" "Okay, 'Rillo, whatever you say." We stop in a little downtown jeweler, and I pick out a gold and onyx ring for $62 bucks. "Fits like it is made for me!" It is a symbol of our toughness, and its gonna look pretty cool when I am smoking too!

Walking in the river area, we see there is an open-air theater with some limestone bridges and a few little joints around. This is the first time the city ever tried to float anything on that river or showcase it, and we didn't want to miss it! It is March 14, 1941. Me and Grins are walking the limestone paths and looking around. Its real peaceful round here. It reminds me of Glen Rose. We get us a couple of beers and walk the sidewalks. Some ladies in real pretty dresses are on floating barges waving at us. Some single ladies are standing around watching the parade. Grins waves in a couple of real 'lookers', and off we head up to find us a honky-tonk or two for the night.

After a two-week stay at Ft. Sam Houston, all uniformed up, I am ready to take on my assignment. I know must seem stupid, but I am looking forward to this. I want to serve my country. America is climbing back up on her feet after the Depression almost leveled us from the inside. I want to be there to protect her from any harm lurking outside. I alongside my brothers, profess our allegiance to this great county and are formally enlisted. Trembling, I repeat these words, *"I, Houston Edward Lowe, do solemnly swear that I will support and defend the Constitution of the United States against all enemies, foreign and domestic; that I will bear true faith and allegiance to the same; and that I will obey the orders of the President of the United States and the orders of the officers appointed over me, according to regulations and the Uniform Code of Military Justice. So help me God."* Grins gets his assignment. He is staying stateside, headed to Hamilton Army Airfield near San Pablo Bay, California. Seems this smart ass is gonna get skilled in bomb building! I will be shipping out to the Philippines. We slap each other on the back. "Rillo, you take care." "You too. Don't go and blow yousef up now!" We threw our duffle bags over our shoulders and looked at each other knowing; we would probably never see each other again.

Houston E. Lowe and CCC Buddy (Unknown), CCC Camp, San Antonio, Texas, Circa 1939, Courtesy Houston E. Lowe, personal collection

Houston E. Lowe, Early Army Air Corp photograph, circa 1941, Courtesy Houston E. Lowe, personal collection

Chapter Four

The World Goes to War

Miracle Four–Corregidor Island – 'The Rock'

On the 22nd of March, 1941, I was assigned to Battery E., 60th Coast Artillery, Ft. Mills, Philippines. I am going to serve under one of the greatest military generals of all time, General Douglas MacArthur. Even though it is very humbling for a simple country boy, I remind myself that I serve a King first.

> *"Ye shall walk after the LORD your God, and fear him, and keep his commandments, and obey his voice, and ye shall serve him, and cleave unto him."*
> *Deuteronomy 13:4*

Getting on a big ole Navy tanker was a thrill for me. Me and all the guys are in our shiny new uniforms and spit-polished shoes. We are swinging our canvas duffels, as we board the big steel monster, the U.S.S. Republic. She was mighty decked out too! Built in Belfast, Ireland, in 1907, this ship is loaded. She was originally named the President Grant. She was used for transatlantic passengers until she was seized as a troop transport ship in WWI. In 1941, she was commissioned the Republic. She was a monster with an armament of one five-foot, and four, three-foot gun mounts.

After a couple of weeks at sea, the Republic dropped anchor off the coast of Corregidor Island, Luzon, Philippines. This is where my story really begins. I was twenty-one years old, just a kid with country smarts; and my Mama's prayers in my back pocket. We took PT boats over to the rock, Corregidor, or 'the tadpole'; as it is called. The local Filipinos came running from every direction from the jungles and beaches. They were waving their arms and whistling. They handed us small packages of pandesal rolls filled with sweet coconut, a local bread the natives bake in open fires. They are so happy to see us, and they know we are here to work alongside their boys.

Corregidor Island is shaped like the little tadpoles I used as bait when I was a kid. Corregidor has a mighty reputation as a fortress, and is nicknamed the 'Gibraltar of the East'. She is situated in Manila Bay, just a bit south of the peninsula known as Bataan. Little did I know, that the little peninsula would soon become the location of the deadliest jungle march of men in the history of humanity. Even though it was just a small island, accordin' to our briefings, Corregidor was gonna serve as a key fortress in the allied defensive plans for the Philippines. Not sure how this raggedy ole island is gonna do that, but my superiors know what they are doing, and I trusted them with my life. I was ready to serve, and my days in the CCC's had me in tip-top, soldier shape. I was willing to defend it with my life if it would keep old glory flying over our great country another day.

Corregidor had a power plant that provided all of the island's pumped water and electricity. A critical part of defending this ole rock is our ability to keep the power plant running and protected from attack. The hospital is underground, just like an underground ant hill. There is a system of tunnels and offshoots that would lead to storage rooms, bunkers, and outside access. When I am down there, I often think of the red ants back home in Texas. It might look like an innocent knob of dirt, but it is seething with an army prepared to fight to the death to protect the queen. The queen, just happened to be a king, named MacArthur. General McArthur moved his personal and military headquarters to Malinta. We got word that some of the troops on Bataan nicknamed him 'Dugout Doug' for that move. Only seems to make sense to me he would fortress up inside a rock. That's what red ants do, and they been around, I reckon, since the dinosaurs. I guess this is gonna be the island I told Miss Carvet I was gonna live on some day. Don't look like I will be seeing any hula girls for a while!

Because I could cook, a skill highly needed when you have over four-thousand men to feed, I became a part-time chow cook, a 'stew burner'. The Mess Hall was the place I was the most at home. You can make a lot of friends or enemies real quick like if you control the chow. I began to meet some of the guys and settled into my new life here.

Our training on this island was daily from 0600 hours, chow, to 1600 hours, for weapon clean-up. We were in physical training on an obstacle course outside most of the time. We marched, climbed over rocks, crawled on our bellies in and out of ground holes, and ran for miles. We were required to complete squat jumps, pull-ups, push-ups, and sit-ups. We also had to run three hundred yards in under a minute and ten seconds. At night, we read and memorized books containing the basic military general orders, conduct, terms, and all of the required drills. We learned uniform care and prepared for inspection. Some of the technical reading was hard for me with my sixth-grade reading level, but I got along by taking good notes. Most of the big words were the names of drills or weapons. Heck, we had a nickname for all of them! A lot of the guys were just like me, country kids who have scrapped to stay alive. We have lived through the Depression. We know how to do "without", and to be thankful when you "with"! "Hey, what's your name?" "Houston, Houston Lowe." I meet up with a few fellas and begin my life on the rock. We had a few ole mules on the island that helped us move supplies around. I was shore glad to see them! Just like my best girl, Waitus, back home, these ole mules pulled their weight around here. I got to know a couple of them as we were moving rations across the island. Their sure-footedness was the ticket for long-haul jobs on a craggy island.

Every day we practiced our assembly, cleaning, and utilization of our standard issue weapons. You never knew when an inspection would be ordered, or a new training procedure would be introduced. Sometimes in the middle of the night, we would be ushered out in our skivvies just to go stand out in the rain. Everything had a purpose I suppose. I guess we all needed a bit of discipline, and this would prepare us for the upcoming monsoon weather. One afternoon when we were just coming in from a hike, our sergeant came in. "Alright Swinging Dicks, line up! Now you are in full uniform and gear, just in case of a little water emergency; let me introduce you to Miss Mae!" The sergeant threw inflatable rubber life belts in a pile on the floor. "This is your own personal Mae West. In the event of a water evacuation, strap her on and grab on to her tits real tight! I guess there is no need for me to explain to you where this equipment gets its name from huh boys?! Ole gal will pull your ass straight out of the water!"

Private Dead Eye

Every day we went to the weapons qualification course with our 30 caliber carbine rifle. Thanks to my Daddy, I was a pretty clean shot. We took rotations on field and air targets and turned in our daily results. Every program had a 'master', and I wanted the rifle bad. Marksman Qualification Badges (MQBs), were especially sought after, and nobody wanted to be in third place. Country and farm kids depended on our shot to eat. If my shot was now gonna keep me and some other Joe alive, I wanna be the best at it. You gotta shoot and load in a set time. For an Expert, you gotta hit thirty-six out of forty targets. Some targets would be in the air, hidden in the ground, and some were human silhouettes. I go out with my regiment and set up for the daily targets. I hit thirty-three out of forty, day one. My sergeant says, "Damn son, you got a steady shot!" We continue in our daily routines building our skills and our bodies in preparation for an enemy attack. I practiced my shot, sometimes on my time off. Uncle Sam could afford the ammunition if it was gonna keep us alive, and I liked challenging myself to get better. Sometimes, they would fly a small plane with a flag behind it. The drill is designed for us to get used to shooting the big guns at a flying target. That is a lot harder than the rifle targets and I almost blowed the tail off one plane!!! After a week of field training, we moved to gas mask training and procedures. A new poisonous gas could be churned up out there. I was not ready to fight an invisible enemy. Seems all kinda evil to use a weapon against a man that you can't even see.

> "For we wrestle not against flesh and blood, but against principalities, against powers, against the rulers of the darkness of this world, against spiritual wickedness in high places." Ephesians 6:12

Master Rifleman

Chow 0600 – Flapjacks, sausage links, black coffee, eggs over-easy. I am nervous. The lists are going to be posted for each of the field requirements and the exams. I have had to take many tests that I did not know a lot of the words. Through the swinging doors of the mess hall, enters our sergeant, and time stops. "Alright ladies, the lists are up. Time to pull your skirts up and see what kind of soldier you are!" I slowly walk to the wall where each test is posted. Military General Orders – passed! "Thank you, Jesus!" I was most worried about that test cause it had the most reading and memorizing. "Whew," I was relieved. Physical training, Field marches– passed! Uniform Inspection – Passed. Weapons Assembly and Cleaning – passed. I slowly walked toward the sheet on Weapons Qualification. I could taste that badge. I take my finger and run it down the list looking for my name and serial number. There it is! Master Marksman! I got it! I am a Master Marksman in the Army Air Corps! I know my Daddy would have been so proud of me. I stop for a minute knowing I owe it all to him, and I can never tell him that.

I have completed my training, and I am in the best shape of my life. It is time for me to take this training to the dirt, and payback Uncle Sam for all the hospitality he has given me.

Betle Nuts

Sometimes for some 'R and R' time, we would go to the small villages around the area. There was always a little shack selling some fermented concoction of some kind. You can make hooch outta' bout anything that will rot. Roots, potatoes, yams, berries, coconuts, anything will do in a pinch. The local people have had centuries of recipes passed on to them, and they are known for some powerful firewater! Being in uniform got the locals' attention, especially the women. They loved American men. It didn't take long afore we would get approached about taking one on in the back room, or to be asked if we "wanted marry pretty young girl." Everyone was trying to get off this rock! We sit around in a little bamboo shanty and have a few shots of God knows what before we would wander off to check the area out around the village. We come across some little kids all in a circle just a whooping up a storm. Some are half-naked little boys and girls just having a great time. They must be playing some game for money, cause they are sure kickin' up some dust and raising their fists. The older kids are collecting coins as they are yelling over the ring of kids, barking like stock brokers. Across the middle of the circle on either side, two girls in little floral dresses are holding each end of a long bamboo stick. On each end, are these hairy looking, brown spiders. This is a local derby they play and bet on, kinda like cock fightin' back home. The owners of the spiders goad them along to get them to engage in 'legs to legs' combat in the middle. It is a blood sport of sorts. The locals call it *'pahibag sang damang'*. The younger kids hunt for the female spiders in the morning while they are out making their webs. The spiders slowly move toward each other as the kids are hollering out at them, and their handlers are coaching them along. Them spiders is mighty pissed! The faster of the two spiders clings to the bottom of the pole. She scurries underneath to the middle, clamping down, getting a big lethal bite on the other female right above her. Their bites are mighty poisonous and cause the losing spider to be paralyzed, and then quickly die. The kids all scream out, and coins are exchanged. The whole thing is over in no time. The crowd does hang around to pay respect to the losing handler and the spider. He wraps the spider up in some silk and a leaf, to carry her off for an appropriate warrior's burial. I hand the kid a dime for his loss as he turns and bows my way.

On our way back to base, a bunch of the old men are sitting around a fire pit cussing and laughing, just like back home. They smiled a big ole mule grin at us as we walked passed them. That's when we noticed they had no teeth, none of them! They was spitting some red stuff out that looked like blood. "Lordy, they must be powerful sick, got the T.B. I have seen that before back home, coughing up blood and all." Getting in a bit closer, I see they are chewing on something and spitting, like spitting tobacco back home. I see they have teeth; they are just in stages of brown, reddish-brown, or in the case of the oldest guy, black as coal. He smiles a big ole goofy grin showing all his black teeth and gums. He waves us over to offer us a chew of his plant. The locals know the troops are here to protect this island from invasion. They don't want to lose their homes and families, and they have a powerful regard for the 'Kawal', solider. Their sons are out here fighting right alongside us. He continues to raise and lower his hand and his head, offering the big nut-thing wrapped in a leaf, to me. I don't know a thing about these people, or this thing he is handing me, but I do know he is sharing a custom and offering his goods to me. You don't offend a man offering you some kindness and a tradition. I take it, nod my head to him, and put it in my mouth. It tastes plumb awful! My mouth started to tingle right away. After a while, I feel like I am ten feet tall and bulletproof. I have the energy of a bull calf in the springtime! Everyone is laughing as I pull back my fist to my waist, and raise my knee; signifying this is some strong stuff. The men around the fire think it is pretty funny that this tall drink of water has felt the effects! This little 'chaw' bundle is a local concoction they make up from a nut called the betel. The nut grows on some of the palm trees here. They chew it to get the 'high' of energy and stamina. It can sure take a headache away too. I am sure they must think it will put some lead in your pencil too! Most of the elderly men here chew it every day. Ole Black Teeth showed us how they mix in spices, tobacco, and lime, to mask the bitter flavor. We sit and laugh with these guys till after midnight when we have to wave off to our new friends and head on back to the base. I do know enough about plants to know, if they have been chewing that stuff long enough to blacken their teeth, it must have some powerful effects. Good God man! I didn't sleep a wink all night in my bunk!

Just a Good ole 'Joe'

I became quick friends with a guy named Joe Romanel. He was a short little man with a nose like a Roman statue. His big ole mouth of perfect white teeth lined up like headstones. We would sit sometimes and listen to the 'Voice of Freedom', a radio broadcast that played records and news. It was on the air about three times a day. We enjoyed getting to catch up. It was one of the few times it felt like home. Joe etched my name on top of my old aluminum mess kit. Some of the boys did that to pass the time, but Joe was the best at it. He had a special style. Guys would leave their names on pieces of paper with a number on it, and Joe would stack up the orders. He traded for cigarettes, hooch, or chocolate. Joe loved himself some chocolate! Joe was a funny little man, and we hit it off right away. Me and Joe used to have coffee together after breakfast. He was a hard working fella and needed to stay busy just like me. His people were from Sicily. He is from a long history of strong, loud Italians, who were all in the paper invitation and jewelry business back home. Joe told me that back over a century ago, all the major cities, especially in Europe, had people that their entire life's work was writing on documents, official certificates, and invitations. Imagine that! My people all use their hands and backs moving dirt in the sun, and his people all protect their hands, and stay at a lit desk all day writing! His father taught him, and his grandfather taught him. His great-great-grandfather, Lupito, started the family engraving business inscribing heirloom jewelry in a little cobblestone cellar. Joe had worked for his family's business since he could write. His family immigrated to America to find a better life, and bring the special craft there. Joe's handwriting was the prettiest I have ever seen. Guys would beg Joe to write their best girl love letters, cuz it looked like a store-bought card. Because his people all had beautifully scripted handwriting like those antique Bibles, they are highly sought after for events in his town and area. Joe just took that skill and turned it into scratching on mess kits!

The Water Cooler

On many days after cleaning and weapons inspection, I went out with some other guys to target practice. I needed to keep my sight aligned and my shot more fluid. Holding dead still for a squirrel shot or moving to hit a rabbit, I was able to keep my shot pretty clean. As time went by, I am positioned on a .50 caliber machine gun, known as the 'water cooler'. The 'water cooler' is M1921, one of the heavy machine guns stationed on the rock to protect from low-flying enemy aircraft. I switched between being a water operator and a gun operator. This weapon was an old out-dated gun, but she was still a fire-spittin' beast that could do a lot of damage ripping through her fabric belts at five-hundred rounds, in under a minute. She was a mighty dependable ole gal and pushed through the hours of rounds like an ox. I named her Bessie. The water operator poured water to keep the barrel cooled off while the belts were ripping through it. One of us would be pouring on the water and feeding in the belts, while the other operator would be scoping and firing. You pour that water on there too fast; it makes a mess of steam! Me and this Frenchman named Pacquin worked as a team. We ran drills and practice runs loading and unloading, and cleaning and assembling. We stored water buckets on the concrete base. At night, we would fall asleep leaning up against the gun. We are being prepared for long sessions outside.

December 7, 1941–Pearl Harbor is Attacked

We was just keeping up with what we had, trying to face what could be beyond us. We continued our practice runs and going to the village for a drink or two. We tried to play some cards or roll some bones to keep our wits about us and pass the time. "Paquin, what are the French dames like?" We hear they don't shave their pits or legs, and they smell like a week-old coal miner. You sure they are worth a roll in the sack?" Paquin spins around spitting as he responds, "You stupid Auhmeerecuns…you know nothing about zee womans. This aroma is like good wine." We all laugh at him

92

and make shaving our armpit motions at him. We go on about our business on this rock awaiting what we have all been trained to do.

General McArthur receives a radiogram at 0540 telling him we are officially at war with the Japanese. Precise as any professional chess match, the Japanese strike military target attacks on the island of Honolulu, Hawaii. During this two-hour battle, they struck right in the middle of the island, bombing Wheeler Field, before decimating Pearl Harbor. We lost over 2000 men and women and most of our naval fleet. The Arizona was a complete loss as she sunk dragging souls to the bottom of the harbor screaming. Men were banging metal cups on the walls and screaming as she slowly took in water and drowned them all. God rest their souls. We are under attack on our homeland. Never before in the history of this great nation has any enemy strike landed on the red, white, and blue stained soil. Clark Field is relentlessly bombed, wiping out all of Mac's aircraft.

December 29, 1941

Our very first bombing attacks began. We were as ready as anyone could be. We had been on high alert for a couple of weeks now since Pearl Harbor. We know this island better than anyone, and we have been in constant training. A giant "kaafoom" sound about a mile out is heard, as tails of smoke and dust are settling over us. A low-flying Jap plane is circling the island. "Slow your pour Pacquin, slow your pour!!!", I yelled. "You steam up this hole, and we all gonna get killed!!!!" I grab the handles and begin blasting. A couple of planes circle back. Pacquin and I prepare to fire, as they turn back and head away. Our first run was short, only lasting a few hours. During those few tense hours, we learned to rotate our roles and maneuver around each other, perfecting our timing. We slept on the cement tarmac and kept watch. I know these guys have more up their sleeves. They can't be done with Corregidor yet.

The Depraved Man's Buffet

After that and a few more diverted planes, I am promoted to Sergeant. My job with my brothers on the decking was to defend the hospital located in the tunnels dug out of the rock, deep below us. It was hot as hell around those guns. After a bit of toast and a cup of Joe, we started our morning routine. The Japanese were disciplined and patient. This discipline was their greatest strength, but it also became one of their most significant weaknesses. Their methodical schedule of patterns became easy for us to recognize. Our now, daily attacks, began each morning with one single reconnaissance plane. We all dubbed the pilot 'Photo Joe or The Lone Ranger'. He would loop the rock scheming up his next location for the rain of bombs, before returning to base. He circles us like a vulture after a dead coon on the road. The bastard was summing up the next map location for his next bombing mission. We felt like being some kinda porterhouse steak on a depraved man's buffet. We all knew someday we would be the B-15 on his twisted bingo card.

My back was strong to hold up those hundred-pound guns, but my eyesight was the perfect tool for scoping out those little bastard planes! I could see them a mile away just like the squirrels in the trees back home. "Two o'clock, two o' clock !!!!!!" I would be yelling over the commotion, while Pacquin poured water over the belts to cool down the gun. Steam was only one of the problems out here. You can't just jump out and run for water in the middle of being fired at either! Sometimes me and the boys around had to just piss in that evap can and jacket, just to get enough liquid to keep the gun cool. Your arms would be shaken to sleep most times. Couldn't even open and close your own hands after an attack. Sometimes, when we would be called to the gun stations, ole Pacquin would be MIA. He was off hiding in the rock somewhere, and the enemy would be closing in. I cranked Bessie up and let the gun belts rip. I was so mad at Pacquin and even more at the Japs vulture-circling overhead, I just fired away pissing on that evap can and screaming, "Come on you little bastards, I'm gonna send you straight to Hell wearing gasoline drawers!"

The bombings continued to rain on us. The Japs were relentless. The loaded belts would just rattle off shell casings like firecrackers. The level of noise was unbearable. I thought my skull was gonna explode. You can't hear anything, dirt in your eyes and mouth, and hot shell casings are jumping like frogs on a hot river rock in summer. Sometimes casings would land on your pants and burn a hole right through. Japs would come raining in, dropping bombs, blowing up that ole rock like dynamite to limestone. I'm gonna die hanging on to this gun! Sonny boy gonna die, I thought. It was late March. Sometimes we had passing typhoons that brought days of torrential, relentless rain. You never know what your mind can do to you till you are forced to live outside in a mud-filled, sandbagged trench, with pelting rain on you for days at a time. We were soaked to the bone, sitting in a soup bowl of mud, sweat, and excrement. We couldn't leave to relieve ourselves. We just stayed right there in that muck, holding that gun belt, waiting for the next round of Japs to come our way. They came, and they came like waves of nausea. Bombs were dropping all around, and we are shooting through every belt we had, the whole nine yards of em! As I am manning this gun, I am praying, praying hard. My prayers were the ones my Mama rained on me over and over, from the book of Psalms... I could hear her voice, so I just repeated her words..."*I run to you, Lord, asking for your wings of protection. Come to my rescue. Hear my prayer and keep me safe. You are my mighty rock, and in You, I will trust.*"

> "*The LORD is good, a stronghold in the day of trouble;
> and He knows those who trust in Him.*" Nahum 1:7

Miracle Five—Direct Hit to the Helmet and Six Day Coma

The aerial bombardment of Corregidor usually happened during the day where they could see us like purple-top turnips in the field. But the Japanese were like yard dogs on a meat bone to finally take the Rock. Finally, they switched their approach to bombing us at night. So now, whatever small bit of peace we sucked from a hot cup of Joe and cigarette at night, was broken. The very moonlight we brewed and ran 'shine under, stole a smooch from our sweethearts under, and chased fireflies through, was gonna be the light that hollered down the pathways of deadly bombs. Just like we held a kerosene burning rag stick over the water to draw out the perch and crappy in the creeks, we flashed up our huge searchlights to illuminate those planes before they could accurately release their bombs. It looks like it confused those Jap pilots seeing all those lights. They turned away to approach from another direction, or just left altogether. We didn't see them at night anymore, and that frightened us.

The sounds were deafening. Bombs were blasting this rock to pieces and bodies began to stack up. Pouring water, wiping sweat from my mud-filled eyes, the muddy decking turned red then white. I thought the whole island exploded and was about to sink into Manila Bay. The sky was red with intense white light and puffs of grey smoke. Shrapnel parts, dirt, rocks, and hot metal were spraying us from every side. "She's gonna jam; she's gonna jam!" We are throwing out hot metal, rocks, and twisted steel. A bomb blasts away most of the platform shaking the foundation, and spraying us with hot cement and steel. Debris is covering us as we spit on our hands to clear our eyes. Clearing the area around Bessie, I threw out a big chunk. It is a leg, severed just below the knee, with the boot still on. I had to clear the gun that was protecting us. I hear the loudest of bombs and then "katow", I hear the horrible sound of my skull crack. My head was violently thrown back and hit the broken cement surrounding me.

Miracle Six–The Light

"Mama, those are the prettiest yellow roses I ever saw." "Do you like them Sonny Boy? Jesus has these in his garden you know." Things seemed different between Mama and me. I would talk to her, but she couldn't hear me. I know she couldn't. I was a real inquisitive little boy, and I asked her a hundred questions a day. She always answered me. Well, she almost always answered me. When she got tired of all my questions, she would say, "Because Jesus says so, that's why!" Most Mamas, said, "because I said so, that's why." Not my Mama, Jesus always had the last word in her house. She would reach to hug me, and I would just disappear like a cloud of dust after she beat a rug. She would start praying again right there before me. " I am right here Mama. I can hear you. Can you hear me????" "To you, O Lord, I offer my fervent prayer.

In my God, I will trust". "Mama, Mama, I am here." "Shhhh, sit Sonny Boy, whilst I hang these sheets. I see a red sky and a deep black hole filled with water. It looks like the womb of a woman in travail. Mens are being killed in their Mama's womb. Guns are shooting fast. Not like your Daddy's gun, with a one-shot chance to feed your family. The sky is black, filled with locusts. They are destroying everything. He is my refuge and my fortress; My God, in Him I will trust. He is my refuge and my fortress; My God, in Him I will trust. He is my refuge and my fortress; My God, in Him I will trust." "Mama, Mama!" I am screaming at her, but she isn't listening. She is still praying, "Surely He shall deliver you from the snare of the evil one. Cover him with Your mighty wings, Lord. Shield him from harm, my Sonny Boy. No evil will cover you. I pray a holy hedge of protection over you. I am circling the walls of Jericho for you." Now she is marching, talking to Jesus. It must be something fierce she is wrestling with. Mama doesn't walk the walls of Jericho praying unless it is.

I ran through the fields of dandelions making the flowers burst into snowfall and butterflies scatter like little pilots on a mission. I was tired, and my head hurt. I laid down out there in the field crying, asking for Daddy to come get me. I had a big ole swollen, purple eye. Daddy wasn't answering me. He was just talking to himself. "One thing they cannot take away, Houston. You gotta hand it to em yourself, your honor." I didn't want Mama to see me this way. She always told me to be a big boy, and always take care of my family. Daddy was fussing cuz he didn't want to go to church, and my Aunt Gracie was making us late. She was looking for her stocking. It was nowhere to be found in that tidy little house. Women didn't go in public without their stockings. It could have been my dad's escape from church. Right about then, Smartie came running around the kitchen door with it in his mouth. My Mama said, "Praise Jesus, Halleluiah." My Daddy said, "you better praise the dog, he found your stocking!"

I just laid there in that field with the sun beating down on me. I was thirsty, so thirsty. I couldn't open my mouth for all the cotton inside. I felt my heart beat slow down. I counted the beats, kathunk, kathunk,.....kathunk. My tears were like hot lye water pouring down my face. I rolled over and grabbed my knees, and drew them up to my chest. Why was it so bright outside today? The sun was piercing through my eyes. My head was reeling like I took some big swigs of Odell's moonshine. I can't remember why I am out in this field. What happened to the house and going to church? Where is Aunt Gracie?

"Houston, Houston." "Shhhhh, shhhh! Where we gonna find some hooch, Odell? This town is tied up like a slip knot, and we ain't got ten-cents between us." "You come behind me. Keep on up in this clearance here." The moon was shining down between the trees like daylight in that clearing. Odell stood in the shadow behind the big mesquite tree. He picked up some pebbles and started throwing one at a time. "Shit, I don't know where they are! Shit!" He throwed a couple more and then, tink! "Houston, run out there where you heard that sound, and start digging." "What the hell, Odell! Have you flipped your damn, turnip wagon!" "Go, go, 'fore we get caught out here in these woods." I took a little stick and scratched off just a little dirt. And there she was, the silver medallion of home-brewed corn shine! I pulled out the Mason jar wrapped in newspaper buried below. It is filled to the brim with clear corn elixir. It can make you happy as a horse in May, and as stupid as a mule in June! Me and Odell, sitting under the moon that gave this liquid fire its name, are laughing and acting stupid, and smoking rollies. I lay down and look up. The moon turns a bright white, just like lightning. It keeps getting bigger and bigger. Pretty soon, it just takes over the night sky.

I can hear my heart beats, my breaths as they are slowly becoming more distant. I am tired. I see why the light is so bright. Just like Mama said it would be someday, it is Jesus. He is beautiful. His hair is like the colors of an oil slick. His eyes are piercing, and so full of love. He has golden sandals on his feet, and his robes look like fresh sheets on a summer day. He is reaching out his hands to me. Bright yellow rays of the sun are piercing through the holes in his palms. He keeps floating away disappearing in and out of the silver clouds. I wipe my eyes to see him better. Once I finally got a good look, I see that he looks at me just like Mama does. Mama is on her knees praying. "Now through the power of your cross

Lord Jesus, I pray that Sonny resists all forms of sin, sickness, and disease. This is not God's good and perfect will for his life, and I pray the power of the cross upon him right now. By the shed blood of the Lord Jesus Christ, I command all forms of sickness and disease to leave his presence immediately. By Your stripes, he has been healed of his infirmities. He has been ransomed and redeemed, sanctified and set free. Lord Jesus. Amen." Nora Pace Lowe, 1941.

> *"Then they cried to the LORD in their trouble, and he saved them from their distress. He sent out his word and healed them; he rescued them from the grave. Let them give thanks to the LORD for his unfailing love and his wonderful deeds for mankind." Psalms107:19-21*

I wake up vomiting all over my hospital gown. I felt like my head was gonna blow off my neck. The room was blurry and dark. I couldn't hear much. People were talking, but I could only see their lips moving. Their faces were hazy, and it looked like I was seeing everything through a dirty Mason jar. They kept yelling louder, but I couldn't hear a word. It was like being high on moonshine. People's faces look like balloons floating around, and everything seems funny. "Sergeant Lowe! Sergeant Lowe, wake up can you hear me?" I hear a very faint voice, that sounded like an angel. She was all in white, but she was no angel. It was a nurse. "Sergeant Lowe, you have been in a coma for six days." "How are you feeling?" "Well, with my fingers, how 'bout you?" She laughed. That sweet angel of mercy laughed. I have a five-inch gash in my head, matching the five-inch dent in my M1 helmet she was waving in my face. My eyes are blood red and half swollen shut. Black and blue bruises are covering my face. It could have been much worse. Thank God for that helmet! We were issued the new M1 helmet cuz the old Kelly helmet was retired, making way for this new 'steel pot' model. It is constructed from one piece of manganese steel. That helmet saved my life that day. Well, besides the hard head I got from my Daddy, and the holy hedge of protection prayed over me by my Mama.

> *"The earnest prayer of a righteous person has great power and produces wonderful results." James 5:16*

Spoils of War

It was not uncommon for Mac to come through the hospital and leave the well-earned Purple Heart on the chests of the gravely wounded and dead. I guess it was kinda his way of personalizing the sacrifices we all were making. Some ole guy in the hospital bed next to me told me that he left one on me while I was in the deepest of my sleep. I don't know about that, but I do know it was gone when I woke up six days later. Spoils of war, I'm guessing. Spoils of war!

I found out the bombing had ceased for about ten days, during most of that time; I was in the deepest of sleep. Somehow, the rock had not received significant damage. For how wars add up bodies, we had very few casualties. Mostly this was due to the months we had to prepare, and the skills of our superiors. Now, all Japanese eyes were focused on Bataan, as they are strategically preparing for the final beating. Corregidor licked her wounds, and we set camp back up trying to keep things normal. At least for now, the rock and her sister fortresses were given a breather. The hospital took care of the wounded, and I eventually returned to my solace, my beloved kitchen. I cooked up a mess of mashed potatoes and beans for all us. You gotta keep stomachs warm and filled to give you the guts to crawl back in that hole. It seemed like years, but it was about ten days, that we waited and prepared, cleaned our guns, and threw out debris.

The Starvation Begins

Soon, American rations are being intercepted by the Jap ships surrounding the island. They was having a grand ole time out there eating on the tab of Uncle Sam. Pissed me off fiercely! While we was moving from hash to caribou, and then on to grubs and pigweed; they was eating our rations and treating their men with our medicines and supplies. Days ground on as the food supply dwindled. Some of us were going on down to the waterfront off the slippery rocks, hunting for any little creature we might be able to suck out of their shell. Climbing around the rocks is the first time we began to notice that our muscles are beginning to weaken.

March 11, 1942

In early March, we all heard that Roosevelt had told MacArthur he needed to get himself and his family off this ole rock. That's when we knew then we were in trouble. We had been struggling for some time now to hold off the takeover. We were gonna fight till the last man was standing if we had to, but precious, life-sustaining supplies are constantly being intercepted by the Japs. We couldn't get supplies or troops by them without too many causalities. We were growing weaker, while they were getting stronger on our rations. Pretty soon, we was eating anything we could find, rats, grubs, snails, and roots. We was glad to get any of it. I turned to digging grasses and forging for local plants. It is just too dangerous to get near the water edge now, too many Japs close by. I watched as we began the painful transition from servicemen to hungry survivors. Our issued uniforms begin to sag, and our belts are cinched up tight. Ole' Mac was asked to take a sub off the island, but he refused. I think he just didn't want to slink off the rock under the water, like a lowly Cotton Mouth. He was going out as we all first came in, on a PT. I, along with many others, went off to salute him and say goodbye. We all hoped it would not be our final goodbye. I heard the bthhhh, bthhhhh, bthhhhh, of the boat motor carrying him quickly away from the shore. Off in the distance, that was the loneliest sound I ever heard. It sounded ghostly, just like a coyote call on a hot, dry night. We were waving goodbye to our king. There was no telling who we would be saying hello to.

> *"He controls the course of world events; he removes kings and sets up other kings. He gives wisdom to the wise and knowledge to the scholars." Daniel 2:21*

General Wainwright began the process of scraping up what was left of Corregidor as the Japanese army begin their hot pursuit of the Bataan Peninsula. We are grateful for any intermissions in this horrible movie show, but we are deathly concerned about our troops on Bataan. We thought about our boys down there at the tip of that peninsula, fighting mano y mano in those hot, torrid Filipino jungles. Recon reports told us it was a horrific, bloody, and torturous, jungle battle. Most of our boys were already sick with dysentery or malaria. When they took to the march, they were puking in the cart trenches and falling in. The Japs took our boys over and treated them worse than a swine for butchering. They skewered some of them for no reason at all. They were stacking bodies up like cordwood in blood-filled cart trenches. Countless American and allied corpse are thrown away like garbage, strewn along the dirt roads. The remaining ones that were still alive took that long, horrible walk; the *Death March*. Boys 'ferred to it as 'The Hike'. Word got to us all from the 'bamboo telegraph', about the brutality and inhumane treatment. Boys were being skewered and filleted open like channel cats. They were sometimes taking every third man or so, and just stabbing their sides for no reason. They marched those poor boys to death. With no water and no breaks, they marched for miles in the wet, 100-degree jungle heat. As they were throwing up from dehydration, they couldn't stop to finish. They had to continue on marching, throwing up and pissing themselves to keep from being skewered with a bayonet or Samurai sword. Dengue fever was taking them down. Japs got no care at all, as these jungle diseases are taking them one by one. Their joints and muscles are seizing up on them, their heads are exploding in pain; and they are running fevers of 102, plus. Boys would stop to vomit and they would either kick them in a puke-filled trench stomping on them or just give em a bayonet in the gut. Sometimes guts would be spilling out of guys, and they would be trying to catch them as they fell to the jungle floor, dead. Blood would be coming out of their gums and mouths and their nose. The diseases are ravishing their bodies. They just don't have a chance out there. Those boys got a blade in the gut for not following orders. They were willing to comply, but their bodies are so sick, they just couldn't. Hearing about all the diseases and suffering going on there was awful.

The Final Assault

The next round of bombings started around May 1, 1942. Corregidor was taking a constant pounding by the Japanese. They weren't gonna stop till the whole island is reduced to powder. Day and night we were being bombed and shelled. The Japs came at us with the ferocity of a junk dog lunging off a chain. They had a special celebration of the Emperor's birthday. The fireworks were the extra bombs on Corregidor. They were not going to let the Emperor's birthday go without a few more casualties. All the remaining animals on the island were not able to take the constant shaking, bomb blasts; and the sounds of enemy warfare. You would find field mice and rabbits lying dead around the compound. The mules took it poorly too. All three of them were found dead on pathways. They just dropped in their tracks where they stood and died. Poor ole things. No matter how steady they can be in times of great distress, they can't take the trauma of these horrible sounds and vibrations. Some were dragged on up to be used for meat to feed us. No matter what happens to me, I can make myself eat anything if I have to. I just could not take a bite of mule.

Tons of explosives were dropped, turning this tropical island into hundreds of burning caldrons. Plumes of fire, ash, and smoke, filled the air. Your eyes would water, and you would be choking to catch your breath. Swallowing ash and cleaning smut from our eyes, we held up. We traded places on the remaining working guns, keeping the freshest arms on the mount. It was clear we could not hold out much longer. Ole Corregidor was like a weakened old dragon. She was belching out her last breath of hot ash and putrid gas, as she slowly melted into the molten rock. The air was thick. The darkening sky cloaked the evil behind a curtain of ash and smoke. It was ominous. It felt like the basement in Hell itself.

"And he opened the bottomless pit; and there arose a smoke out of the pit, as the smoke of a great furnace;

*and the sun and the air were darkened by reason of
the smoke of the pit." Revelation 9:2*

It is enough to make you go mad. We was all waiting out a for-gone fate. Around May 4, it was the worst attack of all. Every few minutes, thousands of shells hit the island as massive explosions sprayed dirt, hot ash, and rocks. Dirt was relentlessly flying in our faces while the deafening bomb blasts were causing ringing in the ears so badly, men are beginning to get 'the stare'. The blaze of bomb cast and the stench of burning sulfur filled the dense air and the tunnels below. We all kept our locations with our machine guns and held up until they were destroyed or could no longer function. We knew we were out of the fight when that happened. When we no longer could keep Corregidor protected, we moved to the tunnels below. We take our places along the corridors. Some guys are just sitting, and others are rocking silently. The officers were preparing for a take-over in the tunnel. If we were gonna get taken in, they sure weren't gonna leave all our classified maps and war strategies laying around for the taking. Soon they began the process of tearing up documents and burning them in the bomb fires. All the equipment is smashed, destroying the chances of any codes, Intel, or radio equipment, get-ting intercepted. I would be lying if I didn't tell you, I am pretty scared too. I am sure we all are. We are on an island surrounded by the Japanese, covered in soot and ash, and weakened from hunger and dysentery. We all foresaw the next chapter for us would come soon; we just didn't talk about it. The Japs slowly weakened us by taking our supplies, food, and weapons. When a man can't hold up a rifle or manage the jerks and bolts of an inoperative machine gun, you just can't defend against a relentless enemy. I close my eyes and think of the many who have faced these fears before me.

*"O our God, will You not judge them? For we are
powerless before this great multitude who are
coming against us; nor do we know what to do, but
our eyes are on You." 2 Chronicles 20:12*

'The Water Cooler' – Marine at Browning .50 – cal (12,7 mm), water-cooled antiaircraft machine gun – Guadalcanal 1942, Retrieved from: https://www.worldwarphotos.info/gallery/usa/pacific/guadalcanal/ guadalcanal-marine-at-50-cal-anti-aircraft-mg-1942/

Chapter Five

My Captivity

Miracle Seven–Captured May 6, 1942–Surrender Without Death

The Last Supper

Around noon, General Wainwright contacted President Roosevelt, notifying him that he would be surrendering Corregidor. With no supplies, broken armaments, and sickly ground troops, he was losing the battle to defend her any longer. The beautiful American flag is slowly lowered as it is replaced with the white flag of surrender. The island is decimated, and the bombing finally ceases. The stillness was bone-chilling. We know what is happening up top. All of us nerve-fatigued, disheveled, and exhausted men, are sitting in the tunnel in a glazed stare. The quartermaster, who oversaw all of the sleeping quarters and food supplies, had held back a few rations for a case like this one. He opened up the pantry and stock rooms for the taking. We all lined the tunnel halls and bunk rooms with our backs to the wall. We sat silently opening cans and eating what was left in our meager rations. It was a very somber meal. No one said a word. Some men just couldn't take a bite. There is a cumbrous void in that tunnel. It pulled at your very being. It felt like we are suspended in a grisly nightmare. I am asking God to spare us. We fought so hard to keep old glory flying. I didn't know if anyone could take it if the Japanese flag ever flew overhead. As hungry as we all are, the food didn't satisfy. We ate what we could, and tried to hide what we could; for God knows what lies ahead. I stared at the paint-chipped, white cement wall in front of me. I tried to calm the fear and millions of thoughts in my head that were whirling like a combine tractor threshing wheat. I felt the anxiety well up, tightening my chest, and causing a lump in my throat. My anxiety built up to raging anger. "Come on you bastards! Get down here and come take us, you damn chicken shits!", I yelled. My voice echoed, bouncing through the tunnel walls. Men are writing notes to home. Some are staring with a still glare, like a porcelain china doll. Some were humming or rocking. Sitting there, we are cottontail rabbits in a hollow log with a coyote on the other end. It is the predator-prey death stare-down. We all felt it, but we knew we had no place to run. Before the panic overcomes me, I prayed quietly – "*Dear Lord, give me the strength to go to battle. Put us under the wings of protection and care. Help see us through another day. Amen.*"

> "*Moreover, no one knows when their hour will come: As fish are caught in a cruel net, or birds are taken in a snare, so people are trapped by evil times that fall unexpectedly upon them.*" *Ecclesiastes 9:12*

First Step on the Wicked Staircase

Pretty soon they did reach us. The suffocating silence is broken with the clattering sound of rifles and bayonets. Steel swords are clanging and scraping along the cement walls. Leather boots pounded the stairs in an organized and haunting cadence. The sounds become louder and louder as they advance toward us in the tunnel. The echo of their boots ricocheted off the walls, and their voices filled the tunnel. In precision speed and accuracy, a swarm of Japanese soldiers waving rifles and shooting off rounds, filled the tunnels and broken rubble, of what is left of Corregidor. They are hustling people in lines, in our faces yelling, and forcing us against the walls. Guys skulls were cracking from the force against the cement walls. The Japanese ground troops had stormed in from the shoreline to find us. Their pants legs and boots are covered in black oil, probably from all the sunken battleships surrounding us. "Te o agemasu!!, Te o agemasu!!,|Raise hands!, Raise hands!| Raising my hands in surrender along with these boys, was the barest naked I have ever felt. The good Lord has seen me stripped down before, but I have never been this exposed. I had never seen anyone from Japan before. They was little bitty fellows, heads about up to my chest, and little squinty eyes. Not a one of them was over about five feet. All of them were about the size of my Mama. Most of us guys just towered over them, and it was clear they did not like it. If I could fight them one at a time, I could take 'em all. Daddy taught me how to protect myself from whiney Mama's boys! That's what they were like. They are just a bunch of Mama's boys hiding behind the flowing, red silk skirts, of their Emperor. They looked at us like we was lowly snakes. They spat at us and laughed, as they used their bayonets to herd us along. As far as I could see, we was just like them. We are all soldiers fighting for our countries and all. But they did not see it that way. A few of their guys brought in the big American flag that was flying over the compound. One guy yelled some profanity at us, as they all stood there spitting and stomping on the flag right before us. "You coward! You coward, dick shit! "You country and you commander leave you here to die!", he yelled. It tore me up real good to have that flag destroyed and disrespected. I had to remain in control. It was a mind game, a chess match in will and discipline. "Get in line flyboy!" A few guys took a hard rifle butt to the face for taking too long. Faces would be dripping with blood as teeth spilled out on the floor. They took their time threatening each of us and making sure we knew we were their property now. They were right in our faces yelling, pulling on our clothes, grabbing any body part of their choosin'. The would pull our faces within inches of them and just stare at us. They are testing us. We all lined up against the tunnel walls as we were 'inspected'. The quarters were all checked and stripped of any usable goods. They are mightily pissed when they see all the broken equipment and destroyed files. A few boys near the office areas took a beating for it. They left us all in a squatting position, backs against the wall, with our hands interlocked over our heads. They rummage through the place like wild boars. My muscles are beginning to burn, and my thighs are quivering from the pressure. I will be damned before I will show it on my face! It was getting hot in the tunnel, and some guys were beginning to pass out. They shot those guys to death right there in that tunnel. This is the first step on the wicked staircase of lessons we had to crawl up to beloved freedom.

> *"Be strong and courageous; do not be afraid nor dismayed before the king of Assyria, nor before all the multitude that is with him; for there are more with us than with him. With him is an arm of flesh; but with us is the Lord our God, to help us and to fight our battles." 2 Chronicles 32:7*

'Bushido'

Their culture ran deep below the surface, and for centuries before us. America is just a young buck compared to this empire. They considered us a bunch of yella-bellied cowards. Back to the days of the Samurai, they have held a code deep inside them about honor and shame. It is burned so deeply in them boys; they would rather die on their sword than to shame their country or be taken prisoner like us. They called it *Bushido*. It means that no matter what happened to them, they would end their life before going home a coward, or surrendering. In America, our soldiers are built on courage, hard work, precise training, a respect for the chain of command, and a love of country. Japanese soldiers work through a fierce and brutal training system. Soldiers are physically beaten, and honor is above everything. Beating us, well, it was just seen as a form of discipline like any Japanese soldier would receive. 'Cept, we was just the scum off the pond to them. Raising our hands meant we dishonored our country too. They saw us as their captives, not prisoners. So, I guess, if we are held 'captive', and not a prisoner, because of our lowly status, they could do what they wanted. When a man has beliefs that deeply rooted, they can do a lot of good, or they can do a hell of a lot of evil. After Corregidor fell, Wainwright summed our final score in three categories: there were around eight-hundred dead, one thousand wounded, and eleven-thousand captured. I was behind bamboo curtain number three.

The Brutality Begins – Twenty-One Days on Corregidor

Many of the Japanese guards they brought in were patients from the psychiatric wards of hospitals, and inmates from the prison system. It is pretty ingenious. The Japs get the guards they need, and they clear their prisons and hospitals for space. Placed in power over us, enforcing a brutal, at-will, code of conduct, were guards, many of whom were criminally insane. The 'Rock' was our home. Our meetings were once held here. Our bellies were filled here. Now, our tunnels, bunks, and buildings, are gathering places for the Japanese. They overran the barracks, the hospital, and the mess hall. They were everywhere. They begin first by taking all of our remaining supplies. They began to strip us, tying some of us to posts at the base gate. The Filipinos who had helped us and passed bits of food along to us as they waved American flags at us are now forced to beat some of us across the face with boards. The Japanese were establishing us as enemy number one to everyone. Command Alpha, the Japanese, established their authority over us and began the first steps to strip away our humanity. Our courage is already disintegrated, and our dignity is about to crawl out on its belly, not far behind. They began our training by slapping a few of us hard, right in the face, for no reason. We was already weak. It didn't take much to put us right on the ground. They didn't care if you were a Lieutenant or a Private. You was in your skivvies, standing at attention in the sun, being slapped or stripped of your stuff and your dignity, equally. I had never seen a superior officer vulnerable. I have great respect for our officers. They are fine military men who keep us well trained. It boiled my blood to see them disrespect our leaders. Now, they reduce us all to lowly equals trying not to anger a common enemy. We are desperate to live another day. They line us all up as they check our heads, our mouths, and our teeth. I'm guessing they was looking for our age like a horse or seeing if we was healthy. They are forcing our heads back and shoving pens in our mouths, slapping our faces when they finish. One poor ole guy had a mouth full of gold crowns. They took some pliers out of a toolbox. One guard threw him down and stepped on his neck. The other guard just yanked his teeth right out by the roots. He is screaming in agony as blood is flowing from his mouth and spilling on to the ground. The guard yanks him up popping his arm out of the socket, as he forces him back in the line. Standing in our army-issued khaki skivvies, they rifled through our uniforms and coats, taking everything we had of any personal or financial value, first. "Watasu! Watasu!!!", [Hand over! Hand over!] First, went our photographs, letters, rings, and necklaces; stripping us of our family and emotional support ties. Then they took pens, lighters, toothbrushes, toothpaste, soap, deodorant, blankets, knives, and any of our rollies, chaw, or tobacco; stripping us of our comforts. They took my onyx and gold pinky ring first. These bastards have no idea what that ring symbolized. They continued to realign us, shoving the butts of guns in our faces, breaking noses and cracking jaws. The pain of these physical wounds is excruciating, but nothing is as painful as the psychological wounds from standing there as they spat and laughed at us and our country.

We lost our unique personhood that day on Corregidor. We forfeited any and all semblance of our humanity. Anything that was left after that inspection raid is not worth taking. Once it is over, we have nothing but our eerie shadows, our army-issued canteens, and our mess kits. Now, we are nothing more than a number, written in a long and blood-stained, rice paper log. My number carved in a bamboo dog tag may be 868.. [八百六十八, Happyaku rokujū hachi], but my name, Houston, is still a child of God; written in the Lamb's book of Life.

> *"Notwithstanding in this rejoice not, that the spirits are subject unto you; but rather rejoice, because your names are written in heaven." Luke 10:20.*

868 [Happyaku rokujū hachi], became my call name. They spoke the words so fast, it always sounded like "aku onno bahn" to me. That is the only way I could ever say it. As soon as we were issued our number, other than an assortment of derogatory names

and curse words, that is the only way we were addressed in camp. Being reduced to a number is humiliating. Ranch cattle have brands and numbers; people have names. They didn't want us associating with our Filipino buddies either. That might make the numbers in our favor, and these boys know this place too well. They wanted all of us to be enemies. Allies do not exist in prison. It is clear; this island is no longer ours. There would be no more sleeping on our beloved bunks, where pictures of our girls are clipped on the springs above. They took over the comfortable barracks and put us out on the broken rubble of the remaining cement tarmac. We were shoved down on the cold cement where we slept out in the open air for a few hours each night. We were left outside with no enclosures, no medical treatment, with no luxury items like mats, blankets, or pillows. Bugs were crawling over us and mosquitoes were eating us alive. Talking was forbidden. They couldn't understand us, and we could be cooking up some scheme to take them over. Intimidation is their first carving tool for the brain. Guards are always walking by, kicking or stabbing legs that roll out of the area they designated as sleeping space. You can't talk, and you surely can't sleep either. Strangely enough, as I was lying there, I was looking at the vast sky of twinkling stars, knowing that somewhere, thousands of miles away, Mama was sharing the same view. When all you have is yourself, and you are in a corner with an enemy, it is hard to focus on the beauty of the night sky. I found a way; I had to. I always thought the night sky was just coal black. But in that vast canopy of distant, murky, blackness, colors like purple, blue, and grey painted the very floorboards of heaven. The millions of diamond-bright stars twinkled in and out becoming dim and then piercing the canopy to bright white. I pondered how vast the universe was and what could make a man evil. I wondered how God could have just flung those stars out there, making such a beautiful shimmering blanket to protect us at night. I nod off for a few minutes out of pure exhaustion.

> *"You alone are the LORD You have made the heavens,*
> *The heaven of heavens with all their host, The earth*
> *and all that is on it, The seas and all that is in them*

You give life to all of them And the heavenly host bows down before You." Nehemiah 9:6

We are all put to work the next day. The first duty assignment was to cut firewood and carry it on our backs to distribute to the guards quarters and kitchen. We worked hours chopping wood in the heat and carrying the heavy loads to stack in piles. A few days later, my work detail is changed to dragging the battle dead off to a hole, and burning their corpses. The guard calls my number, "Hey, Happyaku rokujū hachi, [868], you, stupid, you go! He points me to the death pile. There are plenty of fresh and rotting corpses from the bombing and the beatings we took. After lugging the bodies to trench carts and loading them up, I had to bring them to the 'pit'. The inferno smelled like the dead animal carcasses we used to burn up to keep the coyotes away. It was awful. Guys are slung over each other in stacks like used-up burlap sacks. Their bloated, disfigured, naked bodies were all thrown on top of each other. Frozen, distorted, masks for faces, stared back at you with haunting, white, eyes. The Japs made us strip off all their clothes, shoes, and belts, to use. All of their valuables and weapons were collected. They are naked as they came in this world, robbed of any remaining dignity they may have left. I cover them up as soon as I can.

"The songs of the temple shall become wailings in that day," declares the Lord God. "So many dead bodies!" "They are thrown everywhere!" Amos 8:3

One thing for sure, you can't get the smell of death and burning flesh off you. It was in my mouth and on my hands. The putrid smell was in my hair and clothes, making me puke when I put my hands to my face. After a long, exhausting day of death duty, I have a front seat ticket to a horrific silent movie show of stacking bodies and building make-shift crematoriums. None of the guys wanted to sleep near me because of the smell. On the concrete, I learned how to catch a few winks. But it would soon be interrupted with my gasping and scuffling up on my hands and knees. "Hey get down, get down!" I would be rubbing my eyes trying to scrape the horrible scene away. Bodies stacked in piles would be laying all around me on the cement tarmac. In my slumber, I am hopelessly lost between sleep and wake. Desperate, I slap my face trying to forget thinking I woke up from this nightmare, only after throwing a live man in as he screamed for his life. I think about those guys and their dolls back home. Some would have been doctors, and engineers, and intelligence officers. They would go home, marry their sweethearts, and have a quiver full of kids. I helped the Japs burn that all up. Now they are just ashes. I never got over this duty. I know that many times in my life, this grisly movie will be replayed in my head like a broken reel to reel.

"You will not fear the terror of the night, nor the arrow that flies by day." Psalm 91:5

We are forever being moved from duty to duty. An evil job interview and assessment is taking place daily. Once the battle-dead bodies were taken care of, I along with many other men, had the humiliating task of loading U. S. supplies on Japanese transport ships. We carried tons of canned fruit, meat, milk, soup, and soap. We also loaded life-saving medicines on their ships, only to stand by and watch as all those critical supplies are going off to strengthen the Japanese.

A few guys had hidden some C-rations around the area. We could sneak a few bites now and then, to help keep us strong enough to work the twelve-hour days. One day, I am out getting supplies to load off the docks. Camouflaged in the dense jungle brush, along the pathway, is Ole Black Teeth. His body is painted in jungle mud, and he has tied palm leaves around his body, arms, and legs. He pushes a small bread-like roll in my left hand and disappears. He was hiding right there in plain sight, and nobody saw or heard him. This is how the local villagers did their jungle recon. I swear, I think he just folded himself up like a Sunday kerchief under there, and he was gone. I shoved the bread into my pants and kept loading. Alone that night on the tarmac, I ate it face down, off of the cement. Ole Black Teeth was my angel that day, and I sure was grateful.

*"Be not forgetful to entertain strangers: for
thereby some have entertained angels unawares."
Hebrews 13:2*

We are getting beaten every day now. As more and more guys
are dropping dead, they find new ways to inflict punishment. Day
and night we are interrogated. They continue to ask us about what
we know and slammed a gun butt to the face if they thought information is being withheld. The metallic, salty, taste of warm blood
in your mouth became our routine. For food, we were given a small
bowl of rice soup, twice a day. As a little more of your body ebbed
away, a feeling of aloneness could suffocate you. It could take you
to dark places. Being lonely and feeling alone, are universes apart.
Feeling all alone in the universe with no one to save you, drowns
all hope. You slowly slip into an abyss of desperation. The fear
and panic consume you. I noticed that our younger boys had it the
hardest with this. They were just wet behind the ears, trying to steal
their first kiss, six short months ago. We lost a lot of these young
boys who just slipped away, falling into death's basement.

*"For we are strangers before thee, and sojourners, as
all our fathers: our days on the earth are as a shadow,
and there is no hope of life." 1 Chronicles 29:15*

We had some access to water for our canteens. The food continued to be meager at best. Some guys just couldn't make themselves eat rotting food. They didn't make it long after that. I ate
everything I could. I figure, if I can eat possum guts, I can eat just
about anything. Being poor is good training for being a prisoner.
As each day passed, the cruelty of the Japs got more unpredictable.
Sometimes, just for looking wrong, the Japs would skewer some
ole guy. They were quite skilled with their swords and could slice
through some flesh that you could stick your hand through. They
had such precision; they could cut a skin flap the size of a piece of
country ham, leaving it hanging in its place. Guys still had to work.
They were bleeding from their wounds every time they bent over.
Their swords were so sharp; they could slice off a hand like it was

a stick of butter. Once they stripped Corregidor down to a bucket of rocks and had us schooled in their discipline rules; they began to herd us in lines to march.

> *"It is the Lord Who goes before you; He will march with you; He will not fail you or let you go or forsake you; Deuteronomy." 31:8*

Zablan Air Field–Unknown Time Period

After the twenty-one or so days on Corregidor, under our new Japanese victors, lots of us are taken to Camp Murphy, Zablan Air Field. Zablan was a stopping and processing place for us. The Japs took some photographs of us and processed us here. We are being summed up again and classified in work groups. There are American flags and English materials, and signs here. So much of the Philippines are part of American defense plans. These installations here were once manned by our boys. Zablan Airfield was built to make a strong air-strike for the Philippines. The United States set up the Constabulary Air Corps, or the (PCAC), and trained these Filipino boys to fly. This field is where ole Dwight Eisenhower cut his flying teeth when he was a Major serving on General MacArthur's staff. Some real American military giants have been here on this little airfield. Now, it is a gathering pen, and we are here getting categorized and led like sheep.

> *"Behold, I am sending you out as sheep in the midst of wolves, so be wise as serpents and innocent as doves." Matthew 10:16*

Transported by Boat to Bataan Island

The Japs aren't real sure what to do with us. Lots of arguing and bickering going on between them. We don't know what they are saying, but it isn't hard to understand that they are squabbling with each other. Some of us got loaded on boats. We went to Bataan Island and picked up the remaining dog scraps of American and

Filipino men left over from the transfer of soldiers by the Imperial Japanese Army. These war-torn, are the survivors of the Bataan Death March. These are the guys we heard about back on the Rock. Thousands loaded into boats, half bent over with deep, sunken eyes. Their battered and bruised bodies crawled in, as their ghostly souls were hanging onto the last remnants of their flesh and bone. They are barefoot. They lost their shoes along the way in the cart trenches. Their feet are all swollen up and cut to hell, toenails have fallen off from being in the wet slop. They got the 'rot', and soon they will be losing toes. Their toes look like bloody, gnarled up, tree roots. They look at you, but nothing is there in their eyes. They can barely talk any sense at all. Saliva is all foamed up and stuck around their mouths. They smelled God-awful cause they survived by messing themselves to stay alive. We want to help them, but we cannot. Survival and charity do a complicated waltz in your head. Each takes their turn exchanging who is leading, and who is following. One minute, you are looking for ways to stay alive. Then, you just can't sit by and do nothing, watching a fella die that just marched seventy miles, under the most brutal conditions the world has ever known. We all don't know where these boats are carrying us, but for now, Filipinos, Americans, and Aussies alike are all wearing the same jersey on a broken ragtag team for the Imperial Army.

> *"But if anyone has the world's goods and sees his brother in need, yet closes his heart against him, how does God's love abide in him? Little children, let us not love in word or talk but in deed and in truth." 1 John 3: 17-18*

Caught Unawares

The Japanese army is caught off guard with the numbers of prisoners they captured. Somehow, the military geniuses, Emperor Michinomiya Hirohito, and his henchman, Commander Hideki Tojo, miscalculated the seventy-thousand or so forces on Bataan. They didn't give much thought about our treatment, and they surely didn't have enough provisions, medical supplies, and equipment, to take care of us. They were preparing for around ten-thousand men, the number believed to be the size of the allied forces. The Japs are so engulfed with their complete overtaking of the Philippine Islands, the number of prisoners are the last thing on their mind. The less food, water, and medicine they have to use on us, the more of us will die, leaving more provisions for them.

Transported by Japanese Military Truck to Camp O'Donnell Unknown Time Period

We continued to move by cattle car from place to place. We was all confused and sorely tired. We tried to keep our wits about us as best we could as screams from torture, and haunting death rattles surround us. They throwed us all in the backs of supply trucks like pigs to slaughter. Wooden slats are split, scraping up our legs and arms, while the truck rumbles down the bomb-blasted roads. These trucks transported their supplies too. Boxes would fall and crush you if you weren't ready. The Jap guards assigned to the back of the truck must be their lowest ranking. They look like they just fell off the crazy train. They are jaw-jacking all crazy-like. Two of the guards are talking and pointing at us like we was some special interest to them, in some sick, demented way. We called one fella Mickey Mouse; he looks so goofy. I don't think he has a brain cell in his head. He is just looking at us like a stupid, circus clown. He couldn't muster up a scowl on his face to save his goon-ass if his life depended on it. Sometimes, the guards would just look at you with the crazy eyes. They are just waiting for you to look back disrespectful like, or make eye contact. If you tried to smile, they thought you was making fun of them; and they clubbed you. If you let your face show you was aggravated, disgusted, or mad, they thought you was challenging them with an act of aggression. That could get you killed. If you had anything in between, it could initiate a quick slap, spit in your face; or a gun butt in your back. It was a constant exercise cycle in human body language and psychology. After Camp O' Donnell, I learned to wear my armor mask. It was kinda the face I wore in church with my Mama. No real expression on your face, you just look away, or up to the heavens.

That way, the preacher or the Sunday School teacher wouldn't call on you to recite scriptures. It could keep me safe here, not showing any emotion to these guys. You just never know what is gonna set them off. I used my holy armor face from then on cuz; it didn't get their attention.

"Put on the whole armor of God, that you may be able to stand against the schemes of the devil."
Ephesians 6:11

Camp O'Donnell was also where I cut my teeth in Japanese death camp rules and laws. The Bataan Death March survivors, and guys like me who were at the fall of the Rock, were all together now. I think Bataan fellas were having a harder time cuz they were always looking over their shoulders and seemed more nervous and jumpy. They survived that God-awful march and began to die by the dozens here. Every day, another one was sick, dying, or too weak to carry their canteen to the only water spigot in the camp. One way some of us could help was to carry our canteens along with the canteens of those too weak to do so. We strung them on hollowed-out bamboo stalks. I could tie a few to my belt loops and carry a few more if I needed to. It seems no matter how bad it might be; there was always someone in worse shape than you. Inside the camp, it was awfully crowded. There were just too many men for the facilities to support, and some guys couldn't take it. There were just a few water faucets around, and over a thousand men for each one. A man can get mighty desperate when he cannot get a drink of water. You quickly learn how you can live on almost no food, but you cannot go a day without water. The water shortage led to lots of fights between prisoners, something the Japanese encouraged. Getting sick or wounded was not something you wanted to do at O'Donnell. The stench surrounding the hospital there was horrible. It was the last stop in the train car, O'Donnell, as it puffed down the tracks to death. As bad as the food was in camp if you went to the hospital, they cut your portion in half. They figure you are going to die in there anyway, why waste the food. Guys would be working in full sweats, pale, coughing up blood, running hundred-plus degree fevers, just to stay out of that death locker. There was evil torture in this camp. Guys are constantly interrogated. They would yank guys right off the floor in the middle of the night and drag them off. If there was any chance they might have Intel or information they could use against our allies or us, they are thrown into dark and ghastly places. Deep in underground cells, they are brutally tortured even more. Their wails and moaning are heard throughout the camp. If anyone actually did manage to escape, they would make a game of selecting ten more prisoners at random, to kill in their place. They gleefully would tap their swords on shoulders, and laugh wildly like madmen, as they took their victims to the front to be shot. Death was a wicked chess game, and they were the unlucky pawns moving along their evil chessboard.

Sometimes, the Jap guards would kick or punch a weak and dying man right into the latrine. His last breaths were spent gasping and coughing up shit until it swallowed him. You will never know the depths of your self-control until you have to stand idly by and watch that happen to a man. Approximately 2,300 American soldiers die here in Camp O'Donnell in just the first six-weeks of internment. Some of those poor fellas are forced to dig their own graves right before they pushed them in, and covered them up. They was mostly dead by then. Maybe they got caught with some Japanese yen, and they shot them. Either way, I can't imagine how awful it is to be smothered in dirt, and your last thought on earth is shared with shit and worms. Camp O'Donnell was just one of many hell holes planned and executed by the Japanese, and one of nine locations I learned to adapt to changing rules, guards, and Japanese ranking officers. I guess I am lucky; I have always been able to sum someone up real fast. You can read a man's intentions in his eyes, even if you have to glance quickly so they don't catch you.

Miracle Eight–Malaria

We slept out every night on the tarmac or the concrete blown-out foundation. It was miserable, and the mosquitoes over here are in fighter squadrons. I was bitten all over my legs and arms. Big red whelps were dotted my entire body. They incessantly chewed on us. We would wake up with little blood trails on our arms and legs, where they had sucked out so much blood, they carried it in patterns everywhere. Not long after, I start to come down with some awful headaches at night. My head pounded like the iron hammers in the blacksmith shop. My gut hurt real bad, and I had a blazing fever. In a couple of days, I began the awful cycle of violent shakes with soaking sweats that drenched my tattered and dirty clothes. My brain hurt, and I was sure enough, weak like a kitten. I don't know what God-forsaken, damn disease has hit me, but I sure nuff gotta bad one. Sounds like what the 'Hike' boys talked about that took so many. "Houston, you got malaria. I know it. I have been with the boys on Bataan." One guy, a medic, could read my symptoms real easy. This wasn't his first dance with this killer. On that concrete slab at night, my body began to convulse, beating my skull on the concrete. A couple of fellas laid their hands under my head to keep me from busting it wide open. The only real treatment for this disease is quinine, an anti-malarial drug. It is a medicine made from the bark of the cinchona tree. The U.S. military issued us plenty of these pills to take here as a preventative for this killer. We were all issued packets of quinine from the hospital on Corregidor. But as you can bet, along with everything else the Japs took, they took our quinine too. Now while we are writhing here on the broken concrete, the Japs are administering our quinine to their soldiers, keeping them alive across the way! I stayed low on the concrete and ate what I could to keep my strength up. I got some guys to get me some leaves from some local plants. I had no idea what I might be ingesting, but I needed to try and get these symptoms under control. "Just find anything that looks like a fruit tree or a palm," I told them. I have to try something. I know they aren't gonna let me lie down here long. I chew on a few plant leaves, try to sip water, and get a few bits of food down. After a few days, somehow, my fever breaks; and I hold down some of the crappy rice. I begin to get a little stronger. Once I can sit up, they put me back to work. I guess having the 'gitis when I was a kid, helped me prepare for this crap. Guys were dying every day from this deadly killer. It was impossible to avoid it because we were exposed every day. Without any medicine or medical care, there are more guys dropping dead of malaria than gunshots.

I didn't stay long at Camp O'Donnell. It was maybe just a couple of months before they moved us to the next place. I can only guess, if you still got a back and hands that work, they are gonna find a place to use them. Pretty soon, the guards started checking us over again and assigned us to one of the three, Cabanatuan prison camps. I am assigned to Cabanatuan #3. The once, quiet, little sleepy, fishing town, on the Pampanga River, Cabanatuan City, is a Japanese prison camp location.

> *"Do not fear what you are about to suffer. Behold,*
> *the devil is about to throw some of you into prison,*
> *that you may be tested....and for ten days you will*
> *have tribulation. Be faithful unto death, and I will*
> *give you the crown of life." Revelation 2:10*

Miracle Nine–Marched on Foot Twelve Miles to Cabanatuan, Prison Camp #3

I think sometime around early June they march the American and allied soldiers through a little village named Cebu, which is about twelve miles, northeast of Cabanatuan. The guards are keeping the American soldiers and their allies separated from the Filipino soldiers. We marched through the streets, six men across, with our hands and arms held over our heads the entire way. Marching was another form of mental and physical torture. Guards are prodding and jabbing us along the entire way, trying to get our goat. They are calling us, "Hey Babe Ruth, you shit!" I tell myself, "No eye contact! No eye contact!" Walking for our lives, we are. There is no water and no rest. If you have to piss, you just piss. Keep marching. If you need to throw up, don't stop to do it, or you will get a bayonet in the gut. Keep marching. Guys are dropping like flies out here in this heat. Dry-heaving and wringing wet with sweat, we push on, raising our knees and putting our boots on the ground. With ninety-five percent humidity levels, the temperature is unbearable. Keep marching. I don't know how many we lost along the way, but the guys from the 'Hike', on Bataan, let us know early, you flinch, you die. We was all dripping wet, losing fluids from our bodies at too fast of a rate. Our mouths were all parched, and we needed water badly. If you stop sweating, heat exhaustion has set in. Any of the guys we lost along the way had to be dragged the rest of the way to camp. I had to focus on something else. I had been in the fields plenty of times without water. Somehow, God got me to the next mile and the next.

"If anyone forces you to go one mile, go with them two miles." Matthew 5:41

As I march, I am secretly doing surveillance of the area. We could be here a long while, and I need to know what I might be dealing with. I am looking for any plants we can eat or use for medicine. I know I got to fight to stay alive, and I am as prepared as anyone can be for this sentence. I had gone without a few meals in my day, and now I know I can get some plant medicine around here. As we enter the city, the townspeople were standing paralyzed along the little stick fences. Scrawny, sickly looking chickens were pecking along the rubble pathways. The bombings had badly damaged the town. The entire landscape was covered in holes and broken-up buildings. Roads were blown-up with craters you could sink a truck into. Half-starved dogs scratching at their fleas are laying under any shade they can find. The town folks look like ghosts watching a silent picture show of cows going to their slaughter. No eye contact now. Little boys and girls are saluting the Japanese Officers and throwing little white Sampaguita flowers at them. No more little gifts of cassava cakes or shouts of American flyboy towards us now. We are just filthy swine, taking our last hike to the barn before killing day. The Japs are in control of this island now, and this little village has given way to the Emperor's directive.

"The Lord is a stronghold for the oppressed, a stronghold in times of trouble." Psalms 9:9

'Bahay kubos'

The three camps in Cabanatuan are on about a hundred acres of dusty, scrabble land. Hidden by the jungle foliage surrounding each camp, are tall, razor-sharp barbed-wire fences. This place began as a training camp before it became the home for the Ninety-first Division of the Philippine Army. They captured those boys in the takeover. It is now the 'joint' for this pathetic bunch. Cabanatuan is the largest American POW camp in the Pacific, and it is practically in shambles. It looks like the piss-poor houses and yards, in the backwoods of Arkansas. Everything is in bad shape. We make our way inside the camp as they lead us up to our quarters. Quarters!!? Right away, we was divided up into groups of ten. I am pretty sure by the look of things, we are gonna be shoved in these huts like sardines. Our barracks are Filipino Nipa Huts the locals called *Bahay kubos*. They designed them around their beliefs of 'sawali'. It is their simple jungle form of building and living. Each hut stood on stilts about four feet off the ground. They are built from bamboo with thatched, Cogon grass roofs. Cogon grass grows everywhere around here. It has built up natural fences around the compound from catching all the sand blowing in the tropical winds. Cogon grass is a lot like the prairie grasses back home. If I can get my hands on some, I can eat the sweet white roots, and use the blades for medicine. I see a few straggly fruit trees along the fence lines. I am not sure what they are. I have never seen them before, but one thing for sure; they might be something to eat.

We are taken to the Nipa Huts, separated into groups, and herded inside. The whole hut was about fifty feet by maybe, fifteen feet. It was split up into ten, small bamboo bays, with bunk bed style shelves. Each bay once held only two Filipino soldiers, and the whole Nipa Hut held around forty men. It looked more like a barn with horse stalls, 'cept there was just a small opening at each end. The bamboo was split and tore up, and the grass roof had been leaking. Fleas and bed bugs start gnawing on us right away, and the flies came swarming around like a fighter attack squadron. The Jap soldiers were pushing more and more of us in. "Ugoku !, ugoku!" [Move, Move!!] By the time we all got in, there were about one-hundred of us in that rickety ole hut. It stunk something terrible. It smelled just like the livestock yards in Ft. Worth. Piss and shit smell so strong, your eyes begin to water. It burns your nose to breathe. Flies were flying in and out of the openings. It is unbearably hot and muggy. The thick air feels like a wet wool coat in July. We are pushed to the floor on our knees, shoulder to shoulder, facing the center of the hut. Our arms are forced behind our backs. Swinging bamboo cane poles, they storm through the center of the room. They are smacking us to bow down, splitting the skin on our necks and shoulders. Our first command here, bow to the great Emperor. "Fusu, fusu, fusu nau! fusu nau!" [Bow!, Bow!] We all bow toward the center aisle as the guards stomped back and forth. We accepted our command to bow to our new master in a trade for our lives. I put on my armor face, and think about Mama. I know what she would be saying. "Houston, there is only one God, master of the universe. No matter who you are serving now, one day...every knee will bow, and every tongue will confess, Jesus is Lord." In my head, I whisper, "Mama, my body may be bowing to an emperor, but my mind is bowing to Jesus." They can take everything else from me, but they can't take my honor or my King.

> *It is written; "As surely as I live, says the Lord, 'every knee will bow before me; every tongue will confess to God." Romans 14:11*

The little squatty captain came in swinging his Samurai sword, stepping up on a little wooden box, so he would appear taller. Behind him, was some little fella that could speak a little English; and flanking his sides were his top two guards. Those two both got the crazy eyes. They look like rabid raccoons. Lordy, those two are gonna be trouble! Where did they get these goons to enlist in this so-called 'great Imperial Army'? The first goon steps up and yells out, "Every won, you look eyes at new master! Now, salute big! You are filth; you are coward. You shit! Your country forgot who you aww. You will rot here! Do not try to escape or you will be shot to death! You follow order; you pig now! We drop you in hole, no one find you ever!" He steps down, and they follow him out like ducklings. We scramble to find a spot in this damn lice barn. We are looking for anything that has a break or split board to let some air in. The first night in that old shack, loneliest I ever felt. House full of men, still lonely as a coyote. Men are wailing, praying, and gasping for air. Stomachs are squeaking and grinding. Everyone is laying like cigarettes in a pack, looking up to the pin holes through the thatched roof. The smell of wet Coogan grass, sweat, and feces is suffocating. We shuffle feet to head to make room for our shoulders. Feet stink to high heaven, but they smell better than our breath! I hear some men fussing and squabbling over space. "Don't touch me!; get your ass away from my face!" We was swishing flies and slapping sand fleas all night. Because I am pretty tall, my shoulders took a beating from the caning. I had razor-like cuts across both of them. Flies are coming in those open wounds like planes on runways. They wouldn't stop their incessant landing, circling, landing, and cleaning their feet. Mosquitoes are buzzing by our ears, dirt is lightly raining down from the critters up in the Coogan grass thatch, and we are continually being bitten by bed bugs and fleas. The thatch is infested with lice. Little field mice scurry over us looking for bits of food. Some poor ole fellas are so sick with the fever in their brain; they talked out of their heads all night. Some are catching trains or hailing cabs, and some guys are talking away to their sweethearts. One guy is riding his horse to the country store to get a Coke. You hear the horrible, hollow sound of the 'death rattle'. Men are so sick; they begin the body's involuntary parade of the very last drumbeats of the heart. Their chest sounds are like groaning and shuttering window panes clattering in a storm. Spit and lung mucus are settling in the throat and upper chest, slowly suffocating them. The rattle sound slows to a quiet whirr, and then they suck in real hard before there is silence. You know a new soul has entered the last stop on the life train. I didn't sleep a wink.

A Mad Man's Deranged Railroad Ties

Our first day started about five a.m., when we are awakened by the sickening sound of Jap guards calling, "Dassuru, Dassuru!!" [get out, get out!] I woke up with my eyes crusted over and dirt in

126

my tear ducts. Guards are screaming at us. A man can't even get his thoughts or get out of the nightmare of no sleep before we are shuffled out, and lined up. Going out, I saw about nine or ten men, not moving. Their faces were frozen, eyes fixed with the stare of death. One of the dead guys was still holding the reins of his horse from the trip to town he was taking last night. The guards ordered a couple of men to start dragging the bodies out by the feet. Thump, thump, thump, their heads were cracking against the boards on the stairs until they were lined up like a mad man's deranged railroad ties. We all were ordered to line up in the dirt pathway before the Nipa Huts. Each one of our little bays of ten men had to count off in Japanese to make sure no one escaped during the night. We all filled in the numbers of our dead to make sure we are counted. "Ichi, ni, san, shi, go, roku, shichi, hachi, kyuu, juu." I am roku, number seven in my bay. Over and over, "Ichi, ni, san, shi, go, roku, shichi, hachi, kyuu, juu , Ichi, ni, san, shi, go, roku, shichi, hachi, kyuu, juu , Ichi, ni, san, shi, go, roku, shichi, hachi, kyuu, juu" , was repeated. "Ichi, ni, san, shi, go, hachi, juu." I look over and see the crazy-eyed guards. I was frightened. Sometime during the night three men, numbers roku, shichi , and kyuu, from bay six, did escape. They got out a few miles before they got caught by some Japanese soldiers, and driven back to camp in the night. Those three men were dragged by the neck to the middle of the road and thrown down. Putting their hands behind their backs, kneeling, they begged for their lives. The men succumbed to their fate, as three guards swung their guntō swords, lopping their heads off like spring pullets. It was dreadful. Heads fell in the dirt with an awful hollow thud, spraying blood over our pant legs. Some men just pissed their selves right there, while others, threw up. That got them a gun butt in the face. You could hear their brittle jaw bone crack. The guards took three long bamboo poles with sharp ends. They shoved those guy's severed heads on one end and paraded them up and down that pathway in front of all of us, laughing like demons in the lakes of Hell. They slammed those poles into the ground about ten feet apart. Those poor men were now our depraved gate-keepers. Then, they called the other seven men from that bay to the front of the line, right where the headless bodies were. They lined them up, pulled burlap sacks over their heads, and shot them dead like rabid dogs. There they lay, face down, with their hands behind their backs, lined up like a set of well-worn dominos. We know why we are in groups of ten. This is the size of a 'shooting squad'. The guards called four or five men over. "Horu ikimasu" Horu, Horu!" [Go dig, dig! dig!] Their job was to drag all them boys off and dig a mass grave. Their headless corpses were drained of blood as it flowed from the neck cavity along the pathway. I was glad to be passed up for that duty this time. Once the bodies were matter-of-factly drug off, that was that; our camp morning routine was set. It was our first lesson in group discipline and just a pre-view of the unspeakable cruelties that would play in this horrific moving picture show before us.

> *"And do not fear those who kill the body but cannot kill the soul. Rather fear him who can destroy both soul and body in hell." Matthew 10:28*

At night, back in the hut, it is eerie still. No one is moving or whispering to each other. The hut is dark. A heavy feeling of dread is being sucked through the broken boards with each little gust of the thin air. It is a feeling of doom, helplessness, fear, and loss served with a side of pure anguish. Impending death, fear of death, and seeing death is a lethal concoction, that can mortally wound the spirit. You are privately digging in your well to see if there is an ounce of will left to grasp on to. I know we all have to muster up the strength to continue. I have to muster up the strength to continue. I whisper ever so quietly....*"The Lord is my shepherd; I shall not want. He maketh me to lie down in green pastures: he leadeth me beside the still waters."* Right about that time, I hear the quiet whispers of a few other guys joining in. *"He restoreth my soul: he leadeth me in the paths of righteousness for his name's sake. Yea, though I walk through the valley of the shadow of death, I will fear no evil: for thou art with me; thy rod and thy staff they comfort me. Thou preparest a table before me in the presence of mine enemies: thou anointest my head with oil; my cup runneth over. Surely goodness and mercy shall follow me all the days of my life: and I will dwell in the house of the Lord forever."* No one said another word the rest of the night. The next morning, two more men were dead. I hope those words comforted them as they drew their last breaths on earth.

> *"I am he who comforts you; who are you that you are afraid of man who dies, of the son of man who is made like grass." Isaiah 51:12*

The Disease Pipeline

Since the underside of the huts was full of shit and piss where we slept right above, our first work detail was to dig and build latrines. This is a task we are all happy to do. We don't have any of the proper tools for a job like this. The guards were quite entertained watching us struggle to make a trench. We asked our Japanese captors to give us any working tools and some scrap wood or tin, to support the walls. They mocked us and acted like they couldn't understand us. They would cup their hands over their ears pretending to try and hear us. Sometimes they would just wave hello to us and laugh like we is some kinds ten-cent sideshow. We were committed to getting them dug out anyway. We had no real idea we just built a cesspool, a direct pipeline of disease, right outside our living quarters. Latrines are very close to where our food is prepared. Now, flies had a disease buffet right before them where they constantly swarmed; carrying more bacteria to our open wounds and bits of food. The latrine was a trench about eighteen inches wide, and about four-feet deep. It ran right alongside the Nipa huts. With so many weak and sickly men it couldn't be much farther, or no one would make it there. When the rains came, or the latrine was overflowing, one of the jobs at the camp was emptying the latrine. That would entail using any scrap buckets or bowls, with bare hands, scooping up that God-awful mess, and pouring it into a fifty-gallon drum. You just puked right into it and went on. Eventually, that drum had to be carried out to the waterway where we dumped it.

The guards stand watch as twenty-four-hour sentries in the looming towers above us. We was being watched like buzzards over week-old road kill. Any suspension you was up to something, they would just shoot the guy through the head and demand whoever was closest to him to drag him off to the pile. There were always a few guys who would try their hand at an escape. Even knowing it would mean the other nine would die to pay for you, they were willing. I guess they figured that they would be better off and they would not suffer. So, they switched their methods to torturing guys in some demonic hole, for two or three days. You could hear their screams and pleas to stop all over the camp. Our groups of ten men jokingly became our 'running buddies.' You knew to stay accountable to each other, or risk death. We slept head to foot and kept an ankle over each other at night. We always took someone with us to the latrine at night.

Soon, they sized us up according to their wicked likings. Some of us were builders, repairers, kitchen cooks, gardeners for the guard's abundant vegetable garden, 'woodchippers' woodchoppers, gravediggers, or hospital help. You learned to keep your mouth shut and your eyes open. You did your work and tried not to make any eye contact. We are threatened every day with our lives or limbs. It is a continual barrage of psychological warfare as they wielded their power over us. "We kill you, stupid shit, we kill you!" "Hey, Frank Snottra, you want cigarette?" The boards to the face or bamboo to the back are a constant routine here. You yielded to their power and obeyed, or you died.

> *"But even if you should suffer for what is right, you are blessed. "Do not fear their threats; do not be frightened." 1 Peter 3:14*

Every morning began with the same routine. All the men who were near death were taken to the 'Zero Ward', the hospital for the dying. They were stripped of all their clothing and laid out on the dirty floor, while prisoner medics would try to comfort them and assist in their care. Most of those guys never came back out. Once you got 'summed up', too sick to work, strong enough to work the fields, build a latrine, or hoe in a garden, you were herded off. Each group of men had a guard assigned to them. I was assigned to work in the garden. They knew I was a farm boy [nojo no shonen]. They was gonna get every bit of work and knowledge out of us in forced labor until they either killed us, or we dropped dead. We worked out in the hot Filipino sun about twelve hours a day. Blisters as big as quarters well up on our hands and feet. Once they bust open, we have even more doors open to disease. I decided ifin I was gonna die here, I was ready to die in the farm fields just like my Daddy did, right here in the dirt and plants. Dust to dust and all.

> *"All go to the same place; all come from dust, and to dust all return." Ecclesiastes 20:3*

The Chow Line

Boy, if that isn't the damnedest thing, comparing this skeleton's putrid buffet to chow! They liked using a lot of American words to describe our routines. "Want big chow, flyboy? Come on in and fill up here!" "We got big New York strip fo you!" They would laugh and blow their cigarette smoke in our eyes as we passed by. Guards would be standing around us as they would fill themselves on big meals of fish, rice, and vegetables, cooked in miso broth. The rules are clear; you stand in line to receive your ration. No one stands in for you. You walk here on your own, or you do not eat. The 'mess hall' was a filthy open-air shack where the food is cooked in big iron pots called 'kawas'. Our daily meals consisted of a single cup of old dirty, watered-down, rice soup; called 'luago'. Sometimes we got the remains of a raw fish head or some kelp. We moved from the two-thousand-plus calories of a serviceman's chow to about three-hundred calories a day. The rice was filthy, often swept up off the floors in the packing houses, filled with dirt, little rocks; and who knows what else. It could break your tooth if you weren't careful. Once cooked, it was a slimy soupy, mixture. The texture could gag you. You learned to guzzle it down like bay oysters. Sometimes maggots were swimming about in the bowl. They became our 'protein pellets'. Every three or four days, we might

131

get a bit of caribou meat, or dried fish. That only amounted to about a peach pit size for each of us. We didn't get much drinking water. If we did, it came from an outside faucet that was fed by the dirty wells that are dug close to the huts. There is a lot of sediment in the water, and it tasted like rust and iron. Somedays we would stand in line for hours just to get a bit of dirty water to fill our canteens. The constant gnawing of our stomachs was a daily battle to overcome. The sounds of gurgling and gas can drive a man crazy. You either learned to put your mind over your hunger and fear, you starved, or went plain mad. Starvation debilitates much more than your body. When a man is hungry and starving, your head ain't right. It makes you less able to control your impulses. You are quicker to act out or say something stupid. That was the end of many men who made the mistake of swinging back or trying to catch the butt of a guard's gun. A lot of guys just got depressed, and others were jumpy, nervous, and anxious. I, well, I had a daily talk with myself about my attitude, and what I may be facing each day. I took it one day at a time. Plenty of people in the Bible suffered sorely for thousands of years. The Jews, simple and faithful tribes of families, were beaten, enslaved, and starved. The Egyptians took all their belongings, their homes, and raped their wives. They worked like dogs helping build their empire. Ole Job, well, he done lost everything, his wealth, his wife, his land, all of his possessions, and his whole family. He was covered in sores and sickly. Plenty of suffering in the Bible I knowed. Plenty of good men are put in prison for their beliefs. I knew a few bible verses from Mama. In my head, I recited some of the Proverbs when I knew I was getting low. *"A glad heart makes a cheerful face, but by sorrow of heart the spirit is crushed. Proverbs 15:13."* I knew I had to keep my spirits up. I have seen too many times how that can kill a man. I watched plenty men just lay down and die, just give up. A broken spirit will do that. God is here, even in the deepest ravines of the squalor, hopelessness, disease, and death. His word is clear, no matter how bad it got here, He will never leave me.

"Teaching them to observe all things whatsoever I have commanded you. "And lo, I am with you always, even unto the end of the world." Matthew 28:20

Days went on like a sick ole windmill, turning and spinning, before suddenly changing direction. As bad as the summer heat was, the winter brought on rainy, wet, nights, and winds that cut through the hut. Somehow we slugged through it. With no covers for warmth, we just had to put our skeleton frames closer together. A little bit of body warmth can go a long way when you are this thin. Nights are filled with the same routine. Guys are wailing in pain, stomachs grinding; leading to the release of human mustard gas. Starvation makes your system knot-up, forcing your body to rid itself of waste constantly. You get the runs and a powerful toxic gas that can level a room! My Daddy was always quite the gentleman. Even with four boys to raise, he never let the gas fly in a room with my Mama and sisters. "We go outside to take care of this business, Houston," he would tell me. "It ain't polite, heathen like." With all the sickness and duress, I still couldn't let gas go inside the hut. I would go outside for that.

Joe and I could whisper a bit at night. It helped us a lot to just talk about home. "Ya know, I miss gravy." "Me too Joe, I love me some red-eye gravy!" "Awww, ya putz. Gravy is Italian for tomato sauce!" "Really, Joe...you call tomato sauce, gravy?" "Sure do, it's the old style Italian kind, made from fresh tomatoes, onions, garlic, fresh basil; and cooked all day. We call the noodles macaroni too!" "You give me the recipe Joe; I will have the best mess hall gravy in the universe someday!" Joe told me how to make Italian gravy from scratch. "Ya know Joe; someday I'm gonna write me a cookbook!" We talked about the guava trees outside and some of the healing plants, and of course, we talked about home. I showed Joe how to make a toothbrush from a tree branch and how to brush our teeth with charcoal ashes from the kawa. We had to save ourselves for that big ole Italian spaghetti dinner someday! The night silence is broken by the horrid sounds of beatings outside the hut. Men are screaming in pain as ribs and collar bones are snapping like dead tree branches. The beatings continued throughout the night. "Dear God, they are gonna beat those guys to death!" The sound of broken bones and battered flesh continued as the wailing slowly silenced. In the morning, we find four marines tied to the posts, still in standing positions. They had been beaten to death for an escape attempt.

The Rot

I did end up with some rot in some of my open wounds. Most of the guys did. It is impossible to keep anything clean here. They don't waste any water letting us shower or bathe. If you could get a few cups of water to spare, we would wash our faces and our ass! That is about all we could try to keep clean. It was common to see rotting flesh around open wounds, which would lead to a deadly killer; gangrene. Without any antibiotics, soap, or clean water; even the smallest cut can get madly infected. Red hot streaks would be running up your legs and arms. From the canings I took, I had some open wounds on my back that were beginning to rot and turn black on the edges. The flies were always swarming us trying to get in there. I took some maggots from some of the camp garbage and put them in those wounds, covering them with some cloth. They will do the rest if you let em. They are like little tiny, white surgeons. They will come in and clean out a wound in no time. Joe had pulled off some plant leaves as we talked about earlier. I packed those clean holes with some Bayabas, guava leaves. The guards have completely stripped the trees of any edible fruits that are in season. They don't know to use the leaves. Those leaves problee saved my life a couple of times. I would tell the other guys to use them too when they got the gangrene. If you didn't get any better on your own, it usually led to a trip to the 'medicine hut', where the infected limb was amputated without any anesthesia. You could hear them screaming and begging the Japs to kill them instead. I am grateful I never went there. At night when it is still, sometimes I can still hear their screams.

We did learn to find some bits of joy along the way in our captivity. We made up some games with rocks and shells. I began a cookbook that I hoped to complete over time. I traded some cigarettes for a small black notebook a guy made from scrap paper, string, and leather. I would just jot down recipes that my Mama made, and add some new ones I was going to try someday. It helped me to think of something I loved, healthy food. Using my mind to figure the ratios of the ingredients challenged me mentally. That helped me to keep my mind sharp. I would lay there at night and think of what I wanted to eat. I would make myself write down the steps, the ingredients, and what it took to prepare and cook it. I think mentally walking myself through the ordinary routines and preparing meals in my head kept me from going plumb mad. When I get out of this hell hole, I am gonna get Mama to cook everything in this dang little book! I kept that cookbook hidden in the thatch roof. I needed something to help me hold on another day. This little book gave me the one thing I needed the most to survive – hope.

> *"Hope deferred makes the heart sick, but a longing fulfilled is a tree of life." Proverbs 13:12*

Entry One: Chicken and Dumplings

Catch, wring the neck, pluck, and dress a fat hen
Cut the back in half, split the chicken keeping the back spine and the last thing over the fence intact – throw this in the boiling water to make stock
Cut the pieces – two thighs, two drums, two little wings, two little drum wings, two breasts
Salt and pepper, dredge in flour
Drop in the pot of hot chicken back stock water
Make Dumplings
Flour – 2 cups, cold butter, 1 cup, 1 teaspoon soda, 1 tsp salt, little goat milk
Lightly mix the ingredients, leave in wooden bowl covered
Roll out on floured table, cut into 2-inch squares
Drop into boiling chicken
Remove chicken and debone – save bones for grinding up for the soil
Salt and pepper to taste

Universal Reverence

Some guys made a makeshift little altar and cross from rocks and sticks. We was all amazed that the guards let this happen. Men would walk over to kneel at the fence line. As they was looking toward the moon, they would silently pray. After a while rocks started showing up there. A little stick and vine cross was laid in between the rocks. Pretty soon, it was a little sacred area where conversations with God took place. There was a lot of powerful praying going on here. I learned that even with a starved body and a bruised spirit, you can still muster up enough strength for coming to the throne on your knees. You could see guys kneeling there in the evenings. No loud services, singing, or outward signs of worship were allowed. You could quietly kneel there. The guards do have genuine respect for reverence, and they would not stop a guy ifin he was just kneeling there for a few minutes to pray. We do have something in common with them. They understand the need to talk to an almighty. Not sure who they talk to, but they let us have a little time at that cross if we needed it.

> *"If then, we have a kingdom which will never be moved, let us have grace, so that we may give God such worship as is pleasing to him with fear and respect." Hebrews 12:28*

'Habagat'

In the summers, the southwest winds pick up. This season starts early in June and lasts until late October. The locals call it 'Hagabat' (ha-ga-bat). Monsoon weather is just another brutal event in this place. Mighty strong breezes bring torrential rainfalls. Life in camp becomes like living in a soup bowl. Everything is wet. You may have a grass roof over your head but is not waterproof. The bamboo floors are wet and smell. At night the breezes cool off everything creating a steam bath of humidity in the hut. It is very hot and humid and Westerly wind brings in some mighty rains. Muddy, sloppy, and pelting rains slam this place every day. As a farmer, I can smell it coming in the air. I know the locals are sure glad to have these rains for their rice fields, but the rain brings a whole new problem to us. The latrine trenches overflow on our walkways. For five months a year, and we are walking ankle-deep in watery shit. The slop and smell are horrific. We keep on business as usual here in camp, as our legs and feet slowly begin to rot, turning white and wrinkly. 'Paddy foot' is common to the locals here. They are used to working in the rice fields for months, slogging through the submerged rice crops. Our feet are not used to this kind of exposure, and soon we are all 'pruned up'. Soft white flesh is hanging from our feet. Our immune systems are so weakened; some of us get the 'jungle rot'. Ulcers, open sores, and pustules begin to form on our feet and legs. Once your feet go numb, you will have fungal and bacterial infections setting in. That can bring enough disease to a weakened body that within a week, some guys are dead. The only relief we get to dry out a bit is when we are in the huts at night. Under the broken Coogan grass roof, as drops of rain drip nonstop on us in our sleep; I write another entry in my cookbook.

> *"He gives rain on the earth and sends water on the fields." Job 5:10*

Entry Two: Mama's Country Cornbread

½ cup lard or bacon drippings
1 large yard egg
1 ½ cups of buttermilk
1 cup of fresh corn boiled in buttermilk and butter
2 cups yellow corn meal
1 T baking powder
2 t salt

Rub the cast iron skillet down with lard. It will keep it from sticking and will keep your hands real smooth. Put about half the lard in the skillet and stick it in a hot oven, 450 degrees for 10 minutes

Mix all the wet ingredients together, including the rest of the lard.

Mix all the dry ingredients together real good.
Stir together, mixing well
Pour batter into hot skillet
Bake for 25 minutes until golden brown
Serve with butter. Serve day-old cornbread, pan-fried with honey

'Amihan'

There are only two seasons in the Philippines – really wet and sorta dry. The rainy tropical sloppy season is followed by the dry season, beginning in late November and ending sometime in May. Cool, howling, northeast monsoon winds, called the 'Amihan' (a-me-han), carry off parts of our hut. It is humid, but the constant winds make the heat bearable. The local people's Tagalog mythology, has a great bird 'Amihan', that they believe was the first to inhabit the earth, saving the first human beings. The great winds are carried by the enormous wings of the bird this season is named after. The mildest weather conditions we have are during these months.

> *"While the earth remains, seedtime and harvest,*
> *cold and heat, summer and winter, day and night,*
> *shall not cease." Genesis 8:22*

Miracle Ten–'The Box'

I am out in the gardens doing my job. It is hot out in these beds, but I love it as my Daddy did. I don't have any limestone to burn out here, but I can collect up some of the charcoal ashes from the fires for my teeth. I took my stick and split it up just as I was taught as a kid. I would brush my teeth every day with the charcoal ashes. My gums would be bleeding from vitamin deficiencies, but I wanted to save my teeth if I could. I taught some of the guys to do it too. Out in the fields where the gardens were, I see some Carelessweed! Locals call it Pigweed, but it is just about the same as we ate as kids. I know it will give us some vitamins. I snuck a few stalks and shoved them in my pants just in case it pisses off a guard. I took one quick bite, eating the little white roots, and chewing up some leaves. Pretty soon, that crazed-eyed raccoon of a guard came over to me. We all called him Satan. He was shore 'nuff evil and stared at you with empty windows for eyes. I don't think he was real smart either. He shore didn't like my tall self. He was yelling something and pointing to my pants. "Happyaku rokujū hachi!, Nugu! nugu!" [868!, Take off ,take off!] He wanted me to take off my pants. I knew I was in trouble. Out unrolled the stalks spilling to the ground. He slapped me hard in the face and hit me with a cane pole. " Baka! Kutabare, kutabare!" [Idiot! Drop dead! Go to hell!] He dragged me over to an area in the middle of a field right in the blistering sun. He called the other goon over to get something for him. It was an artillery or shipping container box. I'm guessing it measured around forty-eight inches, by forty-eight inches, square. The top had a hole in it about the size of a man's head. They took off one side, pushing and stuffing my six-foot body in. They prodded me with bamboo spikes forcing me to contort my body to fit inside. I had to squat and balance myself on the balls of my feet. My head was forced through the jagged hole in the top, reopening some wounds around my neck. They nailed the front opening closed. Satan took the butt of his gun and slammed it into my face. "Happyaku rokujū hachi, oroka shinimasu!" [868, die, stupid!] They left me there in that sweat box cooking in my own juices, for a full day and night. The hot torrid sun in the Philippine jungle pounded on me. It is coming in waves where I could hear every artery moving the blood around my body. My leg muscles are locked-up, and my toes are cramping, fixed in place. Every muscle in my body is constricting and soon locked up. I was catching the sweat running down my nose and face just to get some moisture in my mouth. Flies are landing in my ears and crawling in my nose and mouth. Satan came by a few times and threw some water in my face, laughing like a demon as he left. Pretty soon, I quit sweating, and I passed out for a while. In my foggy drifting in and out, I remembered the Bible story and scriptures of Shadrach, Meshach and Abednego, and how they were protected by God when they were thrown in the furnace. King Nebuchadnezzar was so amazed that they came from the furnace unharmed that he praised their

God, our God. I know I have to make it back home. Maybe Satan will see there is something stronger in me too.

> *"They saw that the fire had not harmed their bodies, nor was a hair of their heads singed; their robes were not scorched, and there was no smell of fire on them." Daniel 3: 27*

Every time he came by I lifted my head up, and he would stomp off. One of the other guards is talking real fast to Satan. I wasn't sure what was going on, or if I was gonna be next to get my head lopped off. Satan was pointing out to the fields where I picked the Pigweed, and he is screaming up a storm. The other guard must have told him we were too stupid to know what to eat out there. He knew some of it was poisonous. It is a victory either way. We would probably kill ourselves if they just let us go. That would be fewer people to feed. So far as I know, no one ever got punished for picking weeds again. There was plenty of weeds in this damn place! They were sweet and all afresh in the morning, sometimes with a few locusts clinging on. It was all we had to supplement our diet with any chance of vitamins. It was like manna rained in overnight.

> *"Then the LORD SAID TO MOSES, "I WILL RAIN DOWN BREAD FROM HEAVEN FOR YOU." EXODUS 16:4*

Zero "O" Ward

If a man had 'zero' chance of survival, the death rattle already began, their pulse just slowing to a stall, or they got a fever over a hundred degrees, this is where you went. Nobody wanted to be dragged in there cause you know the only way you will be coming out, is in a burlap sack. It was a sickly place with moans and wails, and blood staining the dirty wooden walls. Hundreds of men went crawling in on all fours and only spilled out in a heap hours later.

> *"When his breath departs, he returns to the earth; on that very day his plans perish." Psalms 146:4*

Miracle Eleven - Surviving Wet and Dry Beriberi

In spite of knowing I could get us a few greens out around, the scorching heat in the box took a toll on my body. I was seized up like a knot on the floor of the Nipa Hut. Satan had reopened my wounds on my neck, and flies were beginning to lay their eggs there. Joe came up to me. "Houston, you ok?" "You need some water; you gotta get some water." I was just too weak to get to my canteen or clean out my wounds. Joe or anyone else couldn't help me without the threat of torture or death. "Get away from me Joe! You gonna get yourself killed!" He moved away. I crawled on my belly to my canteen and took a big drink, sand and all. If you were too weak to work, you had to stay in the Nipa Hut. They are not gonna bring you any medicine or help you. It was just another form of torture for them, 'cept they get two for one in this deal. It was torture for the fallen who are in too bad a shape to get to the little food or water they need to survive, and torture for the comrade who helplessly watches you suffer and die. Pretty soon, my speech was getting slurred. My thoughts were all crazy and mixed up. My legs and feet began to swell. I am just trying to get comfortable so that I can rest, hoping for a few winks of sleep. I kept thinking I can get past this. I woke up in the middle of the night trying to catch my breath. I had such shortness in my breathing; I felt like I was sucking my air through a dirty, wet blanket. Luckily, the night was one of the few times prisoners could get some help to each other. The Jap guards assigned to hut watch got so used to the sounds of the death rattle, moaning and crying, they didn't come in very often. You still had to lay quiet as a church mouse and whisper, or use some hand signals to communicate. One of the guys, Steven, was a medic in my bay. He crawled over to assess me. He listened to my heart and lungs best he could. He saw my incredibly red and swollen ankles and feet, and my neck muscles sticking out and knew right away my diagnosis. "Holy shit! Holy shit! Houston your legs and feet look like rubber truck inner tubes!" "Shhhhh. Quiet down!" "Houston, you probably got Beriberi." I was blazing with fever. I knew I had to get the swelling down and release the rotten fluid out of me if I was gonna survive this. He knew it too, but I don't think he could bring himself to put me through it. "Pull me off a sliver of the bamboo up there." He was able to get me a sliver of bamboo that we could strip away to get a sharp end. "Hold my leg..hold my leg." I took a deep breath, closed my eyes, and jabbed that stick hard in the calf of my left leg, just below the knee. I had to stab it in hard enough to get to the worst of the rot and disease flowing. It hurt like hell stinging and burning all the way in, and all the way out. I couldn't scream without alarming the guards. I clamped my teeth on that piece of bamboo as I watched as all that rotting puss and fluid drain between the floorboards. The release of the pressure gave me some immediate relief. Knowing I had to do it again on the other side sickened me. "Damn, you are some kinda tough soldier!" "I am all country grit with a side of piss and vinegar!", I whispered to him. After about thirty minutes, I mustered up the strength to do it again to my right leg. I moaned real loud as that medic covered my mouth. It was finished now. The smell was horrendous. I lay there on that dirty bamboo floor next to that putrid smell, gagging and coughing. My pain was so intense, I felt it in my groin. Now, I was either gonna lay here and die, or lay here and get well. I had to find a way. I sure as hell ain't gonna just lay down and give em another body to put on the pile. I couldn't let them win. "Hey Medic, tomorrow when you go out, pull up any leafy weeds from the ground. They gotta be from the ground, not a bush or tree unless it is a fruit tree they call guava. Bring them back to me." Steven told me I got to get some more vitamins in me or this shit is gonna kill me. "Damn, you were balled up in that box with the Beriberi!" "That's the reason I got put in that box doc! I was trying to get some vitamins to us. Those fields out there are loaded with vitamins." The next morning, he went out to get some Pigweed. We smashed up some of the weeds into our hands and laid them over my legs and feet. I was hoping somehow I could draw out the rest of my infection. He threw some into my canteen cup and crushed it up with water. It took some time, but I began to get better. I feel certain when I was laying there staring at the thatch roof, swatting off legions of flies, I was being covered in prayer by the best prayer warrior there was.

"And the prayer offered in faith will restore the one who is sick. The Lord will raise him up. If he has sinned, he will be forgiven." James 5:14-15

Cooking in the Enemy Camp

The guards knew I had some cooking skills. They moved me from the garden to the kitchen after I got well. "Happyaku rokujū hachi!!! [868] You cook! You cook!! You try anything, we gut you like rabbit!" From then on, I cooked food for the Jap guards and the other prisoners. They didn't care if I added weeds and plants to the food anymore. It was just less food they had to provide. The rats are pretty brave around here. They had the run of the storeroom where the rice was stored. Sometimes we could catch one that I could skin and boil. That little bit of meat can give a man some protein. As I was preparing meat, rice, and vegetables for the guards, sometimes I could sneak a bone or two in our rice pot. I swept up the floor and took care of the kitchen like it was a Mess hall. It helped me to think of this place as my job. They had a few military-issued supplies for cleaning, food preparation, and cooking. I kept it clean and organized as possible, something the guards highly respected. Over time, they began to trust me more and gave me more time in there unsupervised. Since they no longer cared much about me bringing in plants, I could grab a few and throw them in sometimes. You just had to be on high alert and always respectful, because you never knew what might set them off. As long as I was in the kitchen, they never laid a hand on me in there.

Miracle Twelve–The Gauntlet

About three or four times a week, depending on the mood of the camp guards, we would be ordered out in a marching line. Japs would be lined up on each side with pick-ax handles, baseball bats, or bamboo canes. We had to run through the line, and they would be swinging at us, clubbing our ribs and backs. Crack!, you could hear bones snapping, leading to howls of their demented laughter. Our bones are like brittle, hollow bamboo. It didn't take much to break them. Some guys would break a rib sneezing or from sleeping too long on one side. Those sick bastards just wanna play a game with us! They know broken ribs can conveniently lead to a quick death. Broken ribs cause intense cutting pain, and you can't expand your lungs enough to get a good breath. It wasn't always starvation that led men to the death pit. It could be a broken set of ribs. I was tall enough that most of my blows were to my gut, lower back, and groin. A good strike to the balls led to more waves of laughter. They were especially hell-bent on tall guys like me. I think problee it was because they were all so short. They made us bend over to get the best of us. I had to make myself go to another place during those times. They battered my abdomen and kidneys, leaving huge red and purple bruises on my back, stomach, and groin. I started thinking about Grins and where he was. I thought that little shit is probably screwing every tanned Cali gal out there! He is probably drinking beer and eating a burger on a beach right now. So, that's where I went when it was my turn to run through.... the beach. Grins was sitting at the end with a pretty girl in one hand and a beer for me in the other! I know I should have been thinking about God taking me through the valley of death and not fearing evil and all, but I just needed to see a man being free sometimes.

As days in camp went on, we seemed to move from one cesspool disease to the next. One by one, we watched fellas just fall where they stood. They were so weak from dysentery they couldn't make it anymore. Dysentery wrung their insides out. More and more bodies were found floating in the latrines in the mornings. Some of them would have part of their colon protruding from their rectum, as they floated on the top. Because it was hard to see at night, some guys just fell in and were too weak to crawl out. Any of us pulling up those bodies were just bringing more diseases to ourselves. I continued to write in my cookbook at night, even when the air smelled of death. It was the only thing that kept those images from my mind.

Entry # Three Country Cornbread Dressing

Leftover cornbread makes the best dressing in the world
8 cups of dried-out cornbread crumbs
3 cups of chopped celery
3 cups of chopped onion
6 hard- boiled eggs chopped
2 tsp ground sage
1 tsp ground thyme
¾ tsp rosemary
½ tsp ground nutmeg
½ tsp salt
½ tsp pepper
½ stick of butter
Bunch of chicken parts, wings, and giblets
Mix all the ingredients together with hands gently
Grease up a cast iron skillet and pour in

Pour chicken stock over the dressing and bake for 25 minutes
I think of the days in CCC's and wonder how ole Cookie is getting along. He was a big ole chubby guy. I am not sure Uncle Sam punched his dance card. He is probably a short-order cook in some greasy spoon somewhere. Wouldn't he find it funny I was in this hell hole writing recipes!

The Side Show

Every day was a routine of moving, working, bowing, and finding the will for another hour to survive. It killed every one of us to bow and salute to these guards. It just became part of our daily camp routine. I learned the proper way to bow and show respect. It is a delicate balance of testing your pride and your will to survive. Group cruelties continued as food would be withheld, and much-needed medicines stood on the shelves unused. Beatings would come and go. But, to totally understand the depths of some of their depraved minds, and the level of their bloodlust, a 'side-show', which was usually inflicted on one man, would be the ticket.

145

If you ever were in the camp location and saw a group of Jap guards circled around laughing and screaming, you knew the body yard would have a new partner soon. They would pick out some ole fella, because he talked funny, walked strangely, or whatever they could figure for their demented selection criteria. Sometimes they would force a hose down their throat or up their rectum. They would fill them full of water until their stomachs were raised up. Then one of them would jump hard on their belly forcing the water out like a broken dam. The guards, especially the crazy-eyed stooge, Satan, would just laugh like demented maniacs. You just learned to walk on by if you were around in the area. Helping anyone got you killed. Sometimes they would have two guys stand in the middle and just slap each other hard in the face until they couldn't hold their arms up, or stand any longer. Their faces stayed swollen and bruised for days. Sometimes they would take the weakest fella and make him squat down for hours holding himself up on the balls of his feet. Then, they would put a concrete block on his head. Either he would hold it up and maintain the position, or be kicked or stabbed. We all felt deep shame for walking by and not reaching a hand up to help. It is a shame that a man can't ever forget. It wells up parts of you that no man wants. Walk by or die, walk by or die. It goes against every Godly principle I was ever taught. You just have to keep moving on. If you let those times get to you, or fear it might be you next, you are gonna go plum crazy.

> *"You shall love your neighbor as yourself. There*
> *is no other commandment greater than these."*
> *Mark 12:31*

Survival is an ugly mistress. Her prison camp rules, unbelievable as it may sound, help you in many ways. You help yourself mentally by knowing you was following their orders. Over time, some guys just lost the will to live any longer. They would just lie down and stop breathing. Their body was in such bad shape; it didn't take much for the mind to carry them across the finish line. I seemed the Japs had the least respect for those boys. They believed that we needed to be more hardened to the conditions. We should be able to handle the heat, cold, the discipline, and the lack of food. It was just another example of us being unworthy. Sometimes they would tell us "You need have strong willpower. You need learn like Japanese". "Yowamushi!" ["You weak! You should be shamed!"]

I continued to work in the meager kitchen there at Cabanatuan for about another sixteen months or so. By now, we had been there in that hell hole a total of twenty-eight months and been through two monsoon seasons. Our clothes are rags and falling off. Many of us are in shorts and have used the legs of our pants to repair our remaining scraps of clothes. Shoes have all but fallen apart by now, and our exposed bare feet are wreaking havoc on us. A lot of guys got the 'trench foot'. Their feet are covered in sores, and the skin is falling off in sheets.

> *"From the sole of the foot even to the head, there is no soundness in it, but bruises and sores and raw wounds; they are not pressed out or bound up or softened with oil." Isaiah 1:6*

Gangrene is the ugly companion to rot and is just waiting to take a sore to the bone as it rots away the flesh. This muck we are in just leads to more disease and amputations. If we can keep our feet dry, we can stay away from most of our problems. Boots and shoes have just fallen apart in scraps of string and leather. Most of us are barefoot, or wearing 'clackers': a shoe made by nailing or tying the tops of your boot leather to pieces of scrap wood. These 'designer' shoes protected our feet from the wet slop, worms, cuts, and catching colds in the rainy months. Guys would be clacking about camp like Shirley Temple and Bojangles on the stair steps! At night, I thought about the CCC camp and the great meatloaf show-down. I wrote another entry in my cookbook.

Entry # Four Mama's Meatloaf

2 lbs. ground beef –use the scraps of Sunday roasts
1 1/2 cups real fine chopped onions
½ cup real fine chopped bell pepper

¾ cup stale bread crumbs – soak in 3 T buttermilk
3 large yard eggs
4 slices of thick bacon
½ cup of ketchup
2 T Worcestershire sauce
½ cup spicy dark mustard or T of pickle juice
1 t salt
1 t pepper
2 T dark brown sugar

Gently mix beef, onions, peppers, wet bread crumbs, eggs with ½ of the ketchup and ½ of the Worcestershire sauce.

Put one slice of bacon in the bottom of a hot skillet. Shape meat into loaf and place over the bacon.

Mix the rest of the ketchup, Worcestershire sauce, mustard, and brown sugar and spread over the meatloaf

Put the bacon acrost the top and bake at 350 degrees for about 45 minutes

Serve with mashed potatoes and green beans

Larrupin' good!

Because I was in the kitchen so much, I overheard the Japanese guards discussing the goings-on. Over time, you can pick up a few Japanese words here or there. I listened closely and picked out that some of us would be moving out soon. Maybe we were gonna get out of this damn hell hole! My only fear was that there was a possibility that it could be worse somewhere else, even though I could not conceive how.

> *"Finally, my brethren, be strong in the Lord and in the power of His might. Put on the whole armor of God, that you may be able to stand against the wiles of the devil." – Ephesians 6:10-11*

Miracle Lucky Thirteen–Old Bilibid Prison

Out of nowhere, without any forewarning, one morning we are taken to the gates of Cabanatuan. We are forced into old trucks and the beds of rickety wagons. As ridiculous as it sounds, this awful place had become home. Camp routines, even the cruel ones, became our norm. We were numb to our realities. Not knowing what might be waiting around the corner was unsettling. So many guys are just plum worn out. Moving on, making big changes just weakened them more. We are moved around a hundred and twenty miles to Manilla, where we are marched in the streets to another prisoner of war camp, known as Old Bilibid Prison. It is located in the center of the big city of Manilla, near Santo Tomas University. This was once a place of higher education. Now it is where all of the civilians were kept after the Japanese occupied the Philippines. Ole Uncle Sam himself built Bilibid to house the Filipino criminals when we occupied these islands, before World War II. Now, it is just a processing house where prisoners are transferred to other camps in the Philippines, or on their way to the 'Flaming Asshole', Japan. Some of the prisoners were assigned here permanently to help the Japs run this hell hole. They helped acclimate the other prisoners and move them to other camps, or they did work detail and salvage runs in the city. One improvement made here was under the commandant, Lt. Nogi. He did run the prison, as best he could, according to the Geneva Convention. All he expected was that you salute, or bow to the guards. Considering we have been doing that for a while now, it is a simple request that hopefully will improve our conditions a lot.

Billibid is shaped like a big spoked wheel structure. The buildings and grounds are encircled by a massive stone wall. There are tall guard towers along each spoke that allow the guards an easy pathway to patrol along as they are watching and waving their guns at men in the yard. Billibid is in horrible shape. The concrete walls are broken and damp, and most of the roofs had been damaged by bombings. We are assigned to big concrete rooms about two-hundred feet in length, and around maybe fifty feet wide. Being a prison and all, it did have bars over all the windows. We was grateful for some light and air moving over us.

It rains quite a bit here, so the walls and floors are always wet. Every nasty critter and bug in the universe are basking in their favorite conditions. The place is crawling with bugs. Mosquitoes especially loved Bilibid because of the standing water, but it was infested with roaches, scabies, lice, and bed bugs, as well. It is disturbing and most creepy at night. You can hear the water dripping from the ceiling into small puddles on the floor, as rats as big as possums scurried through them. The constant drip, drip, drip, filled the night hours like an old haunted clock. It wore on my already shot nerves. I had to stuff threads from my tattered uniform in my ears to try to block it out. When guys would be moaning in pain or talking out of their heads in the death locker, their eerie voices danced off the wet cement walls. Their voices lingered in the hallways with hollow, deathly, whispers. You could feel the souls of thousands here. At night, you could swear some of the sounds were their haunted voices. Bug bites in the night are just a part of life. We did have a few beds and some old cots here. Some guys still had to sleep on the floor, and that caused some fights. Clothes, shoes, and bedding are all getting scarce. Some old fellas are just buck naked here. It is plum awful. You have no dignity in Bilibid prison. You cannot care about it, or it will kill you.

Reported a Prisoner of War, January 17, 1943

The news travels slow. Everything was top secret, and America was trying to keep us all safe from further harm. My poor Mama musta been a wreck. She had been on her knees since I was captured and reported MIA, (missing in action). She didn't know ifin I was dead or alive out here. All she knew was her Sonny Boy was at war. She girded up her loins, got on her knees, and orchestrated spiritual warfare on anything she thought might have gotten near me.

> *"For You have girded me with strength for battle;*
> *You have subdued under me those who rose up*
> *against me." Psalms 18:39*

She prayed the 'Holy Hedge' around me as she circled the trees in the yard. She only walked the 'Walls of Jericho' when it was a real serious situation. A perfect seven-foot circle was permanently trenched around the oak tree where she walked and prayed.

She quoted scripture—*"For though we live in the world, we do not wage war as the world does. The weapons we fight with are not the weapons of the world. On the contrary, they have divine power to demolish strongholds. We demolish arguments and every pretension that sets itself up against the knowledge of God, and we take captive every thought to make it obedient to Christ."* 2 Cor. 10:3-5. She continued her walks circling the tree day after day. Church members and neighbors came to join her and bring her food. She was not willing to stop as long as she knew her God would deliver through her faithfulness. "Come in Nora. You have to rest." "As long as my Sonny Boy is out there, I'm gonna pray this hedge around him." *"This is what the Lord says to you: 'Do not be afraid or discouraged because of this vast army. For the battle is not yours, but God's."* 2 Chron. 20:15, I will take this up with God!" Day after day went by as my Mama walked and prayed the Holy Spirit to rain over me. Her little body housed one of the fiercest prayer warriors on the planet, but it was not equipped to pray without ceasing on this level.

> *"Rejoice always, pray without ceasing, give thanks in all circumstances; for this is the will of God in Christ Jesus for you."* 1 Thessalonians 5:16-18

She collapsed in the yard and was carried in the house to rest. Church members stepped in taking her place in the spiritual fight. They came over taking on round-the-clock shifts, marching around that old tree. Soon as she was able, she was right back out there. When you have a group of spiritual warriors together, you have formed a force no man can ever understand. This is the very core of what the church was set up to do.

> *"Again, I say to you, if two of you agree on earth about anything they ask, it will be done for them by my Father in heaven. For where two or three are gathered in my name, there am I among them."* Matthew 18: 19-20

She got a telegram telling her I was a Prisoner of War (POW) in the Pacific Theater, along with nearly thirty-thousand other Americans, interned by the Japanese. She was told that most of us were captured after the fall of the Philippines. Mama and her prayer support team walked that circular pathway and fervently prayed for over two hundred and fifty days. Only time would tell her that we would make American history, with almost forty-percent of us dying here, leaving a blood-stained path to the highest death rates ever recorded in American history.

"The Lord will cause your enemies who rise against you to be defeated before you. They shall come out against you one way and flee before you seven ways." Deuteronomy 28:7

Camp here in Bilibid was made better by all the American and allied prisoners who had come before this ratty detail made it here. They built some pretty good shower systems and a decent latrine. But by the time we are stationed here, food supplies, rations, and American Red Cross drops had all but stopped. One final drop had been made by the Red Cross that had a really big shipment of vitamin pills. We could get those big ole dry pills and try to swallow them down. You know that there is no way they can help us with this level of starvation, but it made us feel better knowing we had something from home. If you weren't sent to the hospital to die, we were forced to labor on Japanese tarmacs during daylight hours. The hot and humid tropical sun made it just awful, backbreaking work. We began our days around 7:00 a.m., where we are awakened by the sounds of boots coming down the concrete halls. We all scattered to get up and ready before the guards came in. At 8:00 a.m., we lined up to get our one canteen cup of gruel rice soup, and a cup of water; before we were off to the tarmac. After a day in the sun, at 8:00 p.m., we got our final meal for the day. It was also a bowl of soupy rice. Sometimes it was green rice because they had thrown in a few greens. You get used to color, texture, smell or any other appearance of food not bothering you. When you get this malnourished, you will eat anything, no matter how bad it looks or smells. I am hungry. For some reason, I cannot get the thought of a good ole catfish fry out of my head. You cannot lay around and dream about these things, or you can go off the rails. I go on back to my cot and write another recipe.

Entry # Five Fried Catfish and Hushpuppies

Catch and clean catfish, remove all bones, filet (6 filets)
Use guts, skin, and bones to grind up for the garden. Bury deeply, or the stray cats will get in it.
Prepare a cast iron skillet with lard about 3 inches deep – heat up real hot
2 Cups of flour
1 Cup and a smidge yellow cornmeal
2 Cups Buttermilk
2 Large yard eggs
1 t black pepper

Mix pepper and 1 cup of flour – drag all the filets through until coated, shake off
Mix rest of flour and cornmeal and place in paper sack or on butcher paper
Mix Buttermilk and eggs together
Drag the floured filets in the buttermilk and eggs and right into the cornmeal bag, shake
Lay out the coated filets for a few minutes on a kitchen towel to drain off liquids that will pop and steam
Fry only 2 at a time to keep oil hot and filets crispy
Hushpuppies
Mix all the remaining flour, cornmeal, and buttermilk and eggs together. Add more flour as needed to get it to scoop out without running. Add 1 t of baking soda. Add some minced onion. Add cornmeal to get texture. Drop by spoonfuls in hot grease until golden brown.

The Chapel

As tired and beaten as we all were when we got into Bilibid, I am amazed to see a little shanty chapel leaning against one of the walls. It was built there by the prisoners before us who were at Bilibid. They held services in it. It was the second time that I saw that religion and faith were respected by the guards, even if this was not what they practiced themselves.

> *"My praise comes from you while I am among those assembled for worship. I will fulfill my vows in the presence of those who respect Jehovah."*
> *Psalms 22:25*

December 13, 1943

The Jap guards bring us in some postcards that are pre-filled in. "Here, stupid dick shits, give me name of assholes you want to know about! We put on caad. You all look healthy and good, we treat you good here, huh, Babe Ruth!?" With that, he slams the gun butt into the back of some guy's head and drops the postcard in his lap. Blood is pouring down his neck. Some guys rip their ragged shirts to make a bandage and put pressure on it to stop the bleeding. This is the first time we have been able to have any correspondence back home. He hands each of us a postcard. They are date stamped, December 13, 1943. They have controlled everything, including our bowel movements, and now they are censoring our mail to our families!

From:
Houston Lowe
Nationality – American
Rank – Sergeant, U. S.A.
Camp – Philippine Military Prison Camp No. 10 – D
To: Mrs. Nora Lowe
Glen Rose, Texas
General Delivery

IMPERIAL JAPANESE ARMY

1. I am interned at: Philippine Military Prison Camp No. 10-D.
2. My health is XXXXXX good; XXXXX XXXXX
3. I am – uninjured; XXXXXXXXXXXXXXXXXX
4. I am – XXXXXXXXXXXXXXX; well
5. Please see that all at home is _____ taken care of.
6. (Re: Family); _____
7. Please give my best regards to_____
   Florine and Odell

All the Xs are marking out any news that would shed a bad light on our treatment. We are all thankful and glad to get any news home, even if it isn't anywhere close to the atrocities we are facing daily. We talk a lot about our families here; it is all we have to keep us grounded. I feel like I know most of these families myself. I can just imagine Mama when she gets this. She is thinking I am at some health spa! I know that is best, but none of us can qualify as being in 'good' health!

Miracle Fourteen – The 'Yella'

After all of this exposure to mosquitoes, I came down with Yellow Fever. It was my time in the barrel I guess, but I could not have picked a worse place to have it. We all knew what to look for by now. It starts with a fever and a headache, chills, vomiting; and body aches. It does look a lot like most of these other damn, jungle diseases. My back was where I felt it the most. With all the mosquitoes in this place, it is a wonder the whole damn camp isn't down with it! Your face gets red, and your eyes are sensitive to any light. They don't care much about all that around here. I went out to the tarmac and worked in the sun in that condition. If you go toxic with the 'yella' you start turning yellow; even your eyes. Most guys that went yella didn't make it. It just starts shutting down your organs until you die. My body has overcome so many diseases and infections by now; I may have built up some strong kinda fighting army inside. I was sickly, sweating and miserable; but I never went

155

yella. One of the Filipino soldiers snuck me in some local weeds called 'Balatong Aso'. It could help if I chewed on the bitter roots. The Balatong Aso has some long seed pods and beautiful yellow flowers. That is how you could recognize it. If you chew on the roots, it could take a fever down overnight. The Filipino soldiers knew all about the native plants here. If we could get to them from information, they would help us along the way when we got down. I lay on that dirty cot breathing in air that was reeking with the stench of death. I wasn't gonna let them take me to the 'hole': the rat-infested hospital ward. I would make up recipes or think about fried pies to keep myself from thinking about how miserable I felt. If you don't go yella with Yellow Fever, it can pass in a few days. You will feel like mule team ran over you, but you will survive.

After I got back on my feet, I was sent to chop wood. Wood was a much-needed commodity to the guards. They needed plenty of it to dry out their living quarters and prepare their meals. They were never happy with a day's worth. They had to have three or four days of wood stacked up by their kitchen. Most days, we chopped wood for seven hours straight. I would go back to my cot, and my arms would just hang like wet bed sheets.

Miracle Fifteen–Final Disposition of Prisoners Final "Kill All Order"

I think it is sometime in August of 1944. We guess Tojo got a gut-full of Uncle Sam relentlessly riding his white horse up his ass. He was getting a lot of pressure to bring this war to a close, and he was sick of hearing from his officers about the work it was caring for the thousands of captives that were still alive. The American allies had really pissed him off, and the war was going on much longer than he had desired. So in his true fashion, he administers a final blow to the remaining bits of the rubble of humanity left in the thousand or so prison camps still in operation. He calls for a *Final Disposition of Prisoners Order*. In this disposition letter, he provides suggestions on how to dispose of the internees. It part, it read:

The Methods.

a. *"Whether they are destroyed individually or in groups, or however it is done, with mass bombing, poisonous smoke, poisons, drowning, decapitation, or what, dispose of them as the situation dictates.*

b. *In any case, it is the aim not to allow the escape of a single one, to annihilate them all, and not to leave any traces."* *EX-POW Bulletin, August 1995, page 34*

So now, as if they ever needed an excuse to kill an internee, they were given carte blanche, license to kill at will, groups or individuals. Some guards took that note as their personal challenge. Immediately following, they chopped a few men down in their tracks like sugar cane.

Houston E. Lowe, Japanese Prisoner Uniform, Circa 1942-45, Courtesy Houston E. Lowe, personal collection

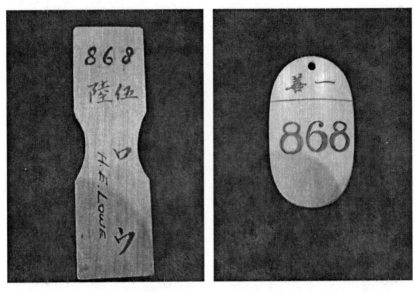

868 Japanese Issued Bamboo Prisoner Dog Tags, Circa 1942-1945,
Courtesy Houston E. Lowe, personal collection

Japanese Soldiers with American Flag being lowered on Corregidor,
Philippine Islands Retrieved from: https://upload.wikimedia.org/wikipedia/
commons/b/bb/Amerflag001_pp1_01.jpg

Surrender of American troops at Corregidor, Philippine Islands, May 1942. 208-AA-80B-National Archives Identifier: 535553 Retrieved from: https://www.archives.gov/files/research/military/ww2/photos/images/ww2-129.jpg

Cabanatuan Prison Camp - Nipa Hut –Retrieved from: https://upload.wikimedia.org/wikipedia/commons/3/30/Cabanatuan_Prison_Hut.jpg By U.S. Army [Public domain], via Wikimedia Commons

American Prisoners Using Improvised Litters to Carry Comrades, Retrieved From: Retrieved from: https://upload.wikimedia.org/wikipedia/commons/d/ d7/Photograph_of_American_Prisoners_Using_Improvised_Litters_to_Carry_ Comrades_-_NARA_-_535565.tif

Camp O'Donnell Mass Grave, Retrieved From: http://www.lindavdahl.com/FrontPage_Links/O'Donnell% 20Mass%20Grave%20Photos.htm, Courtesy Linda Dahl

Old Bilibid Prison, Retrieved from: http://www.lindavdahl.com/Photo%20
Gallery%20and%20Images/Bilibid_Photo.htm, Courtesy Linda Dahl

Bilibid POW Prison Hospital 1945, Retrieved from: http://www.lindavdahl.
com/Photo%20Gallery%20and%20Images/Bilibid%20Prison%20
Hospital%20Photo.htm, Courtesy Linda Dahl

IMPERIAL JAPANESE ARMY

Philippine Military Prison Camp

1. I am interned at _____ No. 10-D. _____

2. My health is — ~~excellent;~~ good; ~~fair; poor~~

3. I am — uninjured; ~~sick in hospital; under treatment; not under treatment~~

4. I am — ~~improving; not improving; better;~~ well.

5. Please see that __ all at home is _____

_____ is taken care of.

6. (Re: Family) ; _____

_____

7. Please give my best regards to ___ Florine and Odell _____

From:
Name

_____ Houston Lowe _____

Nationality ___ American _____

Rank ___ Sergeant, U.S.A. ___

Camp ___ Philippine Military Prison Camp No. 10-D. ___

To: ___ Mrs. Nora Lowe _____

~~Glen Rose,~~ Texas _____

~~General Delivery~~ ___

1311 Lincoln Ave - Fort Worth -

Post Card From Old Bilibid Prison, Houston to Nora Pace (Mama),
December 13, 1943, Courtesy Houston E. Lowe, personal collection

Chapter Six

The Devil's Voyage

Miracle Sixteen–Survival Voyage Aboard The Hell Ship, The Noto Maru–August 27, 1944, to September 5, 1944

Well, sometime in late August, we never really knew what the exact date was....we guessed by the number of moons, and the scratches on our bamboo poles, around the 25th. We were forced to take off all of our clothes. They lined us up naked as jaybirds. The guards wadded up all our tattered scraps of cloth and piled them up to be distributed back to the remaining prisoners. We are issued new woolen Japanese uniforms. These things are itchy, hot, and smelled like a damn goat! But, we had clothes, and some of us had shoes. All the Jap officers started moving us like cattle from Bilibid, toward the docks in Manilla. There was a group of over a thousand of us still alive, ifin you could call it that. We was already thin and gaunt. Most of us already had gone a couple of rounds with some God-awful jungle disease or another. We were to leave the Philippines, and are headed right into the mouth of the devil himself, the flaming red asshole–Japan. We find out it was August 27, 1944.

The Noto Maru

The guards were now bitterly angry and impatient. They were to follow orders to get us to Japan for slave labor as soon as possible. The Japanese industrialists set these voyages of death up to collect and deliver the slave labor they needed. This disheveled bunch is gonna be slave labor! We got to the dock, with the guards herding and prodding us along like cattle in line for a vaccine. Bayonets are swinging and tapping on us. They are yelling "Speedo, Speedo!" [Quickly, Quickly!]. Now we see that this junkpile of a tanker ship is unmarked, no 'flaming red asshole' flag. We know enough that we could be blowed out the water at any time by our pilots or sub crews. In the bay right next to the Noto Maru, was a cruiser and some destroyers. The rickety old gangplank screeched and swung back and forth, groaning out the call of impending death. We stepped into small boats that sped us over to the floating iron demon. The top of the ship's deck is where we found the grave hole we were going to climb down into. The heavy metal hatch door opened and slammed down on that deck, making the haunting sound of a grave door. They were positioning us to climb into the ship hold for transport somewhere.

The cargo hold was a deep framed metal room kinda like a box car on a train, just a lot bigger and a lot darker. Cargo holds were never designed for people; they was for cargo crates, packages, equipment, and bales. There is no place to sit or lie down. The Japanese guards started yelling "Iku!, iku!" [Go!, Go !] Our thin bodies were slithering down that grave hole like worms from a rain bucket. It took a long time, and men just kept coming. We kept being crammed deeper and deeper into the hold, with more and more men just falling in. It is dark, damp, and hot as an old miner hole. We thought there was no way they can get one more of our skeletons down that ladder in that hole, but they did. They kept hollering at us, "koodo!", [pay attention here] "Ugoku!, ugoku!" , [move, move]. They were yelling at us in the hold, to move back to make room for more prisoners. I am thinking, "shit, they can't get any more bodies in this hole." About the last three-hundred men were just heaved down in, falling head first. The Noto cargo hold was maybe big enough for around four-hundred men. The guards were able to pack around a thousand of us in. We was body to body, pressed together like the clove and peppermint sticks, shoved in the big glass jars in the general store at Christmas time. Most of us standing chest to chest. The reeking body odor began to smell like country road kill after three days in August. With the heat, some ole boys are so weak; they couldn't stand anymore. They just fell between us in a heap. With no air down there, it would be easy to suffocate. We just had to move around them best we could. We had to stand most of the time, or sit balled up to the knees, positioning ourselves to keep from falling. It was hot as the infernos in hell. The air was thick with the stench. We stand there locked in a gaze, frozen in place. We fearfully look up and around our surroundings in the hold. The hatch door slammed shut like a prison door, shaking the seams and bolts in this putrid ship. It was immediately dark and eerie. You cannot see anything but shadows. All the rats and roaches began to scurry for a position, running over our legs and feet. We shuffle ourselves and push to get ourselves to any space or air. It is hot and steamy, and I am not sure how we are going to survive in here. The conditions are gonna kill us, but fear will kill us sooner. Our troops have no idea we are in here. They are gonna blow us out of Subic Bay if they see us. The Noto begins to crawl across the bay, wailing and moaning.

There is nowhere to take a piss, except was one Benjo bucket that was dropped down in the front of the hold. It is already filled with puke, piss, and shit. When it is pulled up to be emptied, all that human waste, slop soup rained down on those poor ole sick men right below. Pretty soon the piss soup piled up so high; they threw a few other Benjos down here for us. Some of us are too weak to get to the Benjo bucket. We just had to piss or shit where we stood. If you did, you just let it dry on you, and whatever rags or wool Jap uniform you had for your clothes. The wool uniforms were soon taken off or torn to bits, just to survive the inferno. The shit and urine burned your skin, making you itch and scratch. The nights are miserable. It is hot, but, the dark could take you to some bad places in your mind. It felt like you was in a grave. I guess in a lot of ways we were. Some guys are just going crazy in here. They start screaming or calling they Mama. They start fighting and cussing at each other. Some ole fella just rocked and banged his head against the hold all night. I thought he was gonna turn his head to mush. It was reeking with an odor so befouling; we were puking, making the odor more intense.

Daylight would break, bringing bits of light through the seams and the top of the hold. Our first couple of men were dead by morning. They were kept in their tattered, blood-stained rags, and wrapped in vomit-stained blankets for a shroud. After a couple of days of holding out, the Japanese guards commanded whoever could still crawl out the hole, to come up top and dump their bodies overboard. Prisoners were volunteering to help just to get out on deck and breathe some fresh air. Bodies were bobbing along the watery, foaming wave crests until they disappeared into the dark sea. I am certain more than a few were eaten by sharks. Once a day or so, we would get a small cup of sloppy rice water, and some water. Water was very scarce. If you had your canteen, you might save some when they poured some down. Sometimes during the night, your water would disappear.

When I thought the conditions could not get any worse, the ship took a sharp turn to the left, throwing bodies over in piles. The ship would change direction and course all the time. We could feel the ship swing hard one direction for a few miles, only to be steered the opposite direction soon after. The sea was sliced into ribbons of concrete as we slammed across the choppy waves. The force of the impact raised us off the floors spilling us into each other. We was just like a Cotton Mouth in the river. This constant zigzag across the already choppy seas was just the ticket for making people sick. The vomit began to spew. Men were gagging and heaving. The hold floor was full of human waste past your ankles. If you weren't sick from being tossed around, the smells and sights would make you puke; adding to the human soup on the floor.

The Noto continued to sway and pitch, rolling over the choppy China Sea. You could hear the creaking of the wood, and the old iron plates screeching deathly notes to a miserable song. This ship is a wreck and not seaworthy. She groaned all the way through the China Sea. The constant scraping and high-pitched squealing of the rusty iron are enough to make a man go insane. The dark swallowed us up. I hear my dad. "Only one thing you have to hand them Houston, your honor." The darkness can take a man's soul if you let it.

"Have respect unto the covenant; For the dark places of the earth are full of the habitations of cruelty." Psalms 74:20

Miracle Seventeen–Two Deep-Running Torpedoes are Fired at the Noto Maru

Surrounded by the putrid smells, wearing the coat of death, the wailings of a belly grinding, and men losing their minds from dehydration; we slammed through the China Sea awaiting our fate. The hundred or so Japanese soldiers and crew up top were resting in their comfortable cabins and beds. You could smell their hot tea and rice as guys were suffocating and starving to death down in the iron belly below. It was the devil's voyage, and our captain was Satan himself.

After days of rocking, dysentery took all the fluid a body had left. Organs began to shut down as men staggered, lingering between life and death. The unbearable conditions made some guys plain delirious. They started talking out of their heads, just nonsense. Some others are gazing in a glazed-over expression with no response for days. Some men are crouched in corners like animals who have been beaten. One ole guy has been barking like a dog for hours. We sailed like what seemed forever, but it was just a couple of days. We hear the Japanese guards on the top deck in a hell of a commotion. They are yelling and running; it was madness. Someone is on the radio, and horns are blasting. Word gets down in the hold that two deep-running torpedoes were just fired at us from an unidentified American submarine in a wolf pack. One torpedo actually made a skimming contact with the hull and did not detonate. The other was fired too low and ran just below the belly of the ship. "All you people stupid! See, you people don't want you either! They fire at us!" It seems the whole lot of us just missed a date with death! The guards open up the hold hatch and are threatening us with their rifles. They are angry. I don't know much about American torpedo firing and target contact records, but my guess is, they don't miss real often! I understand that torpedoes were pretty hit-and-miss in the early years of the war before they were better calibrated, and their detonation systems were perfected. By this time in 1944, they are damn accurate! I guess I just got covered in that holy hedge Mama prayed over me again, and He carried the rest of these guys right along with me. That little woman's prayers saved a whole damn ship! I bow my head and thank God for preserving my life. I am fighting off with every inch of my being before asking Him why on earth I am thanking Him.

> *"Though I walk in the midst of trouble, you preserve my life. You stretch out your hand against the anger of my foes; with your right hand you save me." Psalm 138:7*

After being in that cesspool for a few days, we developed a lot of oozing ulcers on our legs and feet. That, of course, attracts flies. I don't know where a bunch of flies come from in the middle of the sea, but it is proof that like my Daddy said, "Houston, you got rot, you got flies." They continued to fly around and land in the wounds carrying their nasty diseases from man to man. Roaches and rats were everywhere in the steel monster. At night, they would crawl over us. You knew a guy just gave up when he let the roaches crawl over him. When bodies are sick inside, they are rotting a bit inside. The smell is unbearable. The worst of the human mess was near the opening of the hold. The men who were the sickest with dysentery and diarrhea were hanging on at the hold opening, nearest to the Benjo barrel. Sometimes they just fell in. When some of them got so bad, they pushed them topside to be sprayed down with fire hoses.

This hellish voyage went on for nine days, including a couple of stops for the Japs to pick up some supplies and other destroyers. We had sores on our legs and feet, and skin was falling off from rot. We have been entangled with each other in such tight quarters our legs and arms are locked in position. We have tried to share our space in the three holds of the ship, but at some point, guys were too tired even to move. The Noto suddenly come to a stop. Engines shut off with a deathly whirr. It is an eerie quiet. We were so used to the rumbling sound of the engine, and the swaying of the hold; that we couldn't get our bearings for a while. We hear more commotion on deck. Jap guards are talking loud again. I thought, well, this is it. They are so pissed the Americans fired at them; they are gonna just drop a cigarette and torch us to death in here. The only reason to keep us alive at this point is for slave labor. Not sure how a bunch of sickly, hundred-pound men are gonna do any good. The screeching hatch opened as a bright ray of sun pierces our dark, death locker. Our skeleton frames were ordered to get out. Stepping across the iron slats in the hold floor, men we sloshing around in the muck. "Dete-Ikiyagare, Usero!" [Get out!, Get out!] We all work to help each other to climb up the slippery ladder. Our muscles are cinched tight, and we are slow to move. The guards are impatient. One guard waves his automatic weapon over the opening threatening to kill us all. The remaining bodies that were not thrown overboard in the China Sea were dragged out to a mass grave site. I have no idea how many men we lost while at sea. No sleep, no fresh air, little food and clean water, crammed down in a hundred-and-twenty-degree hell hole, tossing for days out in the China Sea; created a human gumbo of broken, lost souls.

> *"He heals the brokenhearted and binds up their wounds." Psalms 147:3*

The Watery Bay of Bodies

When the bell tolled on the history of these iron demons, recorded numbers show that of the approximately sixty-two thousand POWs who were transported in fifty-six of these ships, twenty two-thousand men lost their lives in the belly of their chartered sea monster. Most of those fellas had been captured like me for almost three years. After a bombing or torpedo hit, nineteen hell ships sank dragging about nineteen-thousand souls to the bottom of the sea in mangled iron claws. A sadistic typhoon blew another ship off the sea, never to be found again. These iron dragons spewed American and allied bodies up and down the China Sea, swallowing and belching them out in watery, mass graves. When the Noto spit us out, whoever could still walk, were taken to our new camp on

Shikoku Island, Mukaishima, Zentsuji, Hiroshima #4. Of all the camps and treatment over the last twenty-eight months, this one proves to be the worst.

The Noto Maru, Retrieved from: https://upload.wikimedia.org/wikipedia/
commons/f/f3/NYK_Noto_Maru1934.JPG By Unknown Scanning and editing
was done by Ogiyoshisan (Last edited August 30, 2012) [Public domain],
via Wikimedia Commons

Chapter Seven

The Final Camp

Miracle Eighteen–Zentsugi, Shikoku Island, Mukaishima, Hiroshima POW Sub-camp No. 4

Ghostly white, gaunt drawn faces, hollowed out grey eye sockets, bellies sunken in from the years of starvation, hands, and feet are white raisins lathered in week-old shit, vomit, and piss; we walk that wooden plank to march to our next fresh level of hell. March we did. Not to succumb to the mighty Imperial Japanese Army, but to let those bastards know we still can. They are marching us under the fresh yellow-green canopy of wet lotus, banana, and tall palm trees. The locals are watching in horror as we step by. They hide their faces from the guards before being seen as a *Hangyaku-sha, [traitor]*. A tinny radio is playing, and you can smell body odor covered in cheap perfume. There is a shanty building with a rickety bamboo balcony where the guards must keep their 'pleasure girls'. Some of the girls are young, maybe around sixteen or seventeen. I can't tell anymore. They are beautiful little creatures with stark pale faces and jet black hair. The men have them all made up. They are wearing flowers in their hair. Their red lips are glistening against their delicate powder-white faces. They should be home with their Mama, but they are working this camp to keep food on their family table. They are giggling and pointing at us. "Want this flyboy?" Humiliation is a cruel sword that cuts through your soul. They know these wrecks of wasting flesh aren't even capable. They wiggle their little fingers and have them flop over like a wet rag. Their taunts and jeers of "seikou!! mac, mac" are just another cog in their psychological warfare machine.

> *"For a prostitute is a deep pit, and a forbidden woman is a narrow well;" Proverbs 23:27*

We plow on waiting for the next step in this human minefield. Stepping on the broken dock planks, we are immediately searched before we are hosed down with cold seawater. They promptly begin our initiation here with a hard slap across our faces. Each of us, delirious from the voyage, take our humiliating slap across the face. We walk to our huts and bare floors. We know the routine in plank bunks. The weakest take the floors, and the rest crawl in the wooden crates up top. The whole dang camp was infested. It was riddled with swarming flies, gnats, fruit flies, and lice. The damn bedbugs crawled and jumped on everything. You couldn't take a drink, a sip of soup, or a bite of rice without one in your spoon or jumping in your mouth. You know they were just out following caribou or water buffalo in all their droppings, and now they are in your mouth! We look for the latrine and water. We are no longer in the Philippines, our home for almost three years. Now, we are in Japan, in a damn jungle by a shipyard dock. It is all bombed out and scrap iron, and a cement floating dock is about all that is left. Glad our boys took such a toll on this place! We are here to complete the work the Japanese started on their ships, roads, and infrastructure. We begin the dance all over again, a new set of guards, some old guards, new camp rules, and new processes. 'Cept now, the Japs are tired and homesick too. The war has gone on too long now, and they are missing their families. You can see it in their eyes. After thirty-three months in captivity, you can also pick up a few words in Japanese, enough to know; they want to go home. That played out well in some cases with the guards. But for many of them, they were less tolerant than before. Beatings and slaps across the face came with no warning. Everything agitated them. They were angry. We would leave the camp for work duty at 4:00 a.m., and work in the sun or rain until we drug back to our camp around 8:00 p.m. Sometimes we had a small lunch of rice, and sometimes we got nothing. We would forge for a few plants and grubs along the jungle's edge to hold us.

The Ship Yard

Zentsugi is a large ship port for Japanese war vessels. The dry dock is where we will repair rivets on their damaged ships. Damned if we didn't end up repairing rivets on the same hell-hole of a ship we were transported in! We are the Japanese war work-force. We are not just working on projects to maintain a camp; we are helping their war efforts to defeat our own. Days were long, backbreaking, and unbearably hot. On the days we were not in the dry dock, we would be forced to load tons of coal onto the Japanese barges. We stayed filthy dirty. Our bodies were covered in coal dust and soot. It would be in our eyes, mouths, and ears. We would cover our mouths and noses with any dirty rag we could find to keep from breathing in the suffocating dust. In dry dock, we used broken and useless tools. They have no reason to worry about their employee's safety. The remains of machine shops had some metal and wood fabricators working in the drydock, repairing and rebuilding Japanese warships. Many of these ships were welded iron and steel. Mitsubishi was the main builder in Japan at this time. I reckon that is who I was working for. This was the only time I ever received any pay. Just a few yen for twelve hours a day, six days a week. But it was pay, none the less. Of course, we had to spend it in the small store set up in camp by the guards. Mostly there was cigarettes and candy. Most of the prisoners worked on the older ships with riveted hulls. It was a constant process of lining up big steel plates and drilling holes for rivets or replacing the rivets that were already damaged. It took lots of us, some on either side of the plates that we were fastening. Sometimes one of us had to be a driller, holding that heavy machinery up, to drill through the one-inch thick, hull plate. It was punishing work that would turn your arms to oatmeal real quick. It was almost impossible to match the pre-drilled holes, so one guy would ream out the hole, to make the rivet fit. That's where I met Rev. His name was James Revelle, and he was from Schenectady, New York. He shore had an accent that made me chuckle. Rev was a reamer on the ship hold and had already been there a few days. "Damn, bucket of bolts, I'd like to show these boys a real Navy yaaad! "Yaaad!" I loved the way he said yard. "My name is Houston, what's yours?" "My name is James, but people just call me Rev." Rev was a hard worker like me.

The Salt Mine

While we are cleaning the inside hull of a ship in dock, Rev and I noticed rusty looking clumps are growing along some of the walls in the ship hold. We worked a lot of times in the dim lighting. It was hot as hell in there, and it was hard to see clearly. To finish some of the work on the hull plates, we scraped off whatever that stuff was. After scraping a bit, I took a pinky finger scoop and placed it in my mouth. Dear God, it was salt!! The clumps growing alongside the walls of the ship plate seams in the hull were sea salt deposits. We are so grateful. Not only could we possibly get a bit of flavor in our lousy food, but we could also get some minerals from the iron that leeched into the salt from the hull. Rev and I scraped a handful each and hid it wrapped in a palm leaf in our shirts. We were searched at random here, so we had to 'steal' it. We brought back the salt and in secret shared it with our comrades. It is amazing what a little salt can do to raise a man's spirits. The breaking down of this ole ship provided us a lot of joy.

> *"But its swamps and marshes will not become fresh;*
> *they will be left for salt." Ezekiel 47: 11*

When I wasn't riveting, cleaning the ships, or loading coal, the guards assigned me to work in the kitchen. We called one guard Gunso. He calls me over, "Happyaku rokujū hachi!, |868|. I step up and bow as I approach him. He swings back and slams the butt of his rifle in my face. Blood is spilling on the dirt as my face immediately begins to throb. From my concussion in the Philippines, I have instant dizziness and ringing in my ears. I grab my nose. It is broken at the place just between my eyes. I hold my nose and wipe the blood away. Trying to steady myself to keep from falling over,

I bow in submission to him. We lock eyes. I do not flinch. There is an understanding between us. He is in power. I am prodded by his rifle as he leads me to my assignment in the kitchen. I will be cleaning vegetables for the guards. There was even less to eat here. Occasionally, I could find some local jungle mushrooms, pigweed, and snails to throw in the sour rice gruel. If the rice ran out, we were left to eat what we could find. I had become quite an expert by now on the local edible plants. There were always a few mice or rats around; they were just hard to catch. The guards are going hungry too. The camp rations are about gone, and they are left with living off the land like us. One afternoon, most of the guards went on a water buffalo hunt. They knew they needed to survive too, and protein was sorely missing from their diets. It took six guards half a day to corner and kill one. I 'spect it would have taken Rev and me a couple of hours, but they sure weren't gonna put a gun in our hands! They come back into camp and ordered a few of us to go out and field dress it in the swamp where it laid. "Ikimasu, ikimasu," [Go, go!] They pointed to the swamp and handed us guntō swords, and a few knives. Waist deep, out in that mosquito-infested swamp, crawling with leeches and scum, we pulled that thousand-pound animal out on the grassy bank. We were exhausted, lying there on the banks until we could get the strength to break this thing down. It took us until after 6:00 p.m., to completely skin, clean, and dress that animal down to its carcass. After dragging the usable meat and organs in burlap bags to the guard's kitchen, the head guard told me to keep the bones. "Happyaku rokujū hachi, Kokkaku, kokkaku," [868, Bones, bones] He pointed to the swamp, directing me to head back there. Keeping us alive finally began to make sense to them. After all, we were their labor force. Anything we did, they did not have to do themselves. Even, in the midst of all of this bloody battle, if you remove the flags above us, we are just a bunch of men trying to survive. Masked beneath authority, control, and domination, was an act of grace and kindness. I was sure enough glad to be a part of it.

> *"But love your enemies, and do good, and lend,*
> *expecting nothing in return; and your reward will*

be great, and you will be sons of the Most High;
for He Himself is kind to ungrateful and evil
men. Luke 6:35

After searing the buffalo steaks and making a stew with rice for the guards, I chopped up the big bones and put them in the kawa pot. There are a few slivers of meat to eat, and the fresh bones made a decent broth. I know a lot of protein was pumped in that broth, and our battered bodies sure needed it. Everyone ate well that day. The guards are in their hut laughing around a table of steaks and stew, as their captives sit on dirt and bamboo floors, drinking broth in a silent stare of disbelief. We are all just a bunch of hungry men, sharing food at the most twisted of banquet tables. Nourished for another step, another hour, another day; our bodies and our spirits have been given the very prescription to fight on. A feast is being shared in a split universe. Even in their silence and inability to show us, I know the Japs are grateful for what we did for them, and we eat at the banquet table of our enemy.

"You prepare a table before me in the presence of
my enemies. You anoint my head with oil; my cup
overflows." Psalms 23:5

Miracle Nineteen–Elephant Balls

I got sick right away. The swamp was just the recipe for another jungle infection. I began to sweat out of every pore of my body. I knew this vicious cycle too well by now. I hardly got enough water in my body to keep me alive, and now it is pouring out of me like wringing a full sponge. The chills set in, and soon they are followed with a blazing fever. "Shit!, I can't take this crap anymore. My body is ravaged. It seems like it is just fighting me every step of the way. I can't get a damn break!" I lay in my bunk at night trying to get comfortable. Joe, my good buddy from Cabanatuan, gets me a drink from his canteen. We have no idea if what we have can be passed to one another. One of the guys goes out to ask the guards if they have any medicine to give. The guard abruptly yells back, "You stupid fool! You not worth the jaa it store in. Go back to you hut!" I was just laying on that bamboo mat hot as a griddle cake. Joe, my friend, comes over to comfort me. "Houston, you can't take no more of this. You got to lie still and let yourself rest." I was hiding my fear as best I could, but my whole groin and scrotum are swollen as big as two cantaloupes. My penis is burning and hot, stuck inside me. I was in a helluva mess. My legs and feet are swollen again. A medic in the hut told me I problee got one of the worst diseases, elephantiasis. I hear the guards outside casting bets on my life. Cigarettes are being anteed up. Old Satan, who was transferred with us, is standing watch outside. He bet everyone on me. "Happyaku rokujū hachi!, Tsuyoi ishi, tsuyoi ishi!" [868!, Strong will, strong will!] I guess he has seen me through a few episodes, he might as well make a few cigarettes on my behalf. The other guards were sure I was gonna take the next dirt nap, so they bet again me. That just pissed me off even more.

> *"Blessed are you when men hate you, and ostracize*
> *you, and insult you, and scorn your name as evil, for*
> *the sake of the Son of Man." Luke 6:22-23*

That night, I slowly pulled my fundoshi down and showed Joe. A fundoshi is a loincloth that is traditionally worn by Japanese men. "Holy Jehoshaphat, Houston! What the hell are you gonna do now?!!" I know what I have to do, I have done it before in my legs. I just have no idea how I am gonna convince myself to shove that bamboo skewer into my own balls! I laid there all miserable night, fidgeting with sweat and chills. I rolled from side to side trying to get comfortable. When you have a small watermelon between your legs, there is no position that will ease your pain. The pressure became unbearable. I feel the tightness in my groin growing, and the pain is getting more intense. The shooting pains up my groin feel like shots of electricity. My fevered mind is taking me to a deep and deadly valley. My only hope for survival is to punch a hole in my balls! I know I have to do this before I get too weak. The next morning, Joe brings me a torn piece of cloth from someone's uniform. He had soaked it in cool water. "Joe, go find me some guava

177

leaves. You know the little fruit trees around in the fields out back? Just get ya a handful." I stripped off another piece of bamboo and peeled it back until I could get a sharp point. I took a deep breath. Then I begin to question if I am just going crazy. "Joe, are my balls really swoll up, or am I just seeing things?" He knew I was getting delirious from the bacteria and the high fever. "Oh, they are swollen up, Houston, they are sure swollen up!" "Hold my back up Joe. Once I do this, I could just pass plumb out!" I crawled over and sat between Joe's legs, pressing my back against his chest for support. "Shit, Houston, shit!" I grabbed up that damn bamboo stick and jabbed it right into my groin. I knew I had one shot at this, cuz I probably couldn't do it again! That rotten puss and fluid shot like an arrow, spewing out like a fountain. It stung and burned all the way out. I fell back on Joe grabbing my groin as the pulsating pains shot through me. I clamped my teeth on that piece of bamboo as I watched all that rotting, puss and fluid drain onto the dirt floor below. My balls are deflated like two prunes. The pressure was immediately released and the pain subsided. Now, if I don't have enough troubles up in here, I just punched a pipeline for disease in my own balls! Joe gave me the guava leaves. I chewed on them for a few minutes to release the juices where the medicine is. Joe helped me to cover up my groin with the leaves, and we put a damp cloth over it. I got a little relief that night and caught a few winks. The fever broke in the early morning, and the chills were disappearing. In about a week, I was able to eat a little bit; and I did get better. I guess everything is alright, my penis came out of its hut, and my balls were back to normal! The swelling has gone down. I am just weak and need to get my strength back. I am grateful to my father. While I am laying there, I think of him. I think he would be proud of how much I learned from him.

"For the Lord reproves him whom he loves, as a father the son in whom he delights." Proverbs 3:12

I am finally strong enough to get myself up and to the kawa shack. While we continue to be starved to death, in the guard room, they are laughing, smoking, and filling themselves on the remaining water buffalo. They are in a heated conversation. I could only pick up a few words here and there. Three or four guards just cussed up a storm as I passed by. They were throwing their cigarettes at Satan as he collected up his winnings. " Happyaku rokujū hachi!, Happyaku rokujū hachi!, Tsuyoi ishi, tsuyoi ishi!" [868!, 868!, Strong will! Strong will!] "You strong man..you have annah, .I respect you." Then Satan, my tormentor for all these years, looks me eye to eye, man to man. I guess my big ole country grit finally measured up to his damn bushido! That night, being grateful for my life, I wrote Joe's family recipe in my cookbook.

Entry # Six Joe's Italian Gravy – Makes enough for a big Italian Family

10 pounds of fresh Italian tomatoes – peeled – cut an x on top and drop in boiling water for a few seconds and peel
½ cup of olive oil – never used this. Can replace with bacon grease or lard
6 good sized onions chopped up good
2 full bulbs of garlic – minced
2 carrots–minced
1 Cup of fresh basil
4 Bay leaves – take out when finished
2 sprigs of fresh oregano
2 tsp of salt

    Heat oil and add in onions, garlic, and carrots and sauté for about 5 minutes
    Add all the rest of the ingredients and simmer on stove top for 2 and ½ hours
    Check and stir a lot
    Take out the Bay leaves and oregano sprig
    The secret is to add a tsp of honey or sugar and stir in
    Press through a strainer and mix
    Serve over homemade pasta

Miracle Twenty–The Songbird

Sometimes in the hut at night, Rev would sing quietly to us. He would sing a lot of the popular songs of the day like *Only Forever*, by Bing Crosby, or *Back in the Saddle Again*, by Gene Autry. He could sing too. He had a beautiful, deep, tenor voice, just like Frank Sinatra. I always told him that when we get home, he should go sign up for a record label. One day, I was in the kitchen cutting up some scraps of food for the guards. Rev came in singing. Yep, he was singing. In this hell hole, surrounded by death and disease, he is singing. "By the old Moulmein pagoda looking eastward to the sea. There's a Burma gal a settin'; and I know that she waits for me!" "Hey Houston, need some help in here? I can go get you some wadah." "Shhhh, Rev, the guards are in the next room. Don't wanna draw any attention to ya." Rev was a jolly, big ole guy with a manly voice. The guards seemed to like him. I think they were kinda amazed by him somehow. He was a burly ole dude, even scrawny and starved; he still held a presence. And that voice, just resonated in the camp when he talked. I was shewing him off to go get some water when the door opened. "Yo chotto koi!!" [get over here] The head guard called Rev over. "You think you songbird?" "No sir, I just like to sing." "You have strength to sing....you sing fo guards now. You sing dis song now." "Happyaku rokujū hachi!, go conna over dere!" I move to the corner of the hut. The head guard called all his men in the room and pushed Rev to the center of the hut. He poked him in his side with the tip of his sword. "Utau, utau" [Sing, sing]. Rev and I weren't sure what was going to happen. He had only sung in the Nipa hut at night. As unpredictable as these guards are, we are not sure what could happen next. It was just me and Rev, and all the guards in a circle around the room. This really could have been it for us. Disrespecting the guards and their space, was a sure way to get killed. Walking deliberately and carefully towards the middle of the hut, Rev took his place. He positioned his feet and shook his shoulders, before shutting his eyes. He took a long, deep breath. And then, as if it would be the last song his cords ever plucked out, Rev took command of the room. He was the starring first act at the Copacabana on a standing room only

Saturday night. He sang to the guards, drawing them in like smoke from a vintage, Cuban cigar. His booming voice resonated in the room, filling it with beauty and grace.

"By the old Moulmein pagoda
Looking eastward to the sea
There's a Burma gal a settin'
And I know that she waits for me

And the wind is in those palm trees
And the temple bells they say
Come you back you mother soldier
Come you back to Mandalay, come you back to Mandalay

Come you back to Mandalay
Where the old flotilla lay
I can here those paddles chonkin'
From Rangoon to Mandalay

On the road to Mandalay
Where the flying fishes play
And the dawn comes up like thunder
Out of China across the bay

Ship me somewhere east of suez
Where the best is like the worst
And there ain't no ten commandments
And a cat can raise a thirst

And those crazy bells keep ringing
'cause it's there that I long to be
By the egg foo yong pagoda
Looking eastward to the see."

(Lyrics by Rudyard Kipling and Music by Oley Speaks, 1907)
Rev stopped and took a breath. He let down his arms and returned to a position of submission. He kept his head lowered,

making no eye contact. I didn't know what to do. I stood in the corner and looked down at my feet. I was afraid they might take a sword to him and follow with me. The air in the room was still. You could hear the bubbling of the water in the kawa pot, and a few field mice are scurrying in the roof of the hut. And then, one by one, guard after guard, slowly lowered their heads, bowing towards him. They held their position for about thirty seconds. They were showing the highest form of honor for his majestic voice. Rev slowly bowed to each of them in a gesture of thanks. With the utmost reverence, Rev said, "Arigato," [thank you]. The songbird found a way to pierce through the hate. Music was our miracle that day. Music brought two enemies together. It healed a part of us. It built a bridge between us. It fed our souls. For the short two minutes of time, we were just men in a room, appreciating the sound of a skilled voice.

"My heart O' God is steadfast, my heart is steadfast;
I will sing and make music." Psalms 57:7

The Honeypot News

Cleaning the latrine trench out was a weekly ritual. Overflow would be tracked into the hut and left on whatever piece of a shoe you had left. It was powerful smelly and doing nothing but spreading more disease. We took fifty-gallon drums of human waste to the docks to dump in the stream. These are fondly dubbed, 'honeypots'. A local little street urchin sold Japanese newspapers down there every day. By now, a few guys in camp could speak and read enough Japanese that we could get some news, even if it is skewed. We could be tortured or killed for bringing in news to the prisoners. The kid just wanted his yen. He was starving himself, so he would take whatever bits of food scraps, yen, or cigarettes, we could give him. He wasn't gonna turn us in, it would cut off his food supply, probably for his whole family. We would roll that newspaper up tucking the ends inside the rims on the drum bottom, hiding it from the guards. Later on in the curtain of darkness, we would sneak over and get the paper to read by match

182

light. "Son of a bitch!!!" The headlines of the paper around April 8, 1945, read 'Tetsu No Bofu' [Violent Wind of Steel]. Smitty, one of the prisoners, and a lawyer by trade was fluent in Japanese. He was whispering out what it read. He told us that the Japanese air forces and navy ships were all but destroyed; leaving their country devastated and almost broke. We had just taken another island. Battering and slamming into Okinawa Island, were hundreds of allied ships and armored vehicles, engaged in a bloody and brutal battle. The Americans nicknamed the vicious and cruel battle, the 'Typhoon of steel'; which is 'Tetsu no bofu' [violent wind of iron], in Japanese. On April Fool's Day, April 1, 1945, which was Easter Sunday, American bombardments rained fire and steel, destroying battleships and littering the bays. Japan was taking a beating. We can only hope this could be closing in on the end of this hell. Smitty tells us, "Our boys are kickin' some Jap ass in Okinawa!!! Their prize battleship, the Yamato just got sunk!!! She lost most of her crew after being sunk by our red, white, and blue bombers. Our boys are on the beachheads! We are on their sacred soil, and they are mighty pissed! They lost a lot of men, look at all these numbers and names. Their mamas are going to be as proud as peacocks, strutting the honor their sons brought home."

Smitty said the Yamato was one of the heaviest battleships ever produced, and considered by most, the greatest battleship on earth. She was their empress, the lead vessel in their sailing arsenal. Taking her down was a heavy loss for Japan. We know that they must be running low on fuel and their fleet is hobbling by now. We sit in silence, staring at each other. I just pray a silent plea. "Dear God, please let this horror come to an end. Keep us strong to make it home. Amen."

> *"And the God of all grace, who called you to his eternal glory in Christ, after you have suffered a little while, will himself restore you and make you strong, firm and steadfast." 1 Peter 5:10*

The Bloody Tide of Innocence

Over twelve-thousand American soldiers lost their lives in this battle. As military men and women, we are used to the death rolls of our own. No one is ever prepared to deal with the unnecessary casualties of innocent civilians. As our guys are executing the assault called '*Operation Iceberg*', and trying to stop this relentless enemy, the Japanese have convinced the local people on Okinawa that we are all barbarians, waiting to rape their daughters and castrate their sons. These were innocent and meek village people who lived a simple farm life. They are a lot like my upbringing back home. They scratched a life out of the dirt, planting and raising their food, stayed mostly to themselves, and followed their ancient beliefs. They were told that we were such savages, we would kill our own families and ourselves to avoid capture. In the face of Americans coming in their homeland, the poor little village people ran over the cliffsides, plunging to their gruesome deaths on the cutting rocks below. Mothers, swaddling their babies in their arms, would be dragging their teens down the rocky paths, throwing them to their deaths below. Fathers would be pushing their sons alongside their elderly fathers over the cliffs before they jumped to their deaths in mass suicides. Hundreds of bodies were washing up, rolling over the rocks, as the tide tossed them about like ragdolls. Their broken and twisted bodies were wrapping around the legs of our ground forces as they moved on land. Some guys may never get over seeing that horrific scene, as they stepped over dead children still in their mother's arms, to make their way into the caves above.

Daddy Bird

As the food dwindled, so did the men. More and more were found dead in the huts in the morning. Joe finally succumbed to the starvation, and in his weakened state, came down with a high fever. He was just too sick even to get up. His head was burning up, and he was weak as a spring doe. "Joe, Joe, you gotta get up, you just gotta!" "Leave me alone Houston. I can't move. Houston, you can't help me. If ole Mickey Mouse or Satan find you next to me, you will be next." We all knew the camp rules. Everyone had to walk to the kawa hut to get our daily rations. "I am sick of death, Joe, and I am sick of watching good men die. It ain't gonna be you". That little cup of sour, cold rice, gruel is gonna have to do us both. The guards ensured we couldn't sneak food to the weaker prisoners by keeping us under direct supervision as we ate. I sucked that rice water real hard, pasting a thin rice layer up in the roof of my mouth. Our gums and mouths were so white from vitamin deficiencies; it could go undetected if they check me. I am willing to take a chance for Joe. He was my friend. They randomly checked our mouths when we left the hut. " Happyaku rokujū hachi!, Open you mouth!" My heart is racing, and I am trying to control my breathing. The guard pushed my shoulder and forced my head back. We locked eyes with each other. He stuck his pen in my mouth and took a look inside. He locks eyes with me again. I don't move. He signals me to go on. I take a deep breath and walk out. That night, I rolled over next to Joe and had him roll on his shoulder facing me. "Shhhh, you keep quiet you hear me? I'm just gonna hug you to keep you warm." I am frightened. He is so weak. Holding him as he shivers like a newborn lamb, I wrap my legs around him to keep him warm. I gently place my mouth over his as I push the baby food onto his tongue. "Swallow Joe, swallow. Here is some water from my canteen." He is shaking all over. I laid there next to him. I was thinking about what my Daddy told me about baby birds, and I was grateful. It sure showed me how little it took for a man to survive. As long as Joe wanted to fight, I was gonna feed him until he could feed himself again. The bond you forge in captivity is greater than any blood lineage God has graced you with. I was willing to die to keep him alive another day.

"There is no greater love than to lay down one's life for one's friends." John15:13

Walk or Die, Man, Walk or Die

Joe was down for five or six days. At night, I was able to get a little snail to him. Joe got a little stronger each day. When his fever broke, he was able to sit up. On the seventh day, the guards called him outside. He couldn't lay there any longer unless he couldn't get up or dying, I was worried he would be too weak or dizzy to stand up and walk. Walk or die, man, walk or die. Joe pulled hisself up the bamboo wall and held on to the stair rails with a death grip. He throws up all over himself, beginning to slip back down. He knows he has to walk. He pulls himself back up and slowly works down each step. Once on the path, he has to make it alone to the kitchen. Walk he does man! He slowly creeps his way along the path to the kawa hut. He looks like a doe fawn in spring. Over time, Joe got better. He was put to work in the camp after that. He ended up sweeping out the stalls and the bays where he could catch some rest.

The Yellow Rose Life Raft

Almost losing Joe put me in a dark place. You can only push the limits of your mind so far. I am not sure what internal mental cliff I was close to stepping off. I began my very first thoughts of "Why push on, for what?" I could never bring myself to think that way before. I knew if I did; I was finished. I had a Mama back home praying her tail off, and I had to do my part here. I would focus on her face and the Paluxy River days. I finished cleaning the kawa pot and walked back to the hut. "Hey, you stupid dick shit, I left you gift in hut!" Goofy, the guard kicks gravel at me laughing at me as I race back to the depilated bamboo coffin we live in. "Happyaku rokujū hachi! [868], Stupid, asshole!" He is dangerously psychotic, so I avoid provoking him in any way. Any small act can unhinge him. He cocks his rifle as he sadistically laughs my way. I am hoping and praying my friend Joe was alright. "Joe, Joe, what the hell is going on. He points to the mat in the corner where another prisoner was laying on his stomach. He had the open bleeding flesh of a fresh bamboo caning, acrost his face and back. "Dear sweet, Lord! What the hell happened Joe?" "He just asked about our mail." "Mail! A letter got through here!" "All he was asking was when it was going to be passed out, and Goofy just went off the rails. They must have hated giving us mail. It could deliver the one and only thing they worked so hard to take away – hope. Poor fella was dead.

186

His withered body couldn't take another blow. I rolled him over, covered his face with a mat, finding a stash of letters below him. All the guy wanted was to know about the good news from home. A small tattered envelope with my name on it was on the bottom of the stack. It is August 28, 1945. The postmark is January 22, 1945, Glen Rose Texas. The good Lord let my Mama find me. Dear God in Heaven, she knows where I am!

Re: Sgt. Houston E. Lowe 180448878
United States Prisoner of War
Zentsuji Prison Camp
Island of Shikoku, Japan
Via: New York, New York

My darling boy,

Trust you are well. Jake is in Nevada, Leon is in Denison, Texas, Ruth and Deannie are here. We are thinking of you. Mother

Pressed to the bottom of the note is a single, dried, yellow rose. A rose from the garden I left her with! She is alright! That little woman of God is alright! The yellow rose from Glen Rose, Texas, made it halfway across the world, oceans away, to this rotting and filthy place. I know my Mama well enough to know she would have put a scripture at the bottom to keep me pulling, but these bastards control every word. That single yellow rose lifted me to a high place, my earthly home. I closed my eyes as I smelled that withered, pressed, rose. It still has a sweet aroma! It smells like home. The warmth of home rushed over me like a soft breeze. I could smell catfish frying and clean sheets flapping in the wind. The laughter of my sisters filled the air. You will never understand the power of your childhood home until you no longer have any hope of getting back there. It is your very foundation. I quickly put that letter under my mat. They may have to deliver these notes, but that doesn't mean they won't just tear them up when they get the chance. I laid on my mat that night. I had worked enough by now that I could have a few cigarettes now and then. I lit one up and looked between the grass and bamboo slats to the heavens above. It had been three years since I thought about Mama looking at the same stars back home. Somehow, that letter made me feel like a normal Joe. I was just a guy, finished with his day's work, smoking a rollie and looking out to the vast universe. I pick up my little leather cookbook and scratch out this recipe:

Entry # Seven Collard and Mustard Greens

1 bunch collards, washed real good, lots of sand hides in there, pat dry
1 bunch mustard greens, washed real good
Chop up in piles
Heat the skillet with some lard and pork sides
Stir in the greens until they darken and soften
Cover with water and lid.
Boil until soft.

The Day Glowed Eerie

The morning was unnaturally quiet. Japanese beetles are scratching on the hut floor, and a few crickets were still playing their lonesome violins from the night before. The air was thick, and the stillness made the morning dew cover us in a death blanket. Through the thatch roof, we can see the sky is glowing in a strange, ghostly color. The air just got sucked out of the hut in a vacuum, and it became hard to draw a breath. That afternoon while I was working in the kitchen, looking up at the Coogan grass roof, I noticed even the field mice were still. We are in an eye lock with each other. Their little faces are fixed in a warped expression. Their tiny, beady, jet black eyes fixed on me. Small, grey, furry bodies stood there in twisted, unnatural positions. The rest of the morning as we are passing by and seeing each other, somehow we all sense the drop of the universe. There is no explanation for the feeling that morning. It was like the earth stood still and the planets were slung from the heavens. It was sinister. We were in the presence of a deathly evil spoken only by demons. I felt it in my spirit.

*"But when He, the Spirit of truth, comes, He will
guide you into all the truth; for He will not speak
on His own initiative, but whatever He hears, He
will speak; and He will disclose to you what is to
come." John 16:13*

Around noon, the guards begin to scurry about the camp. You
hear chatter everywhere. They run in between the huts and are
yelling at each other. They is mighty pissed. You can see it in their
faces. They were repeating over and over, something like *'Doroppu
Bakudan'* [drop bomb], while they clenched their fists in the air.
Soon, we are all forced in lines as the guards assembled on either
side of us. They were carrying boards about four-feet long. We
were forced to run through as they each took a swing at our backs.
It is on the afternoon of August 6, 1945.

The next morning when we get up for our morning work detail,
I notice that our skin looks pale and dry. Our bodies are lightly
dusted with a very fine, silky, powder. It is almost impossible to
detect, but you can feel your skin changed overnight. By that time,
most of us are only dressed in a fundoshi. Our uniforms had long
since tattered and fallen to pieces. We are ghostly and gaunt, slowly
walking about like fog resting over a pond.

August 9, 1945, 11:02 a.m.

At exactly 11:02 a.m. the final blow to the Imperial Japanese
Army was delivered. *Fat Man*, the plutonium implosion device,
was delivered to Nagasaki. It was directed at the shipbuilding
center in Japan. It hit in the area of Mitsubishi steel and arms fac-
tories. The bombs were ghastly and destroyed thousands of lives.
As much as I have grown to dislike my treatment by the Japanese,
I would never wish any harm on innocent civilians.

August 10, 1945, 6:00 a.m.

Things do not seem right in camp. There was a stillness outside the huts. The constant jabbering in Japanese is silenced. There

are no guards gambling lots on which one of us was gonna be thrown on the burn pile today. The atmosphere is silent. Tokyo Rose sweetly stabbing you in the gut with her verbal assaults on the radio, is gone. We are in our huts, laying on the floor mats. No one moves. There is no sound, no moving air. There is a mysterious void encircling a bunch of corpse-like men in cloth diapers. We hang in suspended reality. We get up for morning roll call awaiting the dreaded sound of a gun butt in someone's head, or the dragging of bodies out to the trench. "Houston, there is something fearful wrong out here," Joe said. The camp was still. Rev runs up from his hut. "Houston, Houston, not a damn Jap in the yaaad!" Men begin to run about. We are fearful of the next imperial move in this evil game of chess we have all been the pawns in. Doors are thrown open, showing the remains of an overnight looting. The camp was completely deserted. There was not a Jap in sight! It was a ghost town. We step out into the yard slowly, looking for the guards. Walking gently, treading slowly, we look for the guards. We slowly move about the camp. We head to the kitchen, the guard hut, and the grounds, where we have been held captive in for eleven months. Finally, someone climbs up to the guard tower, their personal shooting gallery loft. No one was there. There wasn't a guard in sight. During the night, they packed up camp, hightailed it, and left. They took everything. Every scrap of food, every gun, every pot, and all of their maps and Intel. All gone. "Holy Jesus Joe, they are gone! The bastards are gone!!!! They left us in this jungle to rot and die!" "Son of a bitch!" We are hugging and celebrating, but it did not last long. We have no idea if they would be coming back or if they were lurking in the jungles just waiting to chop us down as we ventured out. We are on our own now. No one knows the actual coordinates where we are, not even Uncle Sam. I guess that is the second time I was the most afraid. I thought we cannot go through all of this to be left here to die. We couldn't just go walking out of the jungle...it wasn't safe anywhere for an American to be, especially a lowly prisoner. If we are going to survive out here, we need to know what we are working with. We knew for our safety we had to stay put indefinitely. We begin to run through camp like a pack of rabid dogs, looking for food, blankets, fresh water, and anything we could survive with. Like the Jews in the wilderness, we begin to set up a new camp life.

> *"He found him in a desert land, And in the howling waste of a wilderness; He encircled him, He cared for him, He guarded him as the pupil of His eye."*
> *Deuteronomy 32:10*

August 15, 1945, Noon

On a radio broadcast across the world, allied countrymen are receiving word that Emperor Hirohito announced the full and complete surrender of Japan after he sent a cable notifying President Truman the day before. After allied and American soldiers crawled island to island, overcoming a fierce and relentless enemy, this bloody and bravely fought Pacific battle, was finally over. The untold casualties of the war on both sides were devastating. The world at war was no more, and people everywhere were celebrating what was known as 'Victory in Japan Day'. In a short radio announcement, the Imperial Japanese Army came to a complete stop. The relentless rifle and machine gun rounds stopped. The rumbling of tanks, the squealing and roaring Japanese Zeros dropping bombs, spraying blood, bodies, and dirt, stopped. The guntō and Samurai swords ripping through human flesh and bone stopped. The beatings, the torture, starvation, and the cruel and humiliating words stopped. It all stopped. Along with it, the earth uttered a haunting groan. Her majestic mountains were in rubble heaps. Craters pock-marked the streets, roadways, railways, and bridges. Broken iron and steel penetrated her as smoke and fire spewed out from bombed-out ravines. Reefs are destroyed, slick with toxic oils and gas. Lethal spills are washing over her oceans and bays, as fish and fowl choked on black oil and gasoline. Bloody shorelines wrapped every island. The deadly remnants of radioactive fire and waste decimated miles of countryside as it vomited up charred bodies. It all stopped. The frightening calm of the unknown filled the void in the air.

191

> *"And God looked upon the earth, and, behold, it was*
> *corrupt; for all flesh had corrupted his way upon*
> *the earth." Genesis 6:12*

The Signature of Giants

Nestled deep inside our camp on Shikoku Island on Urado Bay, we are unaware that only about three-hundred and seventy miles away, aboard the USS *Missouri* in Tokyo Bay, surrounded by hundreds of allied warships, Japan was formally surrendering; under the hand of Japanese Foreign Minister, Mamoru Shigemitsu. This surrender effectively closed the door on the horrendous war of World War II. 'Mac', our Supreme Commander, signed on behalf of the United Nations. He solemnly spoke, leaving behind these chilling words: *"It is my earnest hope and indeed the hope of all mankind that from this solemn occasion a better world shall emerge out of the blood and carnage of the past."* General Douglas MacArthur (September 2, 1945). The world is watching as this dreadful war comes to a battered and bloody close. Behind the scenes, the U.S. Military and their allies are working to rescue troops and reclaim lives, property, and our freedom.

> *"Your country lies desolate, your cities are burned*
> *with fire; in your very presence foreigners devour*
> *your land; it is desolate, as overthrown by for-*
> *eigners." Isaiah 1:7*

Manna From Heaven

In a few days, we heard the sounds of low flying aircraft. We all took cover where we were, crawling under huts and scrambling to find a place to hide. There is no way of knowing who is flying above us. We are frightened they have returned to finish us all off. Small parachutes attached to army green boxes, were being dropped into the broken-up fields. It was small airplanes full of Red Cross rations! "Dear Jesus, Mary, Mother of God, they are dropping rations!" It was like a caravan of jungle monkeys just got cut loose after captivity in a circus! Crawling, running, or dragging, we were out to the fields grabbing everything we could. Peaches, canned meat, and milk came raining down like manna from heaven. Guys immediately began busting those cans open with rocks and pouring peaches in sugar syrup down their throats like fresh bay oysters. A few of us begin yelling, "Stop, stop!!!" "Don't eat those so fast, stop! You can't handle this food, your belly ain,t right! I am desperately running from man to man. "Stop! Youll be sick I tell ya, sick as a dog!!!!" " Houston! I'm gonna eat dammit! These came from home! We could be here for weeks until they find us in this overgrown, flea-infested hell hole!" "You gotta take it easy if you wanna get home! Start with some milk, I tell ya!!! Some of the medics are pleading with me. "You gonna kill yourself!!! Wait, wait please wait!" Guys keep opening cans. "I've been starved here for thirty-six months. Piss on them all, I am gonna eat dammit!!!" We begged them to stop. They just wouldn't listen to reason. When you are starved this long, your brain cannot comprehend turning down a bite to eat. We ran from man to man begging them to drop the heavy rations. Watching men gulping down those peaches, drinking up that syrup as it ran down their chins; I dropped to my knees in the middle of that field and crumbled in a heap like a paper sack. I began to shake and then cry. It just rolled into a full uncontrollable bawl. It was the first time I ever shed a tear in this place. I don't know where any tears could have come from, but I had them. All the ugly forty months of containment, disease, death, torture, fear, horror, and brutality, came spilling out. My tears were hot and were hitting me on my dirt-filled chest, like splattering weld. We knew our brothers had just sent a torpedo into their own tattered, tissue-frail guts and pretty soon they would explode from the inside out. In a very short time, the unspeakable agony did begin. Men were in fetal positions writhing on the ground. Their faces grimaced as they wrapped their arms around their knees and fought the horrible pain they were in. It didn't take long before their battered organs began just to shut down. There was nothing we could do to save them. Me and a few other guys stayed by their sides and held their heads or hands. They were screaming and grabbing our necks. Their hearts just rapidly thunking away, pounding against their sunken ribcages. You could hear their inflated guts screeching and gnawing. After a while, you could hear a deep, hollow pop. They began bleeding from the rectum and soon drew their last breath. Of all the things I faced, this was the hardest. We were brothers. Watching good men die so close to being rescued, killed a little piece of me. I will never get over seeing this. I am harshly reminded that the good Lord has never kept a thing from us we needed to know.

> *"Have you found honey. Eat so much as is sufficient*
> *for you, unless you will be overfilled and vomit it."*
> *Proverbs 25:16*

PW

We bury our comrades in a make-shift graveyard next to the hut. A week or so later, some flyers were dropped from airplanes, outlining the plans for our rescue. The flyers told us to stay put and eat the rations they were dropping conservatively. We were also asked to write the letters PW using rocks or sheets, as large as possible, to be seen from overhead by pilots circling the area. As we slowly began to gain some of our strength on the rations, we built up a work system. Waiting for rescue was incredibly difficult. We were all ready to get out of this damn jungle. I thought of all those boys we just lost. My heart hurt. I remembered the prayers of my Mama. She has no idea how very close I came to death.

> *"From heaven did the LORD behold the earth; To*
> *hear the groaning of the prisoner; to loose those*
> *that are appointed to death..." Psalm 102:19-20*

I continued as a cook. Our issued rations were brought to me, and we ventured out a bit further in the camp for additional grubs, plants, and local fruits. It was incredible to just walk in freedom around the camp. I realized I did not hear crying and moaning any longer. I also did not hear the butt of a gun to a face or a death rattle. There are a lot of rats and small varmints out and about. Guys built small traps, catching a few. Some of the putrid, rancid dry rice, was left behind. I rationed it out for meals, adding in some crickets and locusts if we could find some. Hell, it was like camping by a river compared to what we had been through!

Sometimes I would lay out under the moon just because I could. We filled our days staying in camp, keeping low. We did not need any attention brought to us, and we knew our boys would find us soon enough. We divvied up responsibilities. The medics got busy helping treat wounds and illnesses. Some of us got together and stitched a ratty American flag from the parachutes dropped with our rations. It was gonna fly over this camp if it killed us all. We built fires and boiled water. We would take rags and wipe off our filthy bodies with warm water. It was amazing to see what a little warm water could do to help a wound heal faster and a body feels alive again. We kept staring at each other in disbelief. We were walking as free men. Joe and Rev and I went to the fence line at the edge of camp and shared a cigarette. We tried to get ourselves prepared mentally for the coming days ahead. "We been in this ole hole so long, I am not sure how I will be out there", Joe said. "We gonna stick together Joe. Ole Rev here will head back to New Yaahhk! He problee will marry his girl and have a gaggle of kids! Huh, Rev?! It will be just you and me going back to Texas." "I got no place to go, Houston. I have no family in the United States, and I have to re-up. I am not sure I can make it alone." "Well, hell Joe, you just gonna come re-up in San Antonio with me! We will be next door neighbors!"

100 American Prisoners of War, Mukaishima, Hiroshima POW Sub-camp No. 4
(Houston E. Lowe, Second Row, Second from Left) Retrieved from: http//:www.
mansell.com/pow_resources/ ©Roger Mansell, Palo Alto, California

Glen Rose Texas
Jan. 18 1945

Sgt Houston E. Lowe
United States Prisoner of War
Zentsuji Prison Camp
Island of Shikiku Japan
Via: New York, New York

My darling Boy: Trust you are well. Jake is in Nevada, Leon is in Denison
Texas, Ruth and Deannie are here. We are thinking of you.

Mother

Letter From Home (Nora Pace Lowe, Mama) with Yellow Rose, Dated
January 18, 1945, Courtesy Houston E. Lowe, Personal Collection

A. General Douglas MacArthur, Retrieved from: https://upload.wikimedia.
org/wikipedia/commons/b/be/DouglasMacArthur.jpg As a work of the U.S.
federal government, the image is in the public domain.

Gen. Douglas MacArthur wades ashore during initial landings at Leyte,
Philippine Islands. Retrieved from: https://upload.wikimedia.org/wikipedia/
commons/f/f3/Douglas_MacArthur_lands_Leyte.jpg By U.S. Army Signal
Corps [Public domain], via Wikimedia Commons

Chapter Eight

The Rescue: Riding the Storm

September 6, 1945

It was about three weeks after the war ended before we hear the faint sounds of small biplanes circling, and trucks coming towards us. We scatter to the huts because we do not know who could be coming for us. U.S. recovery teams of the American Red Cross were waving large American flags as they were coming from the dense jungle along the perimeter of the camp. They had been trained to approach us slowly. Their task was to rescue and take POWs to recovery centers for immediate care in the area before we boarded U.S. Navy hospital ships to come home. From a distance we hear, "Hello, you are safe. We are Americans. You can come out now. This is the American Red Cross." "Dear Jesus, they are here!" It was a moment, a feeling that can never really be explained, or understood. There are simply no words in the human vocabulary to describe this moment. I will not even begin to try. I can tell you that it was the second most difficult part of my journey. I cannot explain why. I fell to my knees in weakness and gratitude. All the horror began to spill from me as if I was being washed from the inside out. I was frozen. Time, sound, smell, and feeling were all suspended. My body locked up and I could not speak. I felt like I was in the presence of something greater than the universe. I just knelt there and stared blankly at the men coming towards me. Images of camp life were slowly floating off. Faces of the guards were evaporating before my eyes. The foggy silence is broken by the sound of an American Red Cross member calling to me. "Soldier, soldier, you ready to go home? What's your name, soldier?" Crouching in a submissive position, I immediately reply, "Happyaku rokujū hachi" |868|. I freeze for a moment not making eye contact. I wipe my eyes and try to focus. "What's that name again?", He asks. A blurry face with protective gear reaches out his hand to help me up. "Ummm." I hesitate for a moment, trying desperately to grasp what is happening. " Ummm, I clear my throat to speak. In a weakened voice, I answer, "I am Sgt. Houston,... Houston E. Lowe, 18048878, United States, Army Air Corps, Sir." " Well, let me help you up!. Welcome to freedom, soldier. Welcome to sweet freedom."

"You have rescued me! I will celebrate and shout, singing praises to you with all my heart.

> *All day long I will announce your power to save. I will tell how you disgraced and disappointed those who wanted to hurt me." Psalms 71:22-24*

The Imperial Red Curtain Closes

> *"Because of your fighting qualities and the fighting qualities of our brothers in arms of all services, our beloved land has not known the ravages of war, our dear ones at home have not been endangered. Give praise to God Almighty for this and give humble and grateful thanks that He saw fit to use us as His instruments."*
>
> *An excerpt from the speech to the POWs, Admiral Halsey, Aug. 15, 1945, 1300 hours*

We are transported by train to Tokyo, Japan. We look in horror at the devastation of war. Watching children walking in the rubble and broken glass killed a piece of me. After a short stay in the hospital which was manned by the Red Cross, we were fumigated and deloused before we are processed and taken by boat back to the Philippines. Everything looks like blown-up ruins. Piles of debris are still smoldering. Buildings and roads are destroyed with rubble spilling out into the streets. Local people are dazed and walking about dressed in rags. Naked children are sitting in puddles on the streets. We drive passed old Bilibid. She looks like a filthy, old woman crouching over in an alley. It is strange to see the empty buildings and streets. Just a few of the locals are walking about surveying the damage. As we pass by Bilibid, we cannot miss the opportunity to 'shoot the bird' together in her general direction! I wish I had a camera there. Me, Joe, and Rev would have had one helluva shot!

> *"You meant to do me harm, but God meant it for good*
> *— so that it would come about as it is today, with*
> *many people's lives being saved." Genesis 50:20*

The U.S.S. Joseph T. Dickman, APA 13

It is around September 23, 1945. We are taken first to be checked at a field hospital before we are taken to the blasted and broken docks of Manila Bay. The U.S. naval ship, the U.S.S. Joseph T. Dickman, APA 13, is anchored out there. Encircling beneath her, under a watery grave below, the remnants of mighty warships are sunken. Small boats called LCVPs are ferrying us from the blasted docks to the floating hospital ship we will call home until we reach the sweet land of freedom. We are headed to the beautiful island of Oahu for a fuel stop, and then to San Francisco, California, and finally, to Letterman Army Hospital where we will be treated and recuperate. I immediately began to think of Pearl Harbor and all the boys who lost their lives there in that surprise attack that started it all. The U.S.S. Dickman had initially been anchored out in the Marshall Islands. She was loaded with two-thousand army personnel preparing to head just northwest for the final invasion of Japan. The bomb drops abruptly changed those plans. I know those men and women aboard her were grateful as all hell and highway to be dropped off at Leyte for some R and R instead! The U.S.S. Joseph T. Dickman was constructed in the early 1920s. At one time she was a Trans-Atlantic Liner, the S.S. President Theodore

Roosevelt. She has a long military history which includes the invasion of Normandy, and Utah Beach, on the 6th of June,1944. She has seen much of our country's history and has had many heroic men and women in her belly. For now, she is a floating military hospital with forty or so doctors and nurses who will be attending to about sixteen-hundred gaunt, pale, shell-shocked, skeletons for passengers.

Angels of Mercy

The military doctors did not know how to treat us. They had never seen 'walking skeletons' before. We were so severely starved, beaten and tortured, swollen with gangrene, infected limbs, head lice, intestinal worms, suffering from so many diseases, they were not sure where to begin. No medical journal could advise them. The severity of our ailments combined with our jittery, jumpy emotional state, was a medical challenge they had not seen. We were unable to connect with anyone but our fellow prisoners. We often huddled together or congregated in small areas. We had gotten so used to seeing our corpse-like apparitions; we had forgotten how healthy American people looked. The medical doctors had never encountered such badly treated people. We had suffered and overcame so many diseases without any medical assistance; the doctors were in awe. They documented each chart as each of us described our symptoms and length of illness. Medical charts resembled a dictionary, as line after line of disease, malnourishment, and wounds were reported. Wet and dry beriberi, amoebic dysentery, severe malnutrition, dengue fever, scurvy, malaria, yellow fever, elephantiasis, acute hematomas, gangrene, mouth ulcers, intestinal worms, trench foot, broken and splintered bones, and psychological trauma spilled on to the pages. Lice and scabies were documented on every chart. I was 6' 1", 210 pounds when I enlisted, and just 6 feet tall, and weighed a little less than 100 pounds at my physical. I had lost forty-eight percent of my body weight.

The people on deck were kind and patient with us. A Yeoman, Clerk Petty Officer, Ed Mergele, is processing us in one by one. "Hey, buddy, what is your name?" He slowly and methodically writes each name, ID number, general condition, and home address, in a ledger. Sixteen-hundred men and women are written in the book when he finishes. He takes down some anecdotal notes as well. He was gentle and had such a kind face. His voice was calming, and he touched each of us gently on the shoulder. We are issued clean clothes, a pack of cigarettes, a Hershey chocolate bar, some bath towels, sheets, and a shaving kit. Soon, we were being led down into the lower hold of the ship towards bunks. I feel a heavy sense of fear and panic climb up through my stomach. I stop on the first stairwell. I feel an unexplainable terror and my mind can only see darkness. "I cannn't, I caaan't!" I quickly turn, heading up to the top deck, bumping a few of my comrades along the way. "I can't do it, get me the hell out of here! Please let me stay up on the top deck." A few of the 'Hell Ship' survivors had the same response. We are not quite ready to go inside the bowels of a big ship, even this floating paradise. "I've been sleeping on the floor of a hut for so long now, sir; I can sleep on a Navy cot on this here deck." A crew member got me a blanket and pillow and set me up on the starboard side so I could see the sun in the morning.

Miracle Twenty-One–Whirling Winds and Fire-Spitting Islands

Once they got all of us all settled in, we were going to stay anchored in the bay for a day or so. Some of the medics told us because of our weakened condition; they wanted us to get our sea legs for a couple of days before we shoved off on open waters. Over the ship loudspeakers, we hear the Bugle: Officers' Call. Assembly. "All Hands. All hands to quarters for muster. All hands to quarters for muster." "We will be pushing out at 2100 hours. A typhoon is heading in our course. All hands remain in quarters. I repeat, all hands remain in quarters until further notice." So, just as we get settled in for a bit, we are setting sail early due to a typhoon threatening the China Sea directly where we are headed! We have defeated the entire Japanese Imperial Army, and now a typhoon is churning up dangerously high seas and gale force winds, right in our watery path! As much as we all didn't want to, we were ushered down in the hold to batten down for the approaching typhoon.

We set sail out through the China Sea, south from Luzon. We are traveling in the area called the 'Pacific Ring of Fire' about thirty miles south of Manila. The Philippines have many islands, mountains, and lakes surrounding this area. The big steel vessel begins to pitch and roll, and it doesn't take much time for us to start puking down below. The winds are howling, and the rain is pelting up deck. Waves are swelling up to fifty-feet, spraying salt water over the Dickman as she plows through her course. Slamming down on the massive waves, howling one-hundred-mile-per-hour winds, ripped equipment, ammunition, and aircraft loose, sweeping them into the sea. This typhoon is packing a deadly punch, and we are gonna go right beside her on the 'dirty side'. Some of the deck hands are coming down talking about the fires off the coastline. "Hey, the Taal Volcano is giving us the greatest fireworks show on earth right off our port bow!" A few of us crawl out on the deck just to see it. In the night sky, rain showering down, a red and orange glow is off in the distance. You can hear the heavy steam loudly whistling and cracking as the molten lava hit the water below. Smoke is filling the air. There it is in the distance off our bow: an angry, active volcano spewing out molten lava, toxic gas, and ash! It is as if the gates of hell itself have opened up denying our passage. So, to get out of this damn place, a typhoon chases us out of the bay, and a volcano kisses our asses goodbye! Damnedest thing I have ever seen!

"His way is in whirlwind and storm, and the clouds are the dust of his feet." Nahum 1:3

After a rough sea voyage, we made it through the storm to smoother waters. I went on back up deck. Every morning, a hot cup of Joe would wind up next to my cot before my feet even hit the ground. In my skivvies, damp from the salty morning dew, I would just sit there enjoying the warm bitter taste of black coffee, smoking American cigarettes, and watching in awe as the dawn is broken open. The horizon is blanketed in a delicate blue-grey flannel shirt that is slowly lifted, exposing the soft pink and yellow sky underneath, formally opening the book of morning. I have never seen anything so beautiful in my life. I had no idea how many colors there were in a morning sunrise. The entire horizon lit up in a blazing hot red-orange. It turned to a hot red and pink, slowly fading to carnation pink and then the glorious yellow of the rose from home. And then, it happened. Like the crescendo in a dramatic movie score, the very fingers of God, hot white swords of light would break through, piercing the clouds. There it was, in all of God's magnificent glory, the morning sun.

"The sun rises, and the sun goes down, and hastens
to the place where it rises". Ecclesiastes 1:5

During our voyage, our doctors wisely and slowly nourished and rehabilitated us. The nurses were angels of mercy. The unselfish care and concern we were given by these men and women healed more than our bodies. When we complained of being cold, they drew us hot baths in big tubs, warming up and soothing our sore muscles, and brittle bones. After we could tolerate milk, oatmeal, and biscuits, we moved to a high-calorie diet. They nourished our bodies and our souls. Hot coffee and donuts were served on deck. We sat wrapped in blankets watching the water as it slowly took us away from that horrific place. Each wave that lapped the sides and rooster-tailed off the bow floated us farther away. We watched our first movie on a little screen downstairs. Our voyage across the Pacific took us about two and half weeks where we rested, treated, ate, and smoked. Our first paycheck in years was issued on that ship! Some of the fellas asked to be paid in silver Liberty, one-dollar coins. They had a whole sack of them in their lockers. If we weren't playing cards or dominos on deck, guys would be making silver rings out of their coins. Rolling and tapping the coins over and over on the wood and iron decks would turn that silver soft and malleable. After a while, they would have them a mighty fine silver ring too. One guy said, " I'm gonna take this ring and put it right on Mary Lou's finger as soon as I get home!" Something we thought might never unfold for us; we watched as our future drew closer. Guys were preparing for their sweethearts. A kind of peace began to settle upon all of us. Nobody was going to kill us. We begin our first few steps without stopping to look over our shoulders in fear.

"Peace I leave with you; my peace I give you. I do not give to you as the world gives. Do not let your hearts be troubled and do not be afraid." John 14:27

Photo # 26-G-12-14-43(4)   USS Joseph T. Dickman, photographed circa 1943

USS Joseph T. Dickman (APA-13) at anchor circa 1943.
Retrieved From: http://www.navsource.org/archives/10/03/03013.htm
A US Navy photo now in the collections of the US National Archives. US National Archives photo 26-G-12-14-43(4) from the US Coast Guard Collection in the US National Archives, courtesy Shipscribe.com.

Chapter Nine

Sweet Freedom

America, The Land That I Love

Over the loudspeaker blasting from the top deck, a voice rings out; "Good Morning soldiers, at 1600 hours, you are about to be back on the soils of freedom, the United States of America. On behalf of the men and women who have treated you, a heartfelt thank you for your service. It has been our honor serving you. Godspeed to you and your recovery, and God Bless America." On October 16, 1945, we sailed through the remaining ocean miles in the Pacific, right into San Francisco Bay. We are all up on deck in our fresh uniforms breathing in the salty, crisp air. Out in the distance, we hear bands playing *the Star Spangled Banner* and *Anchors Aweigh*. We sail right beneath the beautiful Golden Gate Bridge, where crowds of people have gathered to welcome us home! Red, white, and blue streamers, and balloons are showering the decks of the Dickman as people are clapping, whistling, and yelling; "Welcome home boys!" It is such a beautiful sight. We all freeze, trying to breathe the enormity of it all in. The return from hopelessness cannot be measured on any human emotional scale. We are home.

The Lazarus Call

After disembarking, many of us drop to our knees and kiss the docks. We are taken to billets outside of Letterman hospital for further testing and treatment. The first thing I did when we got there, was to place a phone call through to my Mama. The nurse on our floor would take us down the hall in a wheelchair to the army green pay phone on the wall. With the paper of my information in hand, I dial the lengthy set of numbers. "Hello Mama, this is Houston." The phone was silent. "Mama..Mama…you there?" That's when I heard the most guttural scream I have ever heard. It was a cry from her very soul. "Dear God, Sonny Boy, you are delivered! You are delivered from the very claws of Satan! Dear Jesus in Heaven, thank you, thank you." She begins to sob. I hear her screaming to my kinfolk. "He's alive! He's alive!!! Our Lord has brought him from death!!!" We is both snottin' up and crying. I am so glad to hear her voice and know that she is alright. "How is everyone? How is Waitus?" "Sonny boy, come home, come home." "Mama, we got some shots and physicals to tend to here first. They gotta make sure we ain't gonna bring any foreign diseases back to you. It is for your protection, or I would run on back there myself. It will be a few weeks before I get home." "Okay, Sonny. I am still praying for you." "See you soon, Mama." I dropped that receiver in the chrome switch hook with a loud clunk. The nurse starts to wheel me back to my room. "Boy, are you a good liar!" "She would still whip my butt if she knew I did." "You did the right thing soldier. No Mama needs to know what you look like right now." "I don't think I look so bad!" "You need a shave and a bath." "You volunteering?" "Nice try soldier, nice try!"

We all get our individual physical and mental examinations. Doctors are pouring over us, checking every detail of our health. I am weighed in at one-hundred and fifteen pounds, 6'0. The doctor steps in, "Soldier, have you had any nightmares?" "Oh, no Sir. I am doing just fine here." "I am going warn you, what you experienced will continue in your mind and your sleep. You guys are suffering from "Combat Stress Reaction." We call it "Shell Shock." You will need to be diligent about taking this medication when you need it. I cannot take the memories away, but I can help you when you are suffering from one. You will probably experience some panic, anxiety, nightmares, and an inability to cope with situations. Don't you ever be ashamed of needing help or seeking treatment for this, you hear me?" "Yes, Sir." He hands me the 'nerve' pills, and I throw them in my pocket. I just want to get his behind me. After three-months recovering in the hospital, I am placed on several months furlough, during which time I have to make a decision. Either I am going to remain in the military or separate into civilian life. I opt to remain on active duty. I am even more determined to serve my country now. I guess a lot of guys may have gotten out, and I sure can't blame them. The furlough would give me some time to recover, get my life in some order, and get ready for my next assignment.

Coming Home

Joe, Rev and I began preparing for our new lives in our last days at Letterman. Over a hotly contested game of dominoes, we discussed our next steps. Rev was headed home to Schenectady, New York, and Joe was gonna head to San Antonio to re-up, and wait for my arrival. Rev would be hospitalized in New York for the remainder of his recovery. "After my hospital stay back home, I am gonna get the biggest New Yaak strip they got!" "I am gonna get me a girl," Joe said. "I gotta go check on Mama when I get out." They knew she had prayed us all home and I had to make sure she was alright. We nervously laughed and cussed over the game, as we made mental notes for our first steps in society. Secretly, we are all terrified. What are we going to say? How are we going to act? We have been sworn to secrecy about our captivity and treatment. We are all experiencing nightmares, waking up soaking in sweat. I guess we just go on living like nothing ever happened. We all knew getting out in public and around people was going to be very difficult. We promised to call each other every week to check-in. Having a brother in this helped us all.

Along with medical personnel who are treating us during travel, we head to the train station. As we are walking through the crowds of people, we look over at each other. We all feel a welling up in our throats and nervousness in the crowds. We stood at the train station just staring at each other. We do not make eye contact with anyone. Our uniform belts may be cinched real tight, but we were in a clean uniform with spit-shined shoes, about to head out as free men. We were excited to get home but terrified to leave each other. We had literally saved each other's lives in that God-forsaken place. We shared a bond forged in steel from the very cauldrons of hell itself. We stood there unashamed, as we hugged and slapped each other's backs. Rev's big ole strapping self, just welled up big tears in his eyes. Looking away, he said," It has been an 'annah' serving with you. Houston, you are the toughest sommabitch I have evah known!" "Rev, go get you a sweet gal and have a quiver of kids!" We said our goodbyes, and he waved as he boarded his train home. Something told me I would never see Rev again, and I was right about that.

Joe and I took the American Red Cross train to San Antonio where we were taken to Brook General Army Hospital for a treatment and recovery period. Our medical staff are treating our wounds and administering additional vitamin support along our long journey. In San Antonio, we would receive our medical clearance ensuring we were not carrying any of the jungle diseases we had been exposed to. Also, they will be treating and clearing our intestinal worms. We are going there to rest and to eat nutritious meals while building our strength. We had to get our body weight within a more normal range. After a few weeks, we are released. We went to Ft. Sam Houston where we would resume our duties with the Army, after a couple of months of furlough to convalesce. Joe stayed in town while I made arrangements to see Mama.

Sadistic Visions

Mama had moved to Oklahoma with some of her folks. While there, she met and married a man named Frank Dosher. I wasn't happy about it, but I wanted her to be cared for and happy. I wasn't ready to be very social. I was having a very difficult time 'fitting in'. I would catch myself letting my mind wander, even in the middle of a conversation with someone. I was jumpy and jittery. The docs gave me some 'nerve' pills to help me, mostly to help me sleep. I don't like the way they made me feel, so I quit taking em. I figure if I just get on back to my life, I will be alright soon enough. I had to check on my Mama, and I missed her sorely. I

209

caught a ride to Norman, Oklahoma, and was dropped off about a mile from the farmhouse where she lived. On a crisp early fall afternoon, swinging a canvas duffle bag over my shoulder; I walk up to the house. It has a nice white-washed exterior with a front porch. The porch had a swing, and there were two flower beds filled with beautiful yellow roses. Visitors come to the front door in the country; family always goes to the back. I walk around to the back screen door and knock. Mama was standing at the white porcelain kitchen sink, washing dishes in that same yellow print apron I left her in. "Hey, what's a guy gotta do to get a glass of sweet tea around here?" She spins around with a soapy china platter in her right hand. It immediately drops to the floor, shattering everywhere on the pine boards below. She collapses to her knees and begins to thank God. "Dear Jesus – Give thanks to the Lord, for He is good; His love endures forever. Give thanks to the Lord, for He is good; His love endures forever. Give thanks to the Lord, for He is good; His love endures forever." She is reciting Psalm 118, a Psalm we said over and over again in Sunday School. I drop my bag on the porch, swing open the screen door, and run to her, sweeping her tiny frame up in my arms. I lift her little body up off the ground and hug her tightly. She looks older and frailer than before. The weight of forty months on her knees is showing in her sweet face. The endless prayers and silencing her fear deeply wore into her face. It could not hide the joy on her face seeing me alive, and it encircled her with a halo-like ethereal glow. She looked like she had seen a miracle. "My Sonny Boy! My Sonny Boy! The good Lord delivered you from the depths of evil! My God is good! He raised you from the dead like Lazarus!"

> *"Didn't I tell you that you would see God's glory if you believe?" So they rolled the stone aside. Then Jesus looked up to heaven and said, "Father, thank you for hearing me. You always hear me, but I said it out loud for the sake of all these people standing here, so that they will believe you sent me." Then Jesus shouted, "Lazarus, come out!" And the dead man came out, his hands and feet bound in graveclothes,*

his face wrapped in a headcloth. Jesus told them,
"Unwrap him and let him go!" John 11: 40-44

"Look at you; you ain't nothing but a sack of scrawny bones! What on earth! Them folks not been feeding you?" About that time, a tall, handsome drink of water, with a sharp jaw and piercing eyes, was standing in the doorway to the kitchen in a pair of denim overalls and a plaid shirt. He is eating a few pieces of candy corn he is taking from his pocket. "Sonny, this here is my husband, Frank Dosher, your stepfather." "It is a pleasure to meet you son. Your Mama has told me all about you, and what you have done for her and this country." "My pleasure sir." We sat out on the rickety, white-washed porch. Mama is in her rocking chair. I am in a cane seat chair, shelling purple hull peas and drinking her famous sweet tea. Mr. Dosher was a hard-working man, and he loved my Mama dearly. They met in church where Mama was in the Widow's Club. All the single men and widowers in the church would come and help out the widows doing man work around the house. He was helping Mama fix her roof and a leak in the house, and she fixed him a piece of her famous blackberry pie. I guess with her sweet spirit and crystal blue eyes, that pie sealed the deal! They moved on up here to Oklahoma to be near some of their kinfolks. Leon moved on up here too. I wanted to make sure Mr. Dosher was a straight-up guy. He was out in the garden tilling and pulling weeds, so I went on out to help him a bit while Mama was preparing our supper. Getting my hands back in some dirt, family dirt, rested my mind. You can find out a lot about a man working next to him. We cleaned out his garden beds. He had scads of tomatoes, string beans, cabbage, squash, purple hulls, bell peppers, garlic, and onions. He takes out old vegetable peels and coffee grounds and throws them over the freshly watered soil. Surrounding his little garden are garlic and lavender plants. "Your Mama taught me that trick. The deer won't come anyway near those garlic and lavender plants. That's how I keep them out of our vegetables." He hesitates, then he turns around and looks directly at me. "Your Mama is a good woman, Houston. She is godly and kind. I know you have been real worried about her. I promise I will be good to her." He reaches into his pocket and pulls out a small, very undetectable, flask. "Here son, have a swig. You ain't gonna see the light of day of liquor in your Mama's house. I'm guessing you already know that'!" My nerves are pretty jumpy, so I was shore glad to have a little swig. "Yes, sir, I know that. She can rain down from the Book of Nora over that one! You better not let her catch you!" That night, Mama fixed up a helluva larrupin' meal! We had hot cornbread, ham and turnip greens, corn on the cob, purple hull peas, and an apple pie. I was full as a tick at the county livestock show in July! We talked for a bit over some hot coffee. "Mama, did Ruth and Deannie both get married?. "Yes, they did. They both married good men, sonny, good men." "Where are Waitus and Charlie?" "Sonny boy, I had to sell them both. Mr. Bog bought them from me right away when I was moving here. They was both getting older, and it wouldn't have been good for them to make that long trip. I am sorry Sonny." Leon smarts off, "I ain't sorry. Stupid ole mule wasn't worth two-cents!" As much as I would have liked to have slapped him upside his silly head, I let it go. Seems like a pretty small thing to get upset over. I think my last forty months put a lot in perspective for me. After another cup of coffee, we all turned in early. Farmers go to bed early and rise with the chickens in the morning, something I am used to.

> *"In the morning, O LORD, You will hear my voice;*
> *In the morning I will order my prayer to You and*
> *eagerly watch." Psalm 5:3*

That night, I laid on her crisp, white cotton sheets, with the breeze gently blowing through the screen windows. The hints of lavender and yellow roses were filling the air with a sweet calmness. I was lulled into sweet sleep listening to the serenade of the croaking frogs, and the crickets rubbing their legs together. The still is broken when a barn owl cries out in the distance. I was restful, peaceful; as I slowly drifted to sleep remembering my times as a boy. I am in a deep sleep. I see myself in my little overalls with a cane pole on Squaw Creek. I am fishing away and having a helluva day. Catfish are flying off my hook, and my stringer is full.

The sun is bright, and the sparkle of white diamonds are dancing off the river as it slowly moves along its winding path. I feel the sun on my face. I hear the constant babble of flowing waters over the river rocks. I smell the rye and Johnson grass. Grabbing my pole and my full stringer, I begin to walk back on home. I have a lot of fish cleaning to do before supper, and I was getting hungry. One by one, I am counting the fence posts along the path home. A heart with initials of J and A, the schoolhouse sweethearts, Jolene and Andy; are scratched at the top of one. I keep walking and counting, running my free hand along the posts. At the end of the fence line, only four feet away, a bloody severed head is shoved on top of a pole entering the property. The eyes are popping out, and the tongue is purple and swollen. The entire head was covered in flies, and maggots are crawling out of the mouth. The stench of rancid flesh fills my nose. My breathing quickens, drawing in more of the sickening smell. The odor of burning flesh consumes me. Dead bodies are burning in a pile just beyond the fence. My little nine-year-old body drops the pole and stringer. I freeze at the post before I begin screaming at the top of my lungs. I am gasping for air and screaming in between breaths. "Sonny boy…Sonny boy, wake up..it is a bad dream." Frank, go over there and try to wake him." I violently thrust myself up in the bed. Turning my head from side to side, I am grasping the sheets, looking for a hidden enemy. I grab the kerosene lamp next to the bed and raise it over my head. "Dear God, Sonny boy, what those people do to you?" The night clouds have covered the sky, and the room is basement dark. I am covered in sweat, drawing deep breaths as I try to respond. "Frank, get him a cold drink of water, quick now!" Mama lights her bedroom kerosene lamp and very slowly comes to my bedside. "Dear Jesus, Sonny. You lie here and rest." She kneels by my bed and silently begins to pray. "Dear Jesus, take his sleep. Bring him to the sweet waters of the river Jordan, and the tamarisk trees of Beersheba. Let him smell the myrrh and sweet oils. Rest his spirit, Lord. Amen." After about fifteen minutes of blinking and rubbing my eyes, I get my glass of water and go outside to smoke. I walk around for about an hour, touching farm equipment, hoes, picks, and the chicken wire on the little coop. The bumpy textures are awakening my senses. It is real. I am here. The foggy alternate state is lifting like the clouds after a rain shower. I am touching the lavender and bringing it to my nose, drawing in deep breaths; as I try desperately to push out the odor of death. I realize something very powerful is inside my head, a ghastly movie picture in a theater I may never be able to leave.

After visiting with Mama, Mr. Dosher, and Leon for a few days, I tell her goodbye. I know she is gonna be alright. He is a good man, and he will take care of her. I only have a couple of months or so of furlough, and I want to get on back to Glen Rose and see everyone. I traveled on back to Glen Rose and stayed with Uncle Virgil for a while. He was glad to see me alive and stood right in line with Mama on my prayer watch. Uncle Virgil took me on up to the church and showed me two wooden prayer plaques on the wall. One had silver stars next to all the local boys' names who had been missing in action. People were praying for their safety and return. The other one had gold stars next to their names. Those boys weren't coming home. They were praying for their families now. Their Mamas had to watch as their names were moved from a silver star to a gold one. "You see your name up there Houston? You have been prayed for by this congregation every Sunday for four years." I am mighty grateful to be covered by so many warriors. "Thank you, Uncle Virgil." "No, son, thank you!"

> *"You also joining in helping us through your prayers,*
> *so that thanks may be given by many persons on*
> *our behalf for the favor bestowed on us through the*
> *prayers of many." 2 Corinthians 1:11*

Chapter Ten

Glen Rose

Ididn't have a lot of time to enjoy the beauty of this ole town when I was growing up, too busy working. Glen Rose is just a beautiful little town with flowing rivers, creeks, and natural mineral springs. At one time, this sleepy borough was covered in forests and was the roaming grounds of hundreds of dinosaurs. Yes, dinosaurs! I used to go lie down in the riverbeds and stretch out in the massive tracks. I didn't think anything of it back then. I also used to build little stone structures from the petrified wood I found. Glen Rose, the county seat of Somervell County, has the Paluxy River running through the central part. Charles Barnard first settled here in 1849, in an area called Comanche Creek. He opened the first trading post with his brother George. Glen Rose cut her teeth as a town and began to prosper because of the many natural mineral springs in the area. This 'magic' water began to attract healers, doctors, and naturalists. Health resorts sprang up, and soon after, this sleepy little town became a center for recreation and health. Even the 1900 United States Geological Survey labeled the local mineral waters as 'valuable for medicinal purposes'. Lots of great water also brews up opportunities for creating some mighty potent shine! During the days of Prohibition, Glen Rose was a hotbed for moonshine production. We was real popular too! Our dense cedar brakes were dubbed the 'whiskey woods capital of the state'!

The first place on my stops was to see my Daddy. I thumbed a ride on out to Hopewell Cemetery. I slowly walked up to the little rock headstone where he was laid to rest. There are some trees around but not a lot of shade. His gravestone is covered in grass runners and weeds. As I pulled the weeds away and cleaned it off, I began to cry. God, I missed this man! I owe so much to him. I lay down right next to him, letting the sun beat on my face. I pull out a cigarette and light it up. Laying there smoking, man to man, I tell him all about how I used everything he taught me. I told him every detail of the forty months of gruesome hell. I told him about the plant medicine there and how his great wisdom saved me. I wanted him to know how much I had listened to him. "I found some pigweed, and I used the fruit leaves on my wounds. I saved my teeth, Daddy. Your charcoal powder saved my teeth." I cried over that rock headstone, turning the grey rock to black splatter. I stayed there the entire day pouring out each painful chapter of my captivity. Tears streamed down my face dropping to the red earth below. "I never gave up my honor, Daddy. I never gave it up." When I have exhausted myself, I leave a pack of Chesterfields on his tombstone before heading out. "I hope I made you proud Daddy. I hope I made you proud."

Odell and Easy Come Easy Go

Me and Odell met up right away. He came on down from Dallas, where he was working as a long-haul trucker. It was like we never left each other! He was one of the only people I could talk to about what happened to me. Of course, that would be after a few glugs of whiskey! "Houston, what they do to you over there in that hell hole?" "Awwww, shoot, Odie, you don't want to know. I didn't get this sack of bones in a jungle day spa, that I can tell ya! You know what I need? A ride! Let's go get me a car! I got my muster out money! A whole war's worth!" We went to the Chevy dealership in town, and I bought a brand new, mint green body, forest green roof, Chevrolet Stylemaster Town Sedan; for $1,500, drive out. I wanted a green car. It reminded me of the green Ford truck Daddy had. She had beautiful chrome bumpers and hubs and matching side walls. It's got a nice big ole back seat, just in case I put a tear on and need a place to sleep it off! I paid it in full, with cash from my war earnings. The registration papers would be coming soon.

It sure felt good. I felt like a man again. "Breathe in Odie...smell that new smell? I thought nothing would ever get the smell of death out of my nose, but that shiny car started the process. Now I got me some wheels; I wanna put some road under me. "Hhoooo weee'! "She was a beauty!" This is the first car I ever owned. Me and Odie went tearing out on the dirt roads alongside the farms and fences where I grew up. We spun out and spit gravel for miles, just a laughing like hyenas. I was free, and I'll be damned ifin I didn't start stomping and kicking like a jack donkey to prove it! "Come'on Odie, let me buy your skinny ass a drink!" We stopped at a little watering hole outside of town, and I began to drink away the gruesome atrocities that had been my life for forty horrible months. We didn't talk a bunch. I just sat there swallowing down cold tap Lone Star beer. I felt for the first time; I am safe. I am home. The bubbles burned my throat, and the aroma of hops filled my nostrils. The neon beer signs put a rosy glow over the rows of bottles, and smoke filled the air. Odell and I talked for hours catching up on years of girlfriends, Christmases, jobs, and family. You could hear guys squabbling over a game of darts in back. The jukebox was playing *For Sentimental Reasons*, by Nat King Cole. Odell had to get on back for work the next day, so he left me around midnight. I am sitting on the barstool finishing up a beer. "Hey soldier, these are on the house." "Thanks, Barkeep." "My name is Amos, what's yours?" "Houston, Houston Lowe." My frosted, hour-glass stein was never empty and sure wasn't around long enough to get warm. Amos knew I had been through it. I guess my face read like a front-page newspaper headline. It is hard to disguise that kind of horror. The beer kept flowing, and I lit up a few real cigarettes from a pack of Chesterfield. I sat on that old worn, wooden stool, and talked to that barkeep till closing time. Something about barkeeps, all of them should have an honorary degree in psychology. It seems they know how to get quickly to a man's hurt vault. He told me how proud he was of what we did over there, and he was rightly glad to be taking care of me for a few hours. "Let's top you off, soldier." He poured me a shot of Jim Beam, as we clinked our shot glasses to kickin' some Jap ass! That's about all I remember. I went outside to walk back to my car. I stumbled around that area

under the yellow moon and stars for hours. My beautiful Chevy...
well, I had her for about nine hours in total, I reckon! When I woke
up the next day, she was nowhere to be found. The real problem
came about when I realized I didn't have the registration or any
insurance on her! Like shit through a goose, she was gone! Easy
come, easy go..they always say!

Chapter Eleven

The Raven Beauty

Sycamore Grove stood tall on Old Highway 67, on the outskirts of town. The area has a small gas station with some sodas and beer, and a rock and wood, two-story dance hall with a tin roof. During Prohibition, it was tucked in as a little speakeasy. There was a second floor where some gambling took place. The building has white rocks and red mortar. Small trees and vines surround the place, making it look like a secret mansion. The gas station is inlaid with petrified wood. I step into the bar. Across the rickety oak plank floors, I see the most raven beauty I have ever seen. She was laughing and dancing under the string of colored lights. A neon sign is dimly lighting the bar area. The bartender is popping the tops on brown beer bottles, setting them up on the bar as the white foam slides down the necks. I see her shiny, dark brunette hair. It is perfectly coifed around her angelic face, and it captivated me. I felt the strength of my leg muscles go out from under me. My heart was beating out of my chest, and I could barely catch my breath. Her ebony eyes, delicately placed beneath perfectly plucked brows, pierced through me as we caught our first glance. She tossed back her hair as she laughed. She stopped for a moment and repositioned her mother of pearl hair clip. I tried not to stare, but I couldn't take my eyes off her. Those dew kissed lips! Beautifully pursed, ruby-red rose petals! Right above, was a perfect little delicate turned-up nose. Her porcelain face was crowned with a perfect beauty mark just above the left side of her mouth. Her red fingernails were wrapped firmly around a beer bottle, and a cigarette was waving in her other hand as she spoke. I couldn't believe my eyes! Every time she looked across the room, I made eye contact. I did notice she was wearing a small diamond ring on her left hand. "Shit, she is rationed!" I ain't gonna let that stop me. The damn Japanese Imperial Army didn't stop me; I'm not gonna surrender to a little no-nothing engagement ring. I don't care who put it on her! 'Bout that time, some ole guy took her out on the floor to dance. She was a hoofer! She could dance to anything keeping, perfect rhythm as she glided along with her partner, making him look like Fred Astaire. He was no Fred Astaire, and that little lady was struggling mightily to make his moves look good! After a while, he kissed her on the cheek, strolling out with a few of his chugs. He went off to problee raise some cane elsewhere. That is when I got my chance. I had a bit of liquid hops courage, or I might not have done it. "Hey, you can really cut a rug out there. You shore is a ducky shincracker! Where did you learn to dance like that?" "My Mama taught me." "Well, you got some Mama, now don't you! Is she as pretty as you are?" Suddenly, a very sorrowful expression came over her sweet face as she lowered her eyes to the floor. "She died in December just a couple of years ago." "Awww, sweet potato pie, I am so sorry. I can't think of a better way for you to celebrate what your Mama gave you than to get out on that dance floor and cut a rug with me?" "I really shouldn't; I'm engaged to be married." "Yeah, well what kind of respectable man would leave a beauty like you, all alone in a bar? Huh? Sounds like a jackass to me!" I started to walk off, and she took my hand and led me on the floor. The music swirled around my head as Fred Astaire bolted out *Dearly Beloved* on record fifty-eight, in the jukebox. The lyrics rang in my head. *"Tell me that it's true, Tell me you agree, I was meant for you, You were meant for me."* She glanced into my eyes, and I pulled her close. I could smell her perfume on her neck as her hair stroked my face. Dear God, this is like an electrical current to the heart! The room went hazy dark, and all I could see were her ebony eyes, and her red lips glistening in the neon light. "What's your name, beautiful?" "Beth, Lee Beth." "I am Houston Lowe." "Why are you so skinny?" "Oh, that is a story for another day dolly, another long day." We danced that short two minutes. It is like time

220

has frozen us in some alternate state. She told me she better get back to her girlfriend at the bar. "Hey, when can I see you again?" "I, I, I, can't, I can't." "You can't, or you won't?" I told her I would be at Big Rock tomorrow around one. That is a respectable time after church on a Sunday. We will see if she took the bait.

Big Rock Picnic

At 1200 hours sharp, I was set up at Big Rock. I brought a little chest of iced-down beers, some cheese, roast beef and ham, a loaf of bread and some grapes. I put out the full hog; I gotta impress this gal! I put out a red and white checked tablecloth and set up my little picnic high atop the biggest rock, so I could see her coming. I figure ifin she doesn't show up: I will have a nice afternoon lunch and a few beers at the best viewing spot for eyeing beauties in Somervell County! I wait for hours lying in the sun and watching the families play in the river. It is the first time I did not have dark thoughts and memories of my capture. It was normal, peaceful, and filled with the innocence of my youth. The sun was beating on my face and warming my clothes. Old men were puffing on cigars, shaded by umbrellas. Children were splashing in the water and skipping pebbles; while lovers were kissing alongside the banks. I am drawn to the simplicity of joy and the peace of being free.

> *"When anxiety was great within me, your consolation brought joy to my soul." Psalms 94:19*

Time is Ticking

I had never waited on a dame in my life, I never had to! I got a little buzz going and along about 3:30 in the afternoon, I see her coming in from a distance. A girlfriend dropped her off and pointed to her wristwatch as she drove off in her blue Chevy. She begins to walk toward me placing her dainty steps carefully over the riverbed rocks. Oh my, Lord, she was stunning! Her hair was tied up in a pink silk kerchief, and her long, beautiful alabaster gams were waving glory, right below her pleated, cuffed, shorts. She had on a short sleeve, little pink gingham collared shirt, and brown loafers. She was a sight to behold! She pauses for a second, "I didn't think you would still be here." "Well, I can tell you one thing darling, I wouldn't have for just any gal. You ain't just any gal, are you?" She opens her purse to get out a cigarette. I pull out my lighter and offer her a light. She leans over looking over her sunglasses right at me, as I set the tip on fire. We sit and talk for a few hours, drinking and smoking. We laughed away the afternoon as she caught me up on her wonderful family and all of her seven siblings. "I was raised in Dallas, but I moved here during high school. I graduated from Glen Rose High School. I don't remember seeing you." "I took a little detour to Japan for a while." "You were in the war?" "Just a little bit, honey, just a little bit." We talked for hours as she peeled back the first layers of her life. She moved with her family to Glen Rose in 1935. She hung out with the young socialites in Glen Rose, and I can tell she was very popular. When she was just a junior in high school, she worked evenings and weekends as the telephone operator in Glen Rose, for the Tri-State Telephone Company. After she graduated from high school, she became the full-time operator here. You can tell that everyone loved her. She is bright and cheery and has a great sense of humor. She is easy to talk to, and often times she was the town's part-time psychologist. She consoled many people through some tough war news. She ate and slept there during the war, putting many important phone calls through. "There was plenty of company at the office: spiders, roaches, and rats, the size of your forearm!" I am thinking, man, this is one strong woman! I told her about my service experience and downplayed my captivity. I didn't say much. I never do. I do not want to scare her or make myself sound any better than any other Joe. I shore don't want her to think I may be damaged goods! We were requested to keep this military information confidential, and it isn't something I want to bring up in my head ifin I don't have to. I kept thinking to myself, man, this beauty ain't gonna fall for a corncob like me. I shore have had a few babes fall my way too! A few I couldn't get off me... like flies on day-old honey! We talked about her job as a telephone operator in town. "Man, I bet you shore enough hear some gossip round here!" "Oh, I do. Everyone in town knows I know their business!", she said.

The sun is beginning to lower. The reflection on the water and the rocks is changing to pink. I lean in for a kiss thinking she is gonna slap me silly. It was a chance I was willing to take. Our lips meet, and I feel my heart pound. I was so afraid she could feel it through my shirt and think I was a wolf. "I'm a straight-up guy..I tell ya!" Before I was ever ready to let her go, her friend showed up, blowing on the horn and waving her arms. "I can take you home, Beth," I desperately pleaded with her. "Oh, no, I can't. I am supposed to be married in a week." "In a week! What the Sam Hill for! It sounds to me like you got a decision to make, kitten. You can go on and keep your plans to marry that knucklehead, or you can stay around with me. He sounds like he is dead from the ass up if you ask me! Next time I see you in the square, you better have a decision. I ain't gonna wait forever." I kiss her again. I hold her face in my hands and make sure she is staring into my blue eyes. I pull her tight, wrapping my arms around her tiny, twenty-one-inch waist. I am trying not to let her go. "You remember what a prize you are now. Don't you dare settle for less than what you deserve in this life, and everything your Mama would want for you. I can live with your decision. You go on now, don't keep her waiting."

"Wait, wait"…. She turns around and puts her hand on her hip, cocking that beautiful head of hers, trying hard to look annoyed. She looks like Rita Hayworth on her movie poster, *You Were Never Lovelier*! "My God, you are the most beautiful thing I have ever seen in my life!" She smiles with that gorgeous mouth of hers, showing her perfect pearls for teeth. She climbed down the rocks and was gone. I had no idea what was going to happen next. All I knew was I couldn't get her off my mind, and that had never happened to me before. "Damn, I got the sweet ass for her!!!!!"

For the next few days, I couldn't sleep much. I didn't know where she lived, and I shore nuff didn't want to cause her any trouble in her job at the old telephone building. Work was hard to get, and women already had enough problems in the workplace these days. I know she needs this job. I took a chance and went off to that old two-story, brick building, which housed the Tri-State

Telephone Company. It was right above Squaw Creek outside town. I looked up at the second story, dusty window, and saw a dim light. Was she in there all alone? I throwed a pebble at the window. No response. I throwed another one. Pretty soon, she pushed up that solid wood frame window and stuck her glorious head out. "Shhhhh, you wanna get me fired!" "Who's gonna fire you, this scrawny ass polecat, or the coon under the steps!?" "My boss sometimes drives around here at night to check on me, you gotta scat!" "When can I see you again?" "Look, a girl has to protect her reputation around here, and you put me in the middle of a mess. Pretty soon everyone in town will be talking!" I see my strategic moves have made some infiltration inside the enemy's territory! "Oh, so you admit I do have a chance, ifin I put you in the middle of a love mess, huh? I'm gonna give ya a little time doll face, but I won't wait forever. After this furlough is over, I will get a new assignment. There sure to hell ain't no Air Force base here in the cedar brakes, of Glen Rose, Texas! Hey, I am shooting my pistols at you to remind you to fight!" I draw out my hands from both of my side pockets, like two Colt revolvers. Phewww, pheww! I shoot right at her heart. She threw out a beautiful hand- embroidered ladies kerchief, with pink roses on one corner. She took a quick look left and right before shutting the window and drawing the shade. The dainty cotton kerchief smelled like her perfume, and I was immediately taken back to our night on the dance floor.

"How beautiful is your love, my sister, my bride! How much better is your love than wine, And the fragrance of your oils than all kinds of spices!" Song of Solomon 4:10

Every day I trolled the square just in hopes she would show up or come downtown for an errand. I had lost so much time in my life; I was in a hurry to get my life on a regular track. Anyone who knows me knows patience has never been a virtue of mine. I know Jacob waited for Rachel. I can wait for Lee Beth to come around. One thing for sure, I ain't about to wait no seven years!

"So Jacob served seven years to get Rachel, but they seemed like only a few days to him because of his love for her." Genesis 29:20

His Hand or Mine?

On Friday, following our Sunday picnic, I see her across the square coming out of the First National Bank on the corner. I am sitting on the edge of the petrified rock, five-pointed star drinking fountain, where I had watched the ribbon cutting ceremony a few years back. A lifetime had been spent since that innocent day. I wave over at her only to see the guy come strolling out behind her from the bank door. "Damn," I whisper to myself. He looks over and catches eyes with me right before he raises his middle finger my direction. "Used up old war shrapnel, Son of a bitch!" Well, I guess I am about to get into a fight with this ole guy! Those are fightin' words. I was willing to take it all to the street 'cept; I can't afford to get myself wrapped up with the law and get discharged from the military. He starts towards me, and I think I am about to get in the scrap of my life. This guy is gonna kick my ass cause I have stepped over the line with his girl. I know I have really disrespected this guy, but that doesn't mean I am going to concede! He is coming towards me as Lee Beth grabs his arm. "I have made my decision, dammit, and it is final! We are through!" She is standing firm, planting her well-turned little ankles and feet firmly on the ground in front of him. If that guy puts a hand on her, I swear I will kill him! He raises his fist at me, waving the flying middle finger. He stomps into his car, slamming the door. He peels out, leaving smoke and rubber completely around the courthouse square. He circles the square a couple of times. He is cussing up a storm as he pulls past the old ice house, and speeds off. Holy hell, she picked me! I run over to her, and we kiss passionately right in front of the courthouse. She drops her purse and throws her arms around my neck. "You better not make me regret this! I just left a guy I knew, my family knew, and he had a good job. I barely know you!" "When I saw you coming out of the bank, I thought you two were getting money to get your marriage license." "No, I pawned my ring, cashed the check; and gave it back to him."

Wedding Bells Ring

We married on Sunday, February 24, 1946, at 7:00 p.m., in the county courthouse in Cleburne, Texas. It was five short months after my rescue. The officiant was a Baptist minister, Reverend E. J. Locker. Lee Beth was wearing a navy blue suit with fuchsia and tan trimmings. She was the most beautiful doll in the world, and my beloved was mine. After a quick ceremony, we honeymooned in a little rock cabin in Glen Rose. Soon after, I transferred from the U.S. Army Air Corps into the newly formed U.S. Air Force. I am stationed at Carswell, Air Force Base, in Ft. Worth, Texas. Lee Beth and I took up residence near the base. I am immediately assigned to the mess hall. Carswell was officially authorized following the attack on Pearl Harbor where it was assigned as a factory for building bombers. It was named for Major Horace S. Carswell, Jr., a B-24 pilot, decorated, Medal of Honor recipient. The primary mission of this base was the training and support of heavy bombing groups. I was sure proud to be feeding those boys, and I finally had my own kitchen. Our life together was pretty sweet. I had a good, reliable job with good hours. I did take on a few extra odd jobs after work so I could keep that beauty in some pretty things, and so we could go out once in a while. There is always a greasy spoon looking for a short-order cook on the night shift. A lot of those schmoozes are lazy and unreliable. I could use the extra greenbacks, so I worked a few shifts a week. My first horrific nightmare with Lee Beth was here at Carswell. I woke up in a sweat, grabbing the headboard to escape. I saw the charred bodies smoldering as they were lining up along the deep death pit. I am choking, gasping for air. "Dear God, Houston, are you ok?" I try to wake myself as the stench fills my nose. "Houston, Houston," she gently calls to me. I wake up to see her there in her beautiful blue, silk nightgown. She looks like an angel. "Are you okay?" I reach over and pull her into my arms, hugging her tightly. "Just let me hold you, sweetheart." "Was it a bad dream like the doctor said?" "Everything is okay, honey. It is all okay". We stayed wrapped in each other's arms the rest of the night.

THE WHITE HOUSE
WASHINGTON

TO MEMBERS OF UNITED STATES ARMED FORCES BEING
REPATRIATED IN OCTOBER 1945:

It gives me special pleasure to welcome you
back to your native shores, and to express, on behalf of the people of the United States, the joy we
feel at your deliverance from the hands of the enemy.
It is a source of profound satisfaction that our efforts to accomplish your return have been successful.

You have fought valiantly in foreign lands
and have suffered greatly. As your Commander in
Chief, I take pride in your past achievements and
express the thanks of a grateful Nation for your
services in combat and your steadfastness while a
prisoner of war.

May God grant each of you happiness and an
early return to health.

Harry Truman

Harry Truman Letter, October 1945, Courtesy Houston E. Lowe,
personal collection

Lee Beth Peterson and Friend, Big Rock Park, Circa 1938,
Courtesy Houston E. Lowe, personal collection

Lee Beth Peterson, at the switchboard, Tri-State Telephone Company,
Glen Rose, Texas, Circa 1943, Courtesy Houston E. Lowe, personal collection

Houston E. Lowe, Lee Beth Peterson, and friends, Circa 1946,
Courtesy Houston E. Lowe, personal collection

Lee Beth Peterson Lowe and Houston E. Lowe, Wedding Day,
February 28, 1946, Courtesy Houston E. Lowe, personal collection

Chapter Twelve

My Work and Family

Miracle Twenty-Two–My Girls

Not long after my bride and I set up our home in Ft. Worth, we knew it was time to begin our family. She was twenty-three, and I was almost thirty by that time. We were both considered a bit 'long in tooth' for starting a family. We both came from big families, and we wanted our home to be filled with little chubby feet and hands right away. I had been taking care of Deannie since I was a kid. I have always loved the smell of little clean babies, especially little girls. They are so much sweeter than little boys! From the physical exams we took at Letterman Hospital, we knew that due to our severe physical conditions, malnourishment, diseases, and our beatings in the pelvis and groin, our chances of having children could be mighty slim. They still didn't know much about the effects of the dusting of radioactive bomb fall-out on us. Initial reports revealed it would probably not be positive. Many of us did not have any active spermatozoa in the testing. I warned Beth before I married her that it was a possibility. That didn't make me feel any better. The possibility of not being able to give her children weighed on me terribly. She missed her Mama so much, filling her arms with a baby would help her to heal fully.

The 'Flu'

I am getting used to being told that things are not possible by now. It has become a part of my daily interactions with people. Only the good Lord knows how I was able to muster up one little sperm whale to make it to the promised land, but she did indeed! Somewhere around the first of July, in 1947, Lee Beth began throwing up violently. She looked like a wrung-out dishrag by the time I got home from the Mess hall, and she was just too weak to cook much. "Baby, can I get you something?" "No, I will just throw it up anyway." She just lays there weak as a kitten. I take her temperature. "98.6, you is perfect!" She begins to cry. "I'm so nasty. Look at my messy hair! My hair is falling out in handfuls, and I am pale as a ghost!" The next day I get her an appointment to see a doc out at the base hospital. We want to rule out the flu. A couple of days after, we go in for her blood test for the flu; we get a phone call from the laboratory. The nurse tells her she is she knows what is causing her symptoms...she is about six-weeks pregnant!!! We are having a baby in late January! We are just beside ourselves! I did it! I did it! I beat the Japs after all! We are going to be adding a bundle of swaddled up joy to our lives. For the next few months, Lee Beth suffers tremendously through a very tough pregnancy, filled with sickness, nausea, and back pain.

Tojo and Six Other Jap Warlords Die on Gallows! – December 23, 1948

The local newspapers are wallpapered with stories about the capture and death of some of the Japanese top brass. MacArthur ordered the arrest of the General of the Japanese Imperial Army, Hideki Tojo, as well as about forty other suspected war criminals. I am not one to want to wish harm on another, no matter their wrongdoings. I have to admit; I was pretty happy to see him pay for his sins. There was a lot of evil in that man, and he inflicted plenty of it on good soldiers and innocent people. That whole 'bushido' philosophy was the card he would play first. He was not gonna surrender himself. He would rather take his own life to maintain his honor. When the American soldiers got to his house, well, he just up and shot himself right in the chest. Poor SOB missed his own heart! He would not have made much of a foot soldier! Bleeding there sprawled out on the floor, Japanese reporters were capturing his words. He said; *"I am very sorry it is taking me so long to die. The Greater East Asia War was justified and righteous. I am very sorry for the nation and all the races of the Greater Asiatic powers. I wait for the righteous judgment of history. I wished to commit suicide but sometimes that fails."* Well, ain't that something! His actions in the war were justified and righteous! Lord have mercy! My blood just boiled over that! The good Lord is the only one that can proclaim anybody's actions are justified and righteous and within His mighty will.

> *"We have obtained an inheritance, having been pre-destined according to His purpose who works all things after the counsel of His will." Ephesians 1:11*

Before he was hung on December 23, 1948, he was sent to be tried before the International Military Tribunal for the Far East. His trial was because of his directives and actions in crimes during the war. During the trial, he was found guilty of conducting and promoting acts of war that were in violation of international law; and for his direct authorization that permitted and continued the horrendous and inhumane treatment of all prisoners of war. You know, I have always believed every dog would someday have his day, and that was surely true for Tojo. I found out many years later that while he was in American hands in Sugamo Prison, while getting his mouth full of new dentures, the dentist had *"Remember Pearl Harbor,"* secretly inscribed in Morse code inside!

> *"For as through the one man's disobedience the many were made sinners, even so through the obedience of the One the many will be made righteous." Romans 5:19*

Toni Lee – 'Yap Yap'

On January 28, 1948, a few months after my twenty-ninth birthday, and after seventeen hours of hard labor, Toni Lee Lowe, seven pounds, three ounces, eighteen inches long, is brought into this world, under the glaring surgical lights, at 3:07 p.m. She was born through C-section, under the skilled knife of the OBGYN and surgeon. We are smitten. She has a beautiful head of dark hair like her Mama, a little button nose, chubby pink chubby, and baby blue eyes. She was a beautiful baby, and I just couldn't stop looking at her. She is healthy, has all ten fingers and toes, and cooing up a storm. Thank you, God, for giving us this child!

> *"I prayed for this child, and the LORD has granted me what I asked of him." 1 Samuel 1: 27*

I have never seen Lee Beth glow like this. She loved being a mother. It was a role she was born to do. She immediately bonded with that beautiful baby and became what everyone knew as, the 'mother tiger'. This baby filled a very dark hole in her heart and lifted her spirits so high. I was a proud papa and grateful to be able to have a family. Lee Beth talks to Toni constantly and softly sings sweet lullabies. Her surgery was hard on her. The incision cut her like a gutted rabbit, and getting around and holding Toni Lee was more than her body could handle. She would need some help with the baby, and around the house. I know the road to Lee Beth's recovery is going to be tough, so we call up Lee Beth's baby sister, Mattie Jean, to see if she would like to come help out for a while. Mattie Jean was a real swell trooper and came up on the Greyhound bus the next week. I had to sell our car to pay the hospital bill. When we got home, Toni Lee is placed in her crib. It just so happened to be the bottom drawer of our dresser! We lived in military housing. It was tight, but we got along alright. Mattie Jean stayed about a year and helped out so much. It did those girls a lot of good to have each other too. They did each other's hair in pin curls and laughed together. Sometimes they would go out to an afternoon movie or do a little shopping. Toni Lee was a healthy, sweet little thing. She was curious about everything and smart as a whip. She learned everything so quickly. Lee Beth was a wonderful mother. She adored her little girl, dressing her in a little red cowboy hat and boots, pin curling her hair, and sewing her little pinafores with embordered sunflowers. She taught her all the popular nursery rhymes like *Baa Baa Black Sheep, Tom, Tom, The Piper's Son, Pussycat, Pussycat, and Hey Diddle Diddle.* They had pictures made together, baked cookies and pies, and had little picnics on the cement front porch. Soon after, we were assigned to be stationed at Lackland Air Force Base, in San Antonio.

The American Dream House

The military packs up our few little belongings, and we drive on down US 281 the 270 miles to San Antonio. I called Joe Romanell as soon as we got a little settled. He joined the Army and was stationed at Ft. Sam Houston. It was so good to see him healthy and well. He married a sweet gal and lived in an apartment across town. We talked about buying our first houses. "I'm looking in the northwest side, Joe. You interested in buying that way?' "Yep, I have saved up for the down payment. We really will be neighbors, Houston!".

I move my family into a small motel down the road from the base until we found a little one-room duplex to rent on Elsmere Place. Toni's Aunt Jean lived with us too and helped Lee Beth out so much. We lived there for a couple of years until we could save up enough money to put the down payment on a little house. Lee Beth always wanted herself a house. We both wanted a warm place to raise our little family. After a few months of looking, we find a quiet little family neighborhood. It was filled with newly built, little 950 sq. ft., wood framed houses. That little neighborhood suited us just fine. It was located at the southern gate of St. Mary's University, in the northwest part of town, not far from the base. Joe had already bought his place. He lived two doors down from me! There was a great little corner store, Armand's, and a Piggly Wiggly, right up the street. Lee Beth would be able to get to what she needed easily. The house had two little bedrooms, and a larger bedroom for us, a tiny little bathroom, and a kitchen. There was a small dining room and living room, and a magnificent big ole backyard. I could finally plant a big vegetable garden, and peach and plum trees. Lee Beth can put up some pickles, tomatoes, jams, and jellies. The house was a mansion compared to what we was used to growing up, and we were so proud. No more outhouses! The house cost $7220, with a monthly mortgage payment of $65.50. My take-home pay is $200 per month. We are gonna have to be real careful with our money to make that note every month. Luckily, Lee Beth was an excellent bookkeeper. She watched every dime we had, and we never lacked for anything we needed. We closed on that house in May 1950. It is still my family home today.

Lackland Air Force Base, San Antonio, Texas- May 1950 – June 1973

I took up in the Mess hall right away, and it was under my complete charge. I make no excuses for the fact that I run a very tight ship. I don't tolerate any monkeying around, and I have no patience for laziness. You show up on time, work your full shift, follow orders, and take some initiative; and we will get along just fine. My orders were crystal clear. Every task was listed and checked off, with a time the job was completed. All of the steamers, stovetops, counters, mixers, and other equipment were steam cleaned and sanitized daily. All the kitchen mats were washed in hot soapy water and hung out in the sun, after dinner. Floors were swept twice a day and mopped every night. I put a bit of bleach in my mop water, and I polished all other surfaces with a vinegar mixture. The stainless steel counters shined like mirrors. You could literally eat off the floors. Everything was labeled, categorized, and inventoried. All of the can labels were facing forward and upright. I created a separate storage space for the dry goods in a large closet where some of the guys used to hang out and smoke. That did not make me real popular around here. Everything was organized, date-labeled, and could easily be retrieved. I knew when a pound of butter was missing or out of place. My food was fresh, appetizing, nutritious and made you feel like home. I was proud of my kitchen, and I received exemplary annual reviews and ratings, because of it. My greatest joy was bringing good food to the boys who were shipping out. I knew what it took to complete their training. They needed good nourishing food. Over time, my nickname arose from whispers in back, 'Iron Ass'. I was good with that!

The Birthday Wish

Toni Lee is asking for a baby sister. Her *Tiny Tears* doll was in constant tow, as she followed her Mama around, repeating everything she did. We are ready to add to our family. Why not roll the dice another time, and see if this ole guy has another bullet in the chamber! We are celebrating Toni Lee's third birthday. Lee Beth has baked a homemade vanilla cake with perfect swirls and peaks of white, marshmallow Royal icing. Three pink candles crown the top. Some of the little neighborhood babies and cousins, Phyllis and Paul, are wearing small paper cone hats. Joe's daughter, Leesie is there too. "Happy Birthday to You! Happy Birthday to You! Happy Birthday Toni Leeeeee, Happy Birthday to You!" Toni is standing on the dining room chair wearing her favorite red cowboy hat. Little wrapped packages are surrounding her cake. Delight is on the face of every child because they see the hand-cranked ice cream freezer in the kitchen sink! "Blow out the candles, baby!" That little cherub face purses her lips and blows so gently over the candles. "Look, Mama, I getta' wish now wif my cake." "That's right baby, make a wish." " I wanna baby." "You want a new baby doll, honey?" "No Mama, I wanna baby. Can you put one in your tummy so I can have one?" She points to Lee Beth's stomach. Lee Beth gently strokes her curly hair. "Let's have some cake and then we will go outside and play 'Ring around the Rosie'." As she is cutting the cake, a strange look comes over Lee Beth's face. She grabs the screen door flinging it open. She walks out to the yard, bending over to throw up. She knows what is going on this time. She walks up behind me and whispers, "Houston, Toni Lee got her birthday wish."

Katie Beth – My Broken Angel

Lee Beth has a pretty healthy pregnancy. She is gaining the right amount of weight, and her morning sickness subsides after the first five months. The time is moving quickly this pregnancy, Having a toddler to run after is keeping her occupied. Toni Lee cannot keep her hands off her Mama's belly. "My baby, my baby!" She would kiss her Mama's stomach and cup her hands, talking to the baby. Sometimes Lee Beth would let her feel her stomach when the baby was kicking. "Baby, kick hard, Mama." They laughed and played dolls together while Lee Beth was preparing Toni for the upcoming new arrival. Around the first week in August, Lee Beth woke up feeling strange. It was a Saturday morning, the only time we could all lay in the bed and have some time together before I jumped up to make Toni pancakes. Toni jumps off and is playing with her dolls in the other room. "Houston, the baby hasn't moved today. You know this baby is active in the morning." "I am sure it is alright Lee Beth, you are just tired, and the baby is resting." Two days passed and the baby still had not moved. I come home to find her crying on the couch. "Something is wrong Houston. I just know it." "Now Lee Beth, don't go thinking the worst here." "Dammit, Houston! Don't you tell me how to think here! You will never know what I know about what is going on inside of me. I have known this baby a lot longer than you have!" She is obviously very worried. One thing I learned about women....don't you ever be stupid enough with your x and y chromosomes, to think you will ever know what they do about themselves! Ifin I ever wrote a book explaining about women, that would be the first entry. We set the appointment with the doctor for the next week. Lee Beth dresses up Toni Lee in a little navy blue smocked dress, and baby doll shoes, and we head out. I take Toni to the candy machine in the hall while Beth is being examined. Toni is tearing the wrapper on a Bit 'O' Honey bar, and I am smoking, looking at the black and white photographs on the wall. Beth is in there for over an hour before the doctor steps out, calling me in. He sends his nurse out to keep Toni occupied. Beth is sitting on the examining table, white as a ghost. Her face is stained with tears. "What is going on here?" I go over and put my arm around her shoulder. She places her head and face in my shirt, holding on to my waist. "I am sorry Sergeant Lowe, after several thorough examinations, it is my medical opinion, the baby has experienced intrauterine death." I gasp and quickly ask,

"What, what, how can this be? She is passed the time for that... she is eight months along for God's sake!" He states, "We can't always know, but it can be due to many reasons, most likely, the Rh Factor. You and your wife have a toxic mix of Rh-negative and Rh-positive proteins in your blood, creating the Rh-incompatibility. Because she is Rh-negative, when her blood came in contact with the baby's blood that is Rh-positive, her body immediately developed antibodies, attacking the Rh-positive blood. The mother's body thinks it is a harmful material and will begin to destroy the baby's red blood cells faster than the baby's body can replace them. The red blood cells are used to carry much-needed oxygen to all of the baby's body. Without enough, is called hemolytic anemia.". "Why didn't she have this problem when we had Toni Lee?" "When an Rh-negative mother has her first Rh-negative baby, usually there are no problems. This is because the baby is born before the mother begins to produce the antibodies." "Dear God, man, what do we do now? What am I going to tell our daughter?" "The safest and best thing for her now because she is so far along, and the fetus is no longer viable, is to leave everything alone and let nature take its course. We want to do what is the best medical course of action for your wife. The body naturally knows when it is time and the processes will begin to take place then. She will go into labor in a few weeks, and the baby can be delivered then." "So, in the meantime, I have to send this woman home knowing her child is no longer alive, and tell her just to wait!? " "I am sorry Sergeant Lowe, we have no other safer option. The Rh factor can negatively affect the mother's health as well if we try to do any further intrusive procedures. I will prescribe some pills that will help her, and ease her emotional pain. Unfortunately, there is no concern for the effect on the baby. Here is a one month supply of Valium, it is 'Mother's Little Helper', and can help with the emotions and depression." Lee Beth was so devastated she didn't argue. We walk out to the hallway. She couldn't even look at Toni Lee. "Why you been crying Mama?" Toni grabs her Mama's hand, and in typical three-year-old speak, begins to tell her about her candy, and the nurses in white 'swishy' hose, and pilgrim hats. Lee Beth smiles a weak smile, and we head home to face the inevitable: the slow and painful end of our sweet baby's life.

The Pink Box

Lee Beth keeps a straight face and her head up as she goes along her daily routines carrying a baby she knows is no longer alive. She has no other choice. Going to the commissary, to pay bills, or the post office was paralyzing as she is barraged with well-meaning, but painful comments. "When are you due honey?, "I bet you will be so glad to hold that baby soon." "Do you want a baby brother or sister, sweetie?" She gracefully makes her way through four extremely difficult weeks, keeping up a front for everyone, especially Toni Lee. Lee Beth begins her difficult labor on September 8, 1951, delivering our second little girl, Katie Beth Lowe, by natural childbirth, yet stillborn. Beth named her after her mother, Katie Lee Boliver Peterson. As a very unusual step for hospitals at that time, they allowed me to stand in the back, in a white surgical gown. Once she was born, the nurse whisked her away in a blanket weighing and measuring her. Her birth statistics were quickly recorded as her death statistics. I stood helplessly knowing in a week or so I had to take my wife home with empty arms, to an empty pink bassinette. The obstetrician sedated Lee Beth, increasing the dosage as the baby was born. As she is taken to recovery, I am at a loss for what to do. The nurse brings a tiny little bundle over, and gently leans over, placing the tiny baby in my arms. I take off her little blanket to look her over. Her little lifeless body looks like she is in the deepest slumber. She is beautiful, just like the pictures of Lee Beth's mother. I cannot believe it is real; she looks like she is sleeping. She is fully-developed, five pounds, six ounces, and has a full shock of beautiful auburn hair. As I begin to rewrap her unresponsive body, my tears are dropping on her. The nurses are standing beside me crying. I am wiping tears from her tiny arm. I lift her right arm to place it under the blanket. I see that it is curled up, deformed; clenched tightly to her chest. I whisper to her, "My little broken-angel."

Lee Beth was in the hospital for about four days after the delivery. The chaplain came by every day to talk with us. He provided a lot of comfort during those meetings. Lee Beth was going through some tough times, blaming herself for the loss. He reassured her that was not the case. We opted not to have an autopsy on our little one. Because the infant was fully developed and weighed over a pound, a funeral was required. The baby would be handled by the burial services department of Ft. Sam Houston National Cemetery. It is time to go home and pick up our life. We have to accept it; we have a toddler at home that needs us. I am wheeling Lee Beth down the mint green hospital corridor to go home. The head nurse steps around the nurse's station. She hands Beth a small pink box containing a lock of Katie Beth's hair and her hospital blanket. "We are all so sorry Mrs. Lowe." The nurses had all signed a small card of condolences they placed inside. Passing by in another wheel-chair, a young woman coddles and coos at her baby girl, wrapped in a pink blanket. Lee Beth turns her head, and I push on down the hallway. I am thinking how in the world we can explain this to a three-year-old child.

The Tiniest of Caskets

Two weeks later, at Ft. Sam Houston, a few of Beth's sisters and brothers, along with Joe and his wife, were there with us to watch the tiny casket be put in the ground. Beth handed me her handmade pink embroidered blanket, and we draped over the coffin. I knew the road was going to be long for us. Toni Lee would be asking too many questions, and Beth was emotionally too fragile to answer them. It was harder than anything I had experienced in my life. I felt a loss and a yearning for a life I knew I would never know until Heaven. I had to hold to that promise.

> *"See that you do not despise one of these little ones. For I tell you that in heaven their angels always see the face of my Father who is in heaven."*
> *Matthew 18:10*

Coldest Damn Place Ever!

Thule, Greenland Assignment

I got my temporary duty assignment in November of 1951, a few weeks after we buried Katie Beth. Although this is an incredibly difficult time for all of us, all military personnel are aware that they can be shipped out on temporary duty at any time. I was given a few choices of locations that I could select. Because I had never really been anywhere cold or seen real snow or ice, I selected Greenland! I darn sure wasn't going back to a jungle again! I picked the furthest place from a jungle that I could, and I ended up literally at the top of the world! Secretly, the Defense Department was in full deployment of "Operation Blue Jay". The plan was to develop a full-scale military base for the big bombers and place it at the top of the world! After recovering from World War II, we were preparing for any and all threats. They needed a good mess hall sergeant to prepare hearty grub to keep men working in sub-zero temperatures, and I was their man! After packing up a few things, Lee Beth and Toni Lee saw me off at the airport. I kissed those girls goodbye knowing the next eighteen months would be hard on them, and I wouldn't have a toddler when I got back. "Daddy loves you, girls." I kiss them both and let Beth know I would call her every chance that I got. I know it is going to be hard on them, but I married one of the most tenacious women in the world, and she was up for the battle. I have Joe two doors down if she needs anything.

After about a nine-hour flight, the door swung open as the sub-zero wind sliced right through me. I thought my ear was just sheared off! "Good Gawd man!" I just stepped into the meat locker I would be calling home for a while! This place is nothing but frozen tundra. You can see for miles, nothing but ice and snow. Everyone is all bundled up like Eskimos. I make my way to the Quonset hut mess hall to grab an apron and get busy. The mess hall staff there had been shirking off for a few months without any real supervision, so they were none too happy to see me. I made it clear from the beginning that I run a tight operation. "We serve it hot; we serve it fresh, we serve it on time!" That was my first training lesson. "We clean the mats every day and polish the stainless steel every night. Inventory is done every Friday. Any questions?" I overheard one guy whisper, "This guy is an ass!" I spin around, "Iron Ass, son, get it right. I go by Iron Ass! Good thing you got that figured out so fast."

After a couple of days, I try to reach Lee Beth. The reception was pretty bad up here, so after getting a short choppy call to her for a few minutes, we agreed to communicate through letters from now on. Letter writing is a very personal experience. You learn to control your words, and you take the time to say the things that need to be said.

December 12, 1951

My Darling,

I miss you so much, and I hope that you and Toni Lee are doing well. I miss the smell of your beautiful hair, and what you look like when it is wrapped up in a towel after a shower. I will be home as soon as I can get there. Did you get the money I sent you last week? It is still cold as hell up here. Not much to do but work, there sure ain't no place to go! Nothing but ice and snow. I have been playing some dominoes and cards after my night shift. I won ten bucks! How is Toni doing? I know that Jean has been a great help to you. I will send you a check next week. Why don't you go buy yourself something special? I know this Christmas will be hard on you.

I miss and love you,

Houston

January 12, 1952

Dear Houston,

It is so good to hear from you. I miss you too. We are doing well. Toni is growing like a weed! She is talking up a storm and is constantly on the move. The other day while we were napping, she unlatched the screen door, left the house in the cold! She was wearing only her ruffled panties and cowboy boots, and she walked across the street to the Rexall Drug Store! She commenced to climb up to the counter and ordered a chocolate shake! Mr. Wilson called me up and told me he would put it on my bill, and he would hold her there until I could get there! I ran across the street in my robe and curlers. Other than that, things are going fine! Jean and I are taking Toni to see Singing in the Rain on Saturday. I am saving money and putting it in an account at the savings and loan. I cannot wait until you get home. We both miss you very much.

Love you, honey,

Beth

I missed my little family so much it hurt. The base at Thule was desolate and gave a man the clear, clean air and space to uncloud your mind. Once in a while, I would take a truck ride out on the tundra. It was a landscape not quite like any place else in the world. There is nothing but a bay with some ice caps and miles of ice-covered rocks. The air is clean and crisp, and the wind blows the snow into beautiful waves and pillows on the banks. Very few creatures can live here in these conditions. A few native Eskimos live in a village over sixty miles from us. Sometimes you could see them off in the distance with their dog sled teams traveling across the ice. At night, it was especially lonely. On that ice-covered bay, I thought about my wife and how much she was responsible for in my absence. I realize what a lucky man I am. This cold solace gave me the time to think about my life, to grieve the loss of my infant alone, and to put into perspective the plans God has for me. I am at peace, and I miss my wife and child. They are both the rewards of my suffering.

The entire time I was in Thule, I ran the mess hall preparing three meals a day, seven days a week and took an extra job at night at the airmen's bowling alley as a short order cook. The eighteen months were hard and lonely, but they went by pretty fast, cause I stayed occupied working all the time. It allowed me to save quite a bit of money. I sent most of it back home to Beth so she could keep up the household. I only needed some money for cigarettes and a few items. I returned home in May of 1952.

Dancing With My Darling

Having me gone for so long in Thule, Lee Beth suffered through some very challenging times. She was alone, raising a toddler and recovering from the loss of our baby. She had done such a great job taking care of everything and managed to save us up a little cash. After settling back into our life together, I wanted to do something special for her. I set up a date at the Keyhole Club. It was downtown on Iowa and Pine. It used to be the old Ritz Theater until it was converted to the first club in San Antonio with a cover charge. I reserved a table for eighty-five cents to keep any schmoes from coming around! We went with our good friends Perk and Randy. Randy was a police officer and could clear a floor ifin he had to. Beth gets all dolled up, and we danced the night away holding each other tightly. A good dance time can heal a lot of wounds. A man needs to know the power of holding a woman close in his arms and guiding her around a floor. It is secure, it is protection, and it is only for each other. It is a perfect picture of how God intended us to be. The man, leading and guiding, and the woman following next to his rib.

On other occasions when we had a couple of loose bucks, we would go to Floores Country Store, down the road in Helotes, Texas.

It is a honky-tonk and has some of the best names in country music performing there. We danced to Bob Wills and the Texas Playboys and Ernie Tubbs there. If you think you know country music, if these guys aren't in your collection, you don't! Floore's has some great tamales and bread and the coldest beer around. Lee Beth could always muster up the goings to dance. Slowly a few months passed, and I noticed that nothing seemed to keep her spirits up for long, and she was sleeping a lot more. There is no way I can take away the aching in her heart. She longed for another child, and we were never sure I could give her another one. The Rh factor loomed heavy over us.

Terri Lyn – 'Maudie'

In late October of 1953, the morning sickness began, and we were off to the baby races again! Lee Beth was happier than I had seen her in months. There is nothing that will lift the spirits of a woman with an empty heart, than the hope to fill her arms with a baby again. She had a pretty good pregnancy; it just didn't last long enough. The Rh Factor was knocking on the door to take another one of our babies. Lee Beth is writhing in pain. 'It is too early Houston, too early! The baby cannot survive this early." The doctor wants her to go ahead and deliver vaginally. The baby is small enough, and the risk is less than a major operation through C-section. He does not give her any pain medication, and she is in full labor. Exhausted, she does not have the strength to push any longer. The impatient obstetrician yells "Come on now, aren't you woman enough to push this little baby out!" Lee Beth was furious. She snapped back, "You son-of-a-bitch, you watch me push this baby out!" At only the sixth month of pregnancy, Terri Lyn was born on April 7, 1954, in a Quonset hut on Lackland Air Force Base, near what was known as Lackland USAF Hospital. After the influx of wounded from the Korean Conflict, the hospital was under construction; so temporary facilities were set up until the work could be completed. Terri Lyn had very special needs. She was born three-months premature by natural childbirth and weighed in at just barely three pounds. The obstetrician did not give either of us much hope that the baby would survive. Lee Beth was weak and had lost a lot of blood. The Rh incompatibility contributed to the early birth and possibly further health problems. As soon as the baby is delivered, an eerie quiet fell over the room. Lee Beth, even in her twilight condition, knew something was very wrong. "How is the baby,?" she asked breathlessly. The little lifeless, baby doll lay still in the towel in the arms of the nurse. Lee Beth gasped as she saw her for the first time. "Dear God, she is so tiny!" The nurse told her to rest. "You get some rest now honey." Lee Beth began screaming, "Is she alive? Is she alive, dammit!?" Ever so gently, the nurse leaned over and whispered the dreaded word, no. "Little thing never caught her breath, honey. Here, go ahead and give her a kiss on the forehead, her little skin is so fragile." With tears burning down her cheeks, she kissed that tiny baby goodbye, all alone in a cold delivery room, under the glaring lights. The clanging of steel instruments could be heard while the staff was busying for the next procedure. "I will let your husband know, honey. He will be in soon." I was pacing outside the door. I knew she couldn't recover from the loss of another child. I was praying hard in the hallway. "Lord, let this little one live and be strong." I continued to pace as the time passed. No one came out. I had no idea what was going on in there. The nurse came to tell me the horrible news and to show me my little girl. I cried bullets of tears over her as she quickly whisked her away, headed to the morgue in the main hospital downstairs. "Dear God, she looks like a skinned rabbit"! All I could think about was Lee Beth. I just didn't think she had the strength to put another tiny casket in the ground. Within a minute, the nurse had walked the path to the main hospital carrying the tiny bundle. On the elevator downstairs, a tiny cry, like a kitten, comes from the swaddled baby. It was so weak; the nurse thought she heard the squeaks of the elevator cables overhead. She opened the towel to see that her little eyes were open, and she was trying ever so hard to cry. "Dear Jesus! Dear Jesus, Mary Mother of God!" She immediately tears open the buttons on her uniform top and places the baby on her chest for warmth. She covers her with the towel as she hurriedly takes the elevator back upstairs. She calls for the pediatrician on duty, Captain Mark Dine. Suddenly there is an all call on the delivery floor, and Beth's doctor scurries down the hall. I am finally able to see Lee Beth. She was taken to a group room to recover. Women are taken there when the delivery news is not positive. I immediately wrap my arms around her and hug her gently. She is pale and sweaty, and her beautiful head of hair is matted to her head. They have sedated her to help her with the news. "Honey, I am so sorry." "I just don't know why, why..." She is sluggish, and her speech is slurred. "You rest baby. I will be right outside."

The Intercom Miracle

"Sergeant Lowe, Sergeant Lowe, report to the Pediatric Wing, Office B85, Captain Mark Dine. Sergeant Lowe, Sergeant Lowe, report immediately to the Pediatric Wing, Office B85, Captain Mark Dine." On the hospital intercom system, a staffer is barking out my name. "What in the Sam Hill do they need now....haven't we had enough today!" I stomp off to the office. Captain Dine is standing next to a nurse with blood stains on her white starched uniform. He was a man of very short stature, with a confident look and a firm handshake. "Sir, sir, I need for you to see something." "What now dammit, I have a wife over there that I will never be able to console! Ain't this enough for one day!" "Sir, just follow us please." We walked the halls passed the window of all the swaddled babies in little aluminum carts, in hanging canvas beds. They take me to a small room off to the side, and there she was! My little angel, she was alive! "Dear God in Heaven!!!" "She is alive? My little skinned-rabbit is alive?" "Yes sir, she is indeed!" "What the hell happened?" "Do you believe miracles, sir?" "Well, I am getting pretty used to them." Captain Dine begins to unfold the miracle before me. "When the nurse was taking her down the elevator, she began to cry a little. She placed her on her bare chest to keep her warm." The nurse begins to tell me what had just happened. "Sir, the cold air in the delivery room must have been too much for her as small as she is. Poor little thing was cold." "She is not out of the woods yet. We have one incubator from Louisiana. In the meantime, we are keeping her warm by placing heated cotton diapers around her. She is so tiny, and her skin is so fragile, we can only

247

use kerchiefs for her diapers. Every man on the floor has offered theirs up. I need your signature for a blood transfusion right away. We have to take her now, sir. I will get you when she is finished and stabilized." "Thank you, thank you. I have to tell Lee Beth." "Let's give it a couple of hours and let her rest. When she is a little stronger, you can tell her. We will keep a twenty-four-hour watch on the baby. We are using a baby doll bottle and nipples to feed her. I will not let your little one die, Sergeant Lowe. I will not let her die. I will be right here, all night if I need to." Right away he calls for blood. A G.I. was in the waiting room awaiting the arrival of his little one. After securing matching blood types, Dr. Dine hooked that G.I. up to my little doll. He was draining every last drop of her Rh-positive blood, replacing it with the blood of that G.I.

Dr. Dine is a pediatric genius in a child-sized body. He has both the knowledge and passion necessary to safely care for a child as fragile as this one. He is a brilliant doctor with a powerful mind and a servant's heart. The military built him a small apartment attached to the Quonset hut where he sometimes lived twenty-four hours a day. He developed a specialized area for the tinier babies and their unique needs. Before there was a NICU, he developed one. His inquisitive nature led him to many discoveries in early pediatrics. He discovered a connection between the closed incubator and Retrolental Fibroplasia. Many premature babies are either born blind or have blindness early on after birth. He discovered the level of oxygen in the incubator was too high for their systems. In his apartment next door, he rigged up an incubator system that was opened slightly. He attached rubber tubing that was connected to a large bottle of sterile water, where he added moisture to the flowing air. He placed my little Terri Lyn in that rigged up incubator, and she began to thrive. All babies are a unique miracle from God, but she was truly my miracle baby.

"For you created my inmost being; you knit me together in my mother's womb. I praise you because I am fearfully and wonderfully made; your works are wonderful, I know that full well. My frame was not hidden from you when I was made in the secret

place, when I was woven together in the depths of the earth. Your eyes saw my unformed body; all the days ordained for me were written in your book before one of them came to be." Psalms 139:13-16

With Toni Lee in school, Lee Beth went to the hospital when I got home with the car. Terri Lyn was a tiny little string bean, with saggy little knees and elbows. Within about a week or so, she dropped to two pounds, scaring everyone to death. I held my breath every day as I went by to visit her on my way home. Her miniature hands would be clenched into fists next to her face. She had tape all over her face. Her eyes were covered in cotton and gauze; an IV needle was in her little head. "Little skinned-rabbit, this is your Daddy." I would reach into the little plastic box to stroke her tiny arm and put my pinkie finger into her palm. She would grasp my finger tightly. "You get stronger little girl so you can come home and see your sister." I took my wedding band off and slipped it over her little foot. I could slide it all the way to her thigh. As I laid her back in her little incubator, I drew up my imaginary Colt revolvers. "You keep fighting little rabbit; you keep fighting." I thought, how are we ever going to care for such a fragile little thing?

Dr. Dine kept watch over her every day. He added more nutrients to her formula and began propping her up on small towels at an angle, so she would not have reflux and could clear her lungs more easily. He removed the gauze over her eyes. We were able to hold her a little bit as well. Terri Lyn was in the hospital for four months in that incubator. Dr. Dine placed a cot next to her and slept there every night until she was released. She was receiving around the clock care, oxygen, and feedings with a baby doll bottle. Nurses had to keep up with her vitals and report to him, every hour on the hour. There were no sophisticated devices, feeding tubes, or monitors to keep a preemie stable. Dr. Dine wanted his babies nurtured. "Food and medicine are not enough, they must be loved and feel safe," he told his staff. Babies were held and rocked and talked to, in his care. "They need love to thrive," he would say. This dedicated man may be small in stature, but he was grand in everything else. He saved my little skinned-rabbit. He was assigned to

Lackland Air Force Base from 1953 to 1955, before leaving and setting up his practice in Ohio. What conceivable odds do you think, could be placed on him being here during the critical birth and care of my preemie? It may seem like a coincidence to many, but he was an angel, sent directly from God.

> *"Be not forgetful to entertain strangers: for thereby some have entertained angels unawares."*
> *Hebrews 13:2*

After about four months, she began to thrive. At four pounds and six ounces, Dr. Dine felt she was strong enough to come home. I walk in the house to the smell of homemade corn beef and cabbage and find Beth mindlessly pressing clothes at the ironing board. She is sprinkling water from the Coke bottle with the aluminum cap on it, steaming perfect military pleats in my shirts. This has been hard on her. I kiss her on the forehead. "How are you doing sweetheart?" "Fair to middlin', I guess." "When I stopped by the hospital today, they said Terri Lyn might be ready to come home tomorrow." "Oh, my stars and garters!", Lee Beth replied. "We have to get things ready."

Designer Doll Clothes

Lee Beth had made clothes for her using the very patterns she used for Toni's dolls. She had made a few beautiful little dresses, and some sleeveless cotton tops. We used my cotton handkerchiefs for her diapers. We use real cotton diapers for her blankets. Lee Beth had one silver diaper pin made for her, which she clasped right in the middle of her belly, holding the diaper together. She was indeed a little doll! Our house is once again filled with baby bottles and bibs. It amazed us to watch her growth unfold before us. She was a precious child with a beautiful smile, sparkling blue eyes, and a little blond curl on top of her head. She was so tiny and delicate that we had to watch everything around her. Toni finally got her wish. She had the baby she had longed for. Terri Lyn was our little miracle, and we were going to do everything we could to earn the right to this blessing.

"Be Happy with Two"

Due to our Rh incompatibility causing the low birth weight, two premature births, and a stillborn, along with Lee Beth's weakened health, and raising a very fragile preemie; her doctor suggested firmly that we not have any more children. She was medically likely to begin preterm labor at around the fifth month. It would be too hard on Lee Beth's body, and another Rh Factor pregnancy could likely cause her lifelong medical issues, or possibly death. Even the surgery to tie her fallopian tubes was risky for her. The doctors all told us to be happy for having two healthy children and to move on. It always bothered me that people so easily can dismiss your dreams and hopes, especially ones for children. After talking it over with Lee Beth, I decided that it was best I make an appointment in urology and get this risk taken care of for good. I am not willing to lose my wife for the chance to have another child, no matter how much I may want another one someday. The first of May, I went for my scheduled vasectomy. I was glad to have the procedure behind me. We would learn to live with our little family of four.

The Recanalization Failure

Around mid-November, I come home to find Lee Beth on the couch. Terri Lyn is in her little playpen tugging on a rubber giraffe, and Toni Lee is coloring in a book. "I just don't feel well. I am not sure what is going on Houston. I threw up twice this morning." She has 'the look'. I don't know what it is, but women only get 'the look' when they are expecting. I know that cannot be it. "What have you eaten today?" "Nothing." "Let me fix you some chicken soup and rice." Every morning like clockwork, she throws up. We need to rule out the flu or a stomach bug. We do not want the girls getting sick either. Terri Lyn had to be separated from her until we could figure this out. Lee Beth gets an appointment to get her

251

symptoms checked and some blood work done. In a few days, she gets the results. She is six weeks pregnant! I come home to find her crying. She just spits it out. "I am pregnant!" "Pregnant...that is impossible! You cannot be pregnant, Lee Beth. I had a vasectomy, dammit!" "You think I don't know that! It didn't work, I tell you, it didn't work!" "Or, maybe you have been doing more than washing dishes and folding clothes while I am busting my ass in that mess hall!" Oh shit, I said it! I saw the look on her face go from sadness to deep hurt in a split second. She glares over her glasses at me as she shoots the death stare my way, "You son-of-a-bitch, how dare you accuse me of that! You really think I am capable of that? I would never be interested in another man and you, better than anyone, should know that! And if I were, I would probably be too damn dead-tired to do anything about it! You want to see someone bust their ass? You stay around here for a day! And now, since we are on the subject of asses, you can just go on and take yours on out and sleep in your beloved mess hall tonight!" I was still mad and reeling from not knowing how on earth we could be in this position. "I ain't coming home until I get this settled!" "You aren't welcome home until you get this settled!" I take my shaving kit, a clean uniform, and leave, slamming the door behind me. The next day I make an appointment with my urologist. He gets me in for a consult right away, because I told the nurse what Beth told me. I knew in my heart Beth would never betray me, but my head was always full of mistrust for people. It was something I couldn't shake after my captivity. "We will have to run some tests to confirm it Sergeant Lowe, but it is possible. It is not likely, but it is possible." "How is it possible? I thought you told me I would not have to worry about this again. Beth is in no condition to carry another pregnancy! That is why we did this procedure!" "Sir, it is rare, but it does happen. Let me show you some pictures from this book. Soon after a vasectomy, sometimes scar tissue will develop and create a blockage. That tissue is easier for sperm to penetrate because it is softer. See this; it is the vas deferens. The ends may not have meshed back together well. It is conceivable that your sperm worked its way through all that soft scar tissue obstruction. It only takes one determined one! The only way we will know for sure is to test your ejaculate." "Well, let's get this over with doc. I got big decisions to make around here." "We can see a live specimen under the microscope in the lab. You go take care of your part, and I will let you know when the slide is read."

About three hours later I get a call at the mess hall. "Sergeant Lowe, this is Doctor McBixen, I have your results. You have active sperm, sir. The scar tissue did not completely heal, and your vasectomy did not take. The medical term for this is *recanalization failure*." "Well ain't that a doozy of a name for a vasectomy that doesn't work!" I knew I needed to crawl on my belly back home and apologize to my wife. I also knew her doctor said we couldn't let her continue with this pregnancy. It was just too much of a health risk for her. I am torn as to which emotion I can control right now. I bring the lab records and pictures home and go inside to talk with Lee Beth. The girls are in bed, and she is sitting at the kitchen table alone, drinking a black cup of coffee. I drop the report on the table along with the picture. "Honey, I am so sorry. I said some awful things I did not mean. I know I can trust you with our lives." I told her all about the report and what Dr. McBixen told me. "Don't you ever doubt me again. You made me feel like a cheap street tramp!" She picked up the report and went on to bed. I crawled next to her and held her to my chest. I knew we had a bigger issue to deal within the next few days.

The Decision

Her obstetrician called me from his office on the base. I wasn't sure why he would be calling me, but I went over on my lunch break. I knew the conversation had to happen soon. "Sergeant Lowe, your wife has suffered a stillborn, two premature births, low birth weights, and the remnants and complications of her Rh blood issue. We also think during the stillbirth she suffered from pre-eclampsia as well. Her physical state is at-risk for severe preterm labor. She simply will not be able to carry another child to a healthy full term. The consequences for that could be catastrophic for her. I want to be clear. It could include her death." I am stunned. This miracle, a baby that worked this hard to make its way to being, will have to be aborted for my wife to live. How could a decision be any more difficult? I think about how Abraham so trusted God that he was obedient enough to put his son, Isaac, on the alter to be sacrificed. Lord, I know I am no Abraham.

> *"When they reached the place God had told him about, Abraham built an altar there and arranged the wood on it. He bound his son Isaac and laid him on the altar, on top of the wood. Then he reached out his hand and took the knife to slay his son. But the angel of the* Lord *CALLED OUT TO HIM FROM HEAVEN, "ABRAHAM! ABRAHAM!" "HERE I AM", HE REPLIED. "Do not lay a hand on the boy," he said. "Do not do anything to him. Now I know that you fear God, because you have not withheld from me your son, your only son." Genesis 22: 9-12*

The doctor continues. "I believe the best medical course of action is to schedule a therapeutic abortion while it is still early, Sir. It is a relatively uncomplicated procedure, and she could be home in a few days. If you sign this consent, I can get the procedure ordered for next week." I swallow hard and sign the paper. I hope God forgives me. I cannot risk losing Beth and letting these little girls grow up without a mother.

Lee Beth is scheduled to come in and see her doctor. I am at work, so she is coming alone thinking it is a check-up. When she steps into the examination room, I am waiting along with her doctor, to deliver the news. "Mrs. Lowe, as you know, I have completed a comprehensive review of all of your medical history, your labs, stats and infant birth and mortality records. We previously discussed the severe risk that you would be placing yourself, and your unborn child in if you carry another pregnancy. We know we have a positive pregnancy result. You are approximately seven-weeks pregnant." I know my wife very well. She is sure clever enough to see what is coming next. "Is this where you tell me congratulations, gentlemen?" The doctor matter-of-factly replies, "I think you know why we are all here. You are at too high of a risk for another pregnancy. Your husband and I have discussed this. The only viable course of action for you is a therapeutic abortion. We need to get you scheduled right away, while it is early. We have signed the consent form. It is in your best interest to sign it too. We are trying to save your life here, Mrs. Lowe." I stood there looking at her, knowing her response was going to blister the mint green paint right off the walls! She stands up, pushes her chair back under the steel grey desk, and takes her position. "I really do appreciate the concern you two have for me and all, so let me just tell you this once. Neither one of you two bastards are carrying this baby, my baby. When the day comes that either of you can carry and give birth to a baby, then, and only then, can you advise me on what I can do with mine!" She threw the papers back at the doctor and walked out, slamming the door behind her.

Tina Leslie – 'Squall Bag….Buger'

Tina Leslie was born by natural childbirth in the same Quonset Hut as Terri Lyn, on Lackland Air Force Base, August 15, 1955. Defying everything the doctors warned us about, she was a healthy, seven pounds, three ounces, and beautiful. They had no medical explanation for how this could be possible. Based upon the Rh incompatibility factor and the incredible complications with her previous pregnancies, they predicted either an extremely prema-ture birth, (less than six months gestation), birth defects, or another stillbirth. They gave no hope to us we would have a live birth, or a 'normal' child if the baby survived. They had prepared her an incubator in the specialized area for underweight and sickly babies. . The delivery room staff were prepared to give life-saving mea-sures as soon as she was born. Tina Leslie came squalling into this world! She was a beautiful baby, with huge blue eyes and chubby little cheeks. She had a pouty little mouth that always looked like she was about to cry! She was born without a single complication. She did not require a blood transfusion (they are still scratching their heads over that!). Her vitals were perfectly normal, she had a good birth weight, and she was breathing completely on her own. She was healthy, happy, and hungry! They were testing out a new infant scoring system, called the 'Apgar' (Activity, Pulse, Grimace, Appearance, and Respiration), score. A ten was the highest rating a newborn could receive. Tina received a nine. The doctors had no words. If Lee Beth was not so tired from childbirth, I am certain she would have a few things to say to the doctor that asked her to abort this baby. Tina Leslie was moved to the regular nursery where she began with, what became her signature move, the squall! That tiny thing could squall so loud, she kept all the other babies and their mamas up and crying! Everyone on the floor was carrying her around. I am sure we got to take her home a day or so early, so the staff and the new mamas could get some rest!

Houston E. Lowe and Lee Beth Peterson Lowe, First Wedding Anniversary, February 24, 1947, Courtesy Houston E. Lowe, personal collection

Houston E. Lowe – Ice Cap, Thule, Greenland, Courtesy Houston E. Lowe, personal collection

Houston E. Lowe – On Phone in Thule,
Courtesy Houston E. Lowe, personal collection

Houston E. Lowe, Lee Beth Lowe, Toni Lowe, Circa 1953,
Courtesy Houston E. Lowe, personal collection

Toni Lee and Houston E. Lowe on Porch

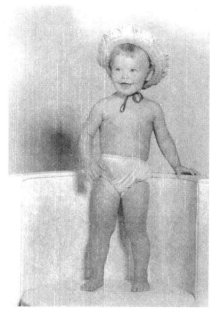

Toni Lee – Yap Yap, Courtesy Houston E. Lowe, personal collection

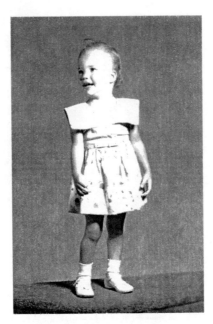

Terri Lyn - My Little Skinned Rabbit at two years,
Courtesy Houston E. Lowe, personal collection

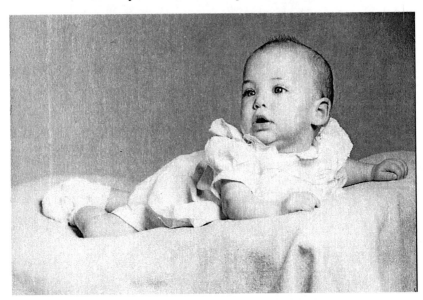

The Recanalization Failure – My Buger at 6 months,
Courtesy Houston E. Lowe, personal collection

Family Portrait, Circa 1959, Courtesy Houston E. Lowe, personal collection

Chapter Thirteen

Miss Carvet's Hula Girl

Paradise: HAWAII

In October of 1959, I receive my orders for a general tour of duty in the newly named 50th state, Hawaii. I was to report to Hickam Air Force Base, Honolulu, in January of 1960. I would be serving a total of four years there, one year, without my family. Even though I was finally gonna see the hula girl Miss Carvet told me about, I was torn up about being away from my family. I knew it was gonna be hard on Lee Beth. The hardest thing I ever did was leave those girls all alone. I packed up my duffle bags and kissed all my girls goodbye. Tina Leslie was squalling away holding on to her Mama's skirt, and Terri Lyn was holding her hand. We all hugged for the longest time until I had to break loose. "I will write you every week, Honey." "I will too, I love you." "You girls, take care of your Mama, you hear me? You better mind her too!" "Yes Daddy," they all replied in unison. "Toni Lee, you help your Mama with the girls." "I will Daddy." Lee Beth stood on that tarmac holding on to those girls, hugging them tightly, as I boarded the Boeing 707, to cross the Pacific Ocean. They watched until it taxied around, quickly disappearing into the clouds after takeoff. I am in the air staring out of the circle windows, not knowing what this next chapter is going to bring for all of us. I fall asleep with a picture of my girls in my hand.

Life and Work in Hawaii

During my year here on the island, I kept mostly to myself, worked in the mess hall and held a part-time job as a grill cook at Ft. DeRussy. I met a local Hawaiian native who became a life-long friend, Tommy Simons. Tommy was assigned to the mess hall and worked for me. We got along just fine because he was a hard-working family man. Sometimes he would come over to Ft. DeRussy and let me fix him a juicy burger after his part-time shift as a barber in the NCO Club. He was a damn good mess hall staffer and was the best barber on the island. He introduced me to his mother Auntie, and his daughter Laura. They took me under their wing and showed me the 'real' Hawaii. The natives pronounce "Huh-vi-eye-ee". On my days off, we had Hawaiian barbeques in his backyard where the whole family would come. We played horseshoes, and he tried to teach me to surf! The native foods here are delicious, and I tried them all. Auntie was an incredible cook and prepared the ancient traditional recipes of the Polynesian people. Dishes like kalua pig, lau lau, lomi lomi salmon, poi, and chicken long rice, were always on the table. Tommy and his family helped ease my loneliness. I could not wait for all of them to meet my family. The end of this year could not get here soon enough.

Miracle Twenty-Three–The Desert Delivery

Lee Beth was poised to join me in Hawaii in 1961. I missed my family so much it hurt. I could not wait to share the majesty of this beautiful place with them. Beth had to travel by car with the three girls, from San Antonio to San Francisco – a total of 1740 miles! I always knew how strong she was. I was about to see how fearless she was as well. She traveled by day, with no air conditioning, stopping in the evenings at small motels along the way. She had to keep a six-year-old, a seven-year-old, and a teenager occupied while she drove the entire way on her own. We had no other options; we needed our car there. She stood tall for the order, and took off across Texas, headed to Arizona. On her first day, she stopped in Dallas and stayed with her brother, Ferol Curtis, and his beautiful wife, Inez. They had a beautiful home in Dallas. Ferol, or 'Brother', as we always called him, was in the Navy during the war. He was stationed at Pearl Harbor, where he and his crew repaired and restored ships, damaged in combat. He was an incredible man, smart as a whip, and had a razor-sharp wit. He was a master electrician by trade and a true authority on American railroading. His hobby in building and collecting miniature railroads was his greatest passion. He had two red-headed teenagers, our niece and nephew, Ginger, and James Steven. The kids were real glad to have some cousin time together. Ginger and Toni loved to talk, and play records. Ginger always called me 'Unc' or 'Unca Hoostun'. Funny how some kids just take a likin to you, and I sure did to her. She has a special, tender heart. I know someday she is going to help a lot of people.

The next day, leaving at four a.m., Beth began the journey across this big state. If you haven't lived in Texas, you have no idea how big it is until you try to drive across it! We had mapped out ten-hour days on a map, with stops in major towns, all the way to San Francisco. As she headed west across the country, she had to make the typical stops, many of which occurred along the roadside; as the girls learned the ways of the outdoors! On day three of her drive, while in the Sonoran Desert, just outside of Phoenix; she encounters a desperate situation. She had let the girls sleep in that morning, knowing the miserable conditions in the desert during the day. It is early evening, and the sun is setting over the mountains. She drives for a couple of hours in that lonely, desolate place. Surrounded by the sounds of the coyotes, with desert tarantulas covering the road, suddenly, the passenger side back tire blows. The car is violently swerving. The entire car is rattling and shaking. She tightly grips the steering wheel, aggressively pulling it to adjust, trying to avoid plowing into rocks and soft sand, along the roadside. The car is careening and fish-tailing, spraying hot sand inside the car. She is fighting it to stay on the road. The girls are tossed and thrown about in the back seat like rag dolls, as the car slams into the soft sands on the shoulder. "Dear God!" Her heart is racing as she braced for impact. The car came to an abrupt stop at a severe angle, with two wheels entrenched in the soft sand.

The other two wheels are balanced on the asphalt highway. The passenger wheels are hopelessly trenched into the deep sand. Lee Beth feels the need to cry but knows she cannot scare the girls. "Girls move to the other side of the car." She is frightened. The car is delicately balanced, teetering on the highway. Nighttime in the desert is lonely and terrifying. It is pitch black, and all of the local inhabitants come out for the cooler temperatures. Scorpions, Gila monsters, and little kangaroo rats are scurrying everywhere. The roadways are covered with scorpions. It is not safe to get out of the car. Coyote are roaming about looking for rabbits and other prey. She is in the middle of literally nowhere with her three girls. There is no phone, and no way to get to help. Bob Jones, Beth's brother in law, had given her a red flare stick to place in the car, 'just in case'. She calmly tells the girls, "everything is going to be alright." "We will just take a break here for a bit." She lights up a cigarette and begins to ponder what to do. They cannot walk in the desert, and the map showed she was at least forty miles from the next town. She knows the tire is blown. The rim along with the other two tires are dug deeply into the sand. It would be impossible for her to change the tire alone. Her best chance is to stay put until daylight. Hopefully, the traffic will pick up, and she will be seen. Relying on a complete stranger to get this family back on the road to California, is her only option. She lights the flare and tosses it out the window on the highway. It was now after eleven p.m., and I had not heard from her. I begin to panic. My wife and my three girls are somewhere in a desert, and I have no way of knowing where. You may not be a praying person, but when you know your entire family is nowhere to be found in the middle of the night, you will find a way. I did pray that night. "Dear God, keep my family safe. Get them to a safe place, and let me hear her voice. Can you make it soon?!" It is balmy. The night winds are blowing hot sand into the car. The coyote calls are getting nearer, and the girls are beginning to cry. Toni is trying to comfort them, as Lee Beth begins to sing quietly, her favorite Patsy Cline song. " I go out walkin› after midnight, out in the moonlight, just like we used to do, I'm always walkin' After midnight, searchin' for yooooooou." "Looky here girls, we are out, after midnight." She opens the little aluminum cooler. She gets Cokes in longneck, green bottles for everyone. It is not a normal practice to let the girls have soda water at this time of night, but Beth was gonna do her best to keep them distracted. "Let's celebrate!" She clinks her bottleneck to Toni's, and together, they all take a swig. Tina Leslie was a known 'Cokaholic', so that worked out real fine for her! "Mama, what are we going to do if we have to go to the bathroom?" "Well, honey, we are going to stick our big ole desert moons out the window, and let it rain!" They all giggle together. The girls curled up together and were resting, as Beth chain-smoked her fears away. In the far distance, through the rear view window, she sees headlights. It is one a.m. A fear comes over her. How can she trust a complete stranger with the lives of her three children? The rumbling of a large truck is coming in, as the squeal of air brakes fills the silent desert canyon. An eighteen-wheeler pulls in behind her, lighting up the entire car and highway in front of her. She is relieved. Truckers are known for their roadside manner, and they come fully prepared to assist in an emergency. He is coming up alongside the car. "Ma'am, what are you doing out in this desert at this time of night?" She is so relieved to see him. "My tire, my tire...I blew a tire out here. My girls are in back, and they are very afraid." He lights up the car with his aluminum flashlight. "You are alone!?" "Let me take a look back there." He surveys the damage to the back tire. He has a hydraulic jack that lifts the butt end of that Chevy like it was a Sunday newspaper. He changes the tire, and shows her how incredibly shredded the tire was. It fell apart in pieces. "You are sure lucky lady. You could have easily rolled this car trying to adjust to the blowout." After he repairs the car, he hooks a chain to the front, and pulls her out of the sandy bog. By now it is three o'clock in the morning. "I am so grateful you came along, thank you so much." "Where are you headed to, ma'am?" "I am going to San Francisco to fly out to Hawaii with my girls. My husband is stationed at Hickam Air Force Base." He clears his throat. "Hickam AFB, you say'?" "Yes." "What is your husband's name?" "Master Sergeant Houston, Lowe, why?" "Ma'am, you are not going to believe this, but I have the entire contents of your household in my trailer!" He radioed one of his buddies up ahead. When he reached a pay phone, he called and gave me the news. That blessed soul followed her all the way to San Francisco! Maybe that is some coincidence in your book, it is divine intervention in mine!

> *"But if I were you, I would appeal to God; I would lay my cause before him. He performs wonders that cannot be fathomed, miracles that cannot be counted." Job 5: 8-9*

ALOHA

I am pacing the International Airport of Honolulu. The greeters, native Hawaiians, are beautifully dressed in colorful floral muu-muus. Their arms are draped in fragrant, plumeria leis. The most beautiful sight I have ever seen in my life, my four girls, walk off that plane dressed in their Sunday best, little white gloves and all. They have all grown so much, especially Toni. She no longer looks like a lanky teenager. She is quickly growing into a beautiful woman like her mother. As they step on the tarmac, they are greeted with 'Aloha', and have leis placed around their necks. By the time they reach me, they are covered to their chins! I grab and embrace Lee Beth. I was so proud of her. She had to endure a lot all alone because of my career. "You all look so beautiful!" Tina Leslie is crying; she is so happy to see me. "Awwww, my little Squall Bag." I pick her up and put her on my hip. We are all so happy to see each other. I take everyone to the little yellow cinderblock building where our military quarters were. We had a little two-story place with three bedrooms upstairs. In September, the girls are enrolled in their new schools. Terri and Tina went to Hickam Air Force Base, Elementary School, while Toni attended Aliamanu Intermediate and then Radford High School. Every summer, one of Beth's sisters or brothers would let one of their kids come over and live with us. Toni was able to have a great three months with her teenage cousins, Phyllis and Fred.

Beaches, Hula Girls, Sacred Waterfalls, and Magical Sunsets

Over the three years they were with me on this beautiful island, we had many wonderful family times together. They climbed and picked fresh mangos from the trees, learned how to crack a coconut open, and how to clean fish. They played in the ocean at Waikiki, and Sunset beaches. We went on hikes up to the beautiful waterfalls and swimming pools of fresh water. Tommy showed us the sacred places like Kukaniloko Birthing Stones, the place where kings were born, and Sacred Falls. He taught us to leave a little offering like fruit, a plant, or a lei, to honor the forefathers. The natives call this a *ho'okupu*. I loved the native Hawaiian ways. They were simple people who lived off the land and oceans, respected their elders, and held tight to their traditions. Sometimes we went to Waimea Bay, to see the beautiful local fish and sea urchins in the tide pools. We camped right on the beach, and the girls learned about sea turtles, sand crabs, hermit crabs, and mongoose. They discovered the beautiful flowers and ate fresh pineapple right out of the fields. We took Toni to see the surfers at North Shore, as we all watched them hand wax their boards before going in. We went to a few luaus and shared in the traditions of their feasts and dances.

My nightmares had subsided a little. Hawaii was such a peaceful place; it may have helped me. However, one night in bed, within a deep sleep, I had a vivid nightmare about my capture. I had a man in my face trying to slit my throat. I reached for my weapon, grabbing the headboard violently shaking it. Lee Beth tried gently to calm me, being careful not to awaken me. She also did not want me to scare the girls. I was having a flashback and only saw an enemy in my face. I grabbed her by the throat, and with my closed fist, I hit her in the jaw and face. Thinking I had disarmed my enemy, I was back in twilight sleep leaving my wife with a bloodied face, broken nose and cracked jaw. She was told by my doctors never to wake me after an intense episode. That steel-framed woman slunk out of bed, wrapped her face in a bath towel, and drove herself to the emergency room. She got home just before breakfast the next morning. You will never understand the depths of your sorrow until you have harmed someone you love. I could barely look at her swollen and bruised face. If my military records were not as thorough as they were in documenting my captivity and reoccurring nightmares, I could have ended up in jail.

After Lee Beth recovered, we continued to explore our beautiful island. Tommy always knew what was happening. We enjoyed many sights and had the opportunity to see so much. We stood behind the tape lines of the filming of *Blue Hawaii*, starring Elvis Presley, and *Ride the Wild Surf*, starring Tab Hunter. Hawaii is a magical place with perfect sunny weather and cool ocean breezes. You could not find a better playground to raise your kids. The atmosphere is kind, and the people are loving. The family is king, as generations of families live together passing on the traditions of their forefathers.

Front Seat Girls

Toni Lee has grown into a beautiful young lady like her Mama. She has Beth's perfect figure and legs. Sometimes, when she would be in the side yard sunbathing, she would about cause a wreck on the street outside! I can quickly see that the boys at the beach are interested in more than the coconut drinks in the stands beside us. I have been around enough knucklehead menfolk to know to be worried about her, and I was fiercely protective of all of them. Her Mama is raising all of these girls to be strong, independent, respectable woman. I figure it will do her just fine to have a man's perspective on these matters. I take her outside on the back patio with a glass of cold pineapple juice. "Toni Lee, I spect' by now you are old enough to understand what I am about to tell you. Now that you have a boyfriend and all, I am just gonna put it to you straight from a man's thinking. There are only two types of girls in this world – front seat girls, and back seat girls." She looks at me like I just came out of a spaceship. "Front seat girls, stay in the front seat. Their suitors open the car doors for them and walk them to the front door. They respect those girls, are willing to wait for marriage for the opening of 'the gift'. These girls meet boy's Mamas and are taken to the movies. They get phone calls, letters, flowers, and marriage proposals. Your Mama was a front seat girl. Then, you have your back seat girls. Boys don't take them anywhere but the back seat! They shore ain't gonna take them to their Mama! They don't want nothing from them but what can be found in the back seat, and they will tell you anything you wanna hear to get you back there! There ain't nothing going on in the back seat any girl of mine needs to be a part of! You copy that!?" Her face was red as a beet, but it was clear we had an understanding between us. And with that, a strong five-minute lesson from a country boy brought a lifetime of training in walking the straight and narrow path. She turned around and passed this knowledge to her sisters too.

> *"Who can find a virtuous woman? for her price is far above rubies." Proverbs 31:10*

Kennedy in a Lincoln

In the summer of 1963, the island was all abuzz with the news that the current president of the United States, John Fitzgerald Kennedy, was coming to visit Oahu. This included an all-scale alert to the military bases, that would be supporting his travel and safe arrival here. On June 8, 1963, he landed at Honolulu International Airport. He had come to pay his respects to the many fallen at the U.S.S. Arizona Memorial, on the following day. It meant a lot to us soldiers who had served in WWII, to have this brilliant man come and honor the sacrifices. Everything on base was in tip-top shape. American flags were waving on every block for miles. During his short time here, he was meeting with mayors from across the United States, advocating for human rights, and the equal rights for black Americans. About one-hundred-thousand people lined the streets trying to get a glimpse of our beloved president. His motorcade slowly drove through downtown Honolulu, as he waved at the crowds. He is covered to his neck in colorful leis. In the front of the motorcade, he rode waving to the crowds. He was riding in that fateful Lincoln convertible that just a few months later he would be shot to death in. He was such a good man. I can't imagine what great things he would have done for our country.

A New Age is Ushered In

The girls all did a good job in school; Lee Beth made sure of that. They all loved their teachers, and they always did their homework. The 60's brought in a new age of understanding for all of us. Lee Beth and I saw the impact right away for the girls. Times were beginning to change. Women were becoming more independent and worked outside of the home. Lee Beth has always been a strong, independent woman. Her job as a telephone operator developed her sense of empowering women to be what they wanted to be. She is a great mother, but she would have been just as great in a boardroom. She is a no-nonsense, no-whining, no-excuses, kinda gal. As a strict disciplinarian, she taught these girls to be respectful. On the newscasts, we would see female lawyers and business owners. One thing I knew we would not negotiate was getting an education. When I was growing up, you could get by without one. There was plenty of hard work available for a strong back. There was a world of opportunity out there for them, but it began with an education. We never wanted them to depend on a man, or to be trapped by one because they had no other options to survive.

They all adapted well to the changes in their lives and school. After our three years on this beautiful island, it was time to pack up and head back to San Antonio, where I would pick up in the mess hall there, and finish out my military career. Hawaii left an indelible mark on all of us. We love the islands and the life we had here. It was hard to leave Tommy and our friends behind, but our time here was over. We moved back home and started all over again.

The Wreck

We return home to find our beautiful little home in shambles. The people who rented it for the three years we were in Hawaii, ran it to the ground. Beth and I walked inside to find open food containers, dog feces, spray paint on the walls, burn marks on the golden oak flooring, holes in the sheetrock, and broken blinds and windows. The front yard was burnt-up grass and littered patches of bare dirt. The backyard was a grown over junkyard. Grass and weeds were standing four to five feet tall. Tires, old paint cans, car parts, and trash are littered from fence line to fence line. Beth immediately broke down in tears. "It is ok honey. It is gonna be ok." I could not believe someone could do this. I grew up with nothing. Having my own home was something I would take care of the rest of my life. I really had no idea how we could recover from this. It was in shambles and totally unlivable. I could not move my little family back in this squalor. We had no other options; we were flat broke. With the cost of living in Hawaii, it took every bit of money we had to live, even with me working an additional part-time job. As good as Beth was with taking care of our finances, at the end of each month, there was not a thin dime to spare. We couldn't afford to put us all up anywhere, and the girls needed to be taken care of. Toni went and stayed with one of her good family friends for a month. Beth asked her brother David, and his wife Mary, if Terri Lyn and Tina could live with them until we could get back on our feet. I am forever grateful for their help. It was two mouths I did not have to feed them. I knew they would be well cared for. Mary was a wonderful mother and cook, and baked the best oatmeal cookies on earth! David made the girls laugh every day.

Lee Beth and I slept on the floors on mats. Our household goods were stored in a small storage house out back that I had built before we left. While I would go to work at the base, and to my part-time job at a local bowling alley, Lee Beth would scrape the thick hardened food and filth off the floors and walls. I hand sanded the floors at night when I was off. A good coat of varnish did the rest. Sometimes we would have a bologna sandwich sitting cross-legged on the floors at night. We laughed about how small and crowded we thought our military quarters in Hawaii were! Over the next couple of months, we slowly got that little house back in shape. A friend of mine did some sheetrock work. I traded him a couple of fishing trips with cold beer to repair and replace our damaged walls. Long-time neighbors and family members brought cleaning supplies, mowers, and helped me throw out over five-hundred pounds of garbage and debris from the backyard. They cut sod squares of Bermuda grass from their yards and helped me rebuild mine. Plants were started from family plants, and roses were taking root in pots on the patio. We had backyard pot-luck dinners where family and friends nourished and restored us. I could bring my girls home now, and my little family would be complete again. I do not know what we would have done without their help.

> *"You shall not see the donkey of your neighbor* or his
> ox fallen on the road and you ignore them; certainly
> you must *help* them *up with him." Deuteronomy 22:4*

Thomas Jefferson

All three girls attended Thomas Jefferson High School. It is a beautiful school with a history dating back to 1932. The entire campus of the school is spectacular, like a Spanish palace. The acreage where it sits is near the original location of the Old Spanish Trail that dissected San Antonio. The architects wanted it stately and in the Spanish Moorish style. It has beautiful, ornate, columns built around two patios with Spanish fountains. Hand-painted tiles cover the hallways, and carved arches crown the doorways. It has a long history of excellence. The girls loved their high school, and we spent many nights at football and basketball games. It is as beautiful today as it was when it was built.

Houston E. Lowe and Lee Beth Lowe, Honolulu Airport, Circa 1962,
Courtesy Houston E. Lowe, personal collection

Girls at Wakiki Circa 1962, Courtesy Houston E. Lowe, personal collection

Houston E. Lowe, Hawaii on Base in Uniform,
Courtesy personal collection, Houston E. Lowe

Kennedy in a Lincoln, Presidential Motorcade, Honolulu, Hawaii, June 8,
1963, Photograph taken by unknown staffer, Hickam Air Force Base, and
given to Houston E. Lowe, Courtesy personal collection, Houston E. Lowe

Chapter Fourteen

The "C" Word

Miracle Twenty-Four–My Cancer and Surgery Survivals

Beginning with my first symptoms around 1965, I began to experience a lot of pain in my lower abdomen, back, and groin. I mostly ignored them and pressed on. I was pretty insensitive to pain. Around 1970, intercourse became very painful, and I had a continual burning during urination. My urine became tinted with blood. For several years, the doctors ran tests, but they were inconclusive. Then a scope was invented allowing a complete examination of the bladder. After a long series of tests and pathology work, my diagnosis came like a bull through a wooden gate – cancer. It was cancer, the kind that can kill you. They predicted I had probably had it for years. I swallowed hard, as the test results were read to me like a grocery list right before Easter. I had Squamous cell carcinoma of the bladder, and possibly the prostate gland. The doctors were not too optimistic about my prognosis. They were extremely concerned that my bladder cancer had already metastasized to other areas. The recommended medical treatment – full radical cystectomy (removal of the urinary bladder), and preventative removal of anything else in my abdomen that I did not need to live. I was not given the option of chemotherapy or radiation therapy. The doctors felt this drastic, forever life-altering surgery, would save my life and that other lesser options might not. Dear Lord, I am only fifty-three! I was given a choice at that time to opt for an external urine drainage bag or to 'hook up my plumbing pipes internally'. I opted for the second choice, for obvious reasons.

My surgery was called a 'pan resection'. The doctors 'cleaned house with my innards'! The surgery took nine hours, where they removed my bladder, appendix, prostate gland, gall bladder, seminal vessels, part of my urethra, the vas deferens, and every lymph node they could find. Yes, the trusty vas deferens, that thankfully, but 'accidentally', allowed my baby girl, Buger, to be born! My doctor did a resection of the ureters and sewed them into a piece of my colon, allowing the kidneys to dump directly into my intestinal tract. I was pieced together like a patchwork quilt! I was going to be peeing through my anus, hopefully for the rest of my long life. I was knocked back pretty good on that one. This surgery would keep me from having an exterior bladder bag hooked to my belly, and I was all for it.

As the doctor was going over causes, trying to answer my questions, it became apparent my past life as a POW had a profound effect on me. Bladder cancer has many causes, but if a human being was going to be at-risk for obtaining this stuff, it was shore gonna be me! Low arsenic content in poor drinking water, not enough drinking water, smoking, workplace exposure to chemicals, fumes, poor oxygen, being a machinist, and just being a male, put me in the bull's eye of the dreaded, deadly target. The sediment in the poor drinking water, and not having enough drinking water to flush the bladder, took a huge toll on my system. The beatings to my gut and lower back didn't help my odds either. The proximity of the bladder to the prostate gave a gateway for the disease to spread. In all of the testing, the docs discovered that one of my kidneys was very 'stunted' in size; about one-third the size of a normal kidney. They think it was injured during my beatings in captivity. My extreme sun exposure while laboring on Japanese tarmacs in the Philippines, and my closeness to the Hiroshima bomb, are responsible for my skin cancers.

'Tough Guts'

My surgery was scheduled right away. I had a full incision from my lower chest to my groin. They cracked me open like a yard egg! As the doctors began the surgery, it became evident that scar tissue had formed a massive web covering my entire abdominal cavity.

They spent the first five hours of the surgery, just cutting through the webs of leathery flesh, encasing the area. The doctors said I had some 'tough guts' to get through and around. All of my pathology reports after this surgery were negative for cancer, except for my bladder. The doctors were enthusiastic about my outcome and felt that they were able to remove all of the cancer.

Recovery was long and hard, and I am sure I was no picnic to be around or take care of. Adjusting to my new life as a male was not easy. Lee Beth was by my side every step of the way as we traveled through unchartered territory together. This was the first time I can remember being angry, really angry, about the effects of my captivity. I would explode in anger sometimes, saying some very cruel things to Beth. I easily lost my patience with the girls. I always felt regret after I did. I took to my room for a while and was a bit depressed at times. For the first and only time in my life, I felt sorry for myself. It is a wonder Lee Beth didn't kill me in my sleep! You really can only say you're sorry so many times before it falls on deaf ears. But, asking for forgiveness is a critical part of any emotional healing. Do not ever go a day without saying you are sorry for something you did to hurt someone.

> "For Your name's sake, O LORD, Pardon my iniquity, for it is great." Psalms 25:11

It's a Boy!–The Birth of a Bladder

Six months later I had a follow-up surgery to completely redirect my entire urinary tract. The first surgery, a trial, was not successful and the complications were too great. My body had begun absorbing the waste products of urine into my bloodstream. I had become uremic, something else that could have killed me. Back on the steel table again, I was reopened along the same scar. This time a piece of my colon would be used to make a 'stoma', a pinkish tube opening just below my rib cage. I would be peeing into a plastic bag attached to my body, for the rest of my life. After cutting through the new scar tissue, changing the resection to my colon, creating the stoma, about eight hours later; the surgeons closed me up. That is when I began my life with my bag, my pet, 'Charlie'. I struggled greatly with the impact. I felt like a waste. I didn't feel like a man anymore. For the sake of my family, I knew it would be something I had to learn to cope with.

Medical Retirement

I retired in July of 1972 after my second surgery, with a full medical discharge. I am 100% disabled, and I began my new life with 'Charlie'. After thirty-one years, five months, and seventeen days, the military career that I was so proud to serve in, came to a close. With full military honors, we all stand together, as Uncle Sam gives me my certificate. My heart is not ready to stop serving my country, but my body cannot take the daily grind any longer.

Unmeasurable Joy – Unmeasurable Pain

Life as it often does goes by in the blink of an eye. If we are not careful, we miss life making a living. I tried to cherish the picnics, birthdays, graduations, weddings, and family gatherings; as I watched my girls grow into beautiful women. Toni Lee met and married her true love, Lt. Roy Lane Nelson. He was a good man with a kind heart. Lee Beth could not wait to have grandchildren. After being stationed in Georgia for a short period, we got the news we were going to be grandparents! Our first grandchild, Shannon Lee Nelson was born! She was adorable! I cannot begin to describe the joy of being a grandparent! We were elated. The year 1971, was a stormy time for our country. The Vietnam war was breaking wide open, and soon we got the call that Roy would be shipped out.

Toni Lee suffered the unthinkable when two men in Army dress uniforms came to her apartment door in April of 1971, to tell her that her husband of only twenty short months, 1LT Roy L. Nelson; was killed in action in Vietnam. It was the darkest time in our family. She was twenty-three years old, with a three-month-old baby girl, Shannon Lee. The guttural, desperate, scream that came from her over the phone dropped me to my knees. It is a sound I will never forget, and one that I hope no parent ever has to hear. We were all devastated. For the first time in my life as a father, I could not take the pain away from one of my girls. There was nothing I could do. Daddy could not 'kiss it and make it all better this time'. When I came to Toni's apartment, after holding her tightly, I told her two things... that I had tried to get orders to go to Vietnam in his place, and if I could have laid down my life to spare Roy's, I would have. She knew that I meant every word. Toni asked me to carry the news of the mantle of honorable death to Roy's parents, along with the two soldiers that had come to her door. It took all of my strength to face them.

When his body was flown in, I went to identify him along with his father. We could not bear to let her or his mother see him. Toni's Uncle David, a decorated WWII hero himself, inspected the body for her. War is ugly, and the invisible and innocent casualties line the streets all across America. My oldest daughter and my first grandchild were now in that line. I was not in a good enough physical or emotional state to help her as much as I wish I could have. I think in many ways, as she navigated through my appointments and procedures, it helped her to heal. In a year or so, she reunited with her former seventh-grade boyfriend, Fred L. Serene Jr., and they married a year later, in April of 1973. I have another military son-in-law, a lieutenant in the Army. This places me on high alert every day knowing, I could get the phone call again.

Miracle Twenty-Five–Death on a Steel Table

As I begin my new life in retirement, it was the first time in my life I was at a loss for what to do. I went back to my childhood love of fishing. Staying out on the Medina River gave me peace. We camped there in the little cabins where I could be out in nature again. I thought of my father and how much he would have enjoyed the beauty here. I still missed him after all these years. Lee Beth and I had some time on our hands, and a little change in our pockets, so we would drive out to New Braunfels or Castroville for the day. I have always loved seeing the beautiful green crops in the fields. I would pull off on the side of the road and lean over the barbed wire fence line, just to get close to the rows and rows of freshly turned dirt, dotted with cabbages and turnip greens. I worked in the yard and planted some more vegetables in the garden out back. I would pick pecans from the tree outside, feeding a couple of squirrels right out of my hand. Sometimes I would just sit and listen to the birds sing. It was peaceful, and I needed the rest to recover fully from my two surgeries. And then, it all changed in a wink. I am out in the backyard clipping the hedges when my guts feel like they are wringing inside out. I fall to my knees at the fence line. Gripping my hand through the chain link fence, I doubled over in excruciating pain. My guts were twisting up, and my head was pouring out sweat. I knew I was in trouble. I stumble inside the house with a ghost-white face. Lee Beth dropped the pen she was finishing up a crossword puzzle with. "Houston, what on earth!?" I went to the bathroom. My urine had turned to the color of black coffee. I grabbed my gut, trying to get a hold of the stabbing pain. Lee Beth rushed me to the emergency room, where the doctors ordered scans and tests. I had a full colon blockage. The doctors could not initially tell what the blockage was, but they knew I was in serious trouble. It could have been scar tissue, but their prediction was it was cancer, that had metastasized from the bladder.

I am so sick, and in so much pain, I would have let them cut me right there. "Sergeant Lowe, if this is cancer, as I predict it will be, our only course of action is to do a full colostomy." "What the hell is that?" "Sir, it is another external bag, it will divert the waste from your colon to a bag on the outside of your body. It will be complicated surgery due to the previous surgeries you have had. There are no guarantees. I know this is very difficult news, sir, but we will have no other choice to save your life." "Dear God, no, man!" I was in shock. I lay there on that table feeling like I just can't go on. How could I take care of two bags? I could not even think about the care and cleaning of a bag filled with shit too!" My head went back to the filthy latrines, and the God-awful stench of the Benjo on the Noto Maru. All the putrid smells suffocated me, causing my stomach to go sour. My mouth filled with warm acid water, as I puked all over the floor below. Sweating profusely, pale as a ghost, and writhing in pain; I gave the doctor the go ahead. Beth signed the Medical Power of Attorney, allowing her to make my decisions

281

for me if necessary. I am immediately rushed into emergency surgery. I didn't know how I would come out on the other side, but I am too sick to worry about that now. It was an extremely long and complicated surgery. Doctors worked to remove the questionable tissue that was causing the stool blockage, while delicately avoiding my bladder pouch and stoma. Contamination of the area causing a septic condition from the colon could have killed me. During the surgery, they literally took the entire contents of my abdomen, all my remaining guts, and laid them on top of me. They gently inspected every inch, looking for the blockage in my colon and any signs of cancer. All of this was incredibly delicate work because they could not damage any of my other surgical work. They found the blockage in my colon and determined it was not cancer. It was a rotting mess of scarred and webbed tissue, right above my pelvic bone. This was the very place I received most of my beatings in camp. Necrosis was quickly setting in as the entire area was beginning to die. After they removed the scarred section of the colon, they performed an 'anastomosis'. They stitched the two ends of my bowel back together, like fixing a flat on a rubber tire!

During the sixth hour of surgery, right before they were to close me up; I went into a full cardiac arrest. My heart stopped, and I completely flat-lined while on the surgical table. Cardiac arrest under general anesthesia is very rare, and my pre-operative tests showed no signs of heart disease. I was laying there in a deep sleep, while my heart was beginning the first stages of death. My brain was only receiving oxygen from the work of the respirator. I was cut wide-open, gutted out like a feral hog; when my heart stopped. Doctors immediately had to move to life-saving measures in and around the open, delicate surgery site. Trying to save my life, with heart compressions and defibrillation, the doctors cracked open my rib cage; desperately trying to massage my heart back into any rhythm. After eleven or so minutes in a death-like state, with a team of medical doctors working, my heart began a weak, subnormal rhythm (arrhythmia). For a few suspended minutes clicking away on a respirator, I am a dead man! I was alive, only at the mercy of machines, and the good Lord above. I was in an extremely critical condition. The doctors relayed the information to Lee Beth, that it was touch and go, and could be for a while. She and my girls were in the waiting room and heard the terrible news.

> *"Have I not commanded you? Be strong and courageous. Do not be frightened, and do not be dismayed, for the* LORD *your God is with you wherever you go."* Joshua 1:9

The heart monitor showed an irregularity known as atrial fibrillation (AFib). My heart was quivering uncontrollably and not beating efficiently enough to move blood around my body. Knowing this could lead to blood clots, stroke, or complete heart failure, my doctors took immediate action to control my irregular heart and put it back in rhythm. All of this is complicated by the extensive and sensitive surgery they just completed in my gut. The doctors eventually put everything back into my bruised and battered abdominal cavity. I am certain they must be scratching their heads over me! They were sorely afraid that due to my very weakened and frail skin, that any traditional sutures would not stay closed. This would cause a major post-surgical complication, an opening of the abdomen; which could also be deadly for me. I was sent to the recovery room with my entire torso split from the chest to my pelvis. The sutures had large orange tubing, holding the wires that were keeping the entire abdominal cavity together. Going into surgery, I feared a colostomy. During the surgery, they were just trying to save my life. My heart rhythm was still off, and they were unable to stabilize me. They knew I was in a precarious spot. At the doctor's request, Toni came into the ICU where I was under continual monitoring. She is a registered nurse, and he knew I might recognize her voice. She spoke directly into my ear. "Daddy, you do not have cancer, no colostomy bag. Daddy, no colostomy bag. It was just scar tissue; you are ok. Can you hear me?" In my deep twilight sleep, I heard her. My heart settled down a bit. It was still a very abnormal beat, but it got strong enough to pump my blood around my body, allowing for me to begin to heal.

I have had an abnormal heartbeat since that day, but; by the grace of God, I lived through the tunnel of death one more time.

> *"But when Jesus heard it he said, "This illness does not lead to death. It is for the glory of God, so that the Son of God may be glorified through it." John 11:4*

I had tubes coming out my nose, mouth, arms, and legs, with IV drips of morphine to manage my pain. At any time I could go into cardiac arrest again. My breathing was very shallow. With a weakened heartbeat, as I was placed in a drug-induced coma to minimize the risks. They let my body rest for a few days while Lee Beth turned in our updated will. All the girls came to visit, but eventually had to go back to school and their lives. When I am awakened after a few days, I remember thinking back on my life and what God has done for me. With all of the miracles He has surely blessed me with, I was ready to go home, my heavenly home. I was tired. My body was tired. I felt like I just did not have the strength to climb back up on the horse one last time. I began to reason with myself. "I just can't take it anymore. What can I do to help my family now? I will be a burden to everyone". For the first time in my life, I lost the will to live, something I never thought would happen to me. I have seen so much death in my life; my own seemed so insignificant. I lay there on that recovery bed contemplating my life. I told myself over and over that all my girls would be better off without me. They were grown now, and I had finished my job. I was weak and tired, and my heart began to slow down in an irregular heartbeat. The doctors told Lee Beth that they had done everything medically they could do. My job was to find the will to fight, and they feared I didn't have any fight left. No one could blame me for that. With my weakening state, she called all the girls back to the hospital. Tina Leslie drove in from the University of Texas, where she was working on her bachelor's degree. "Girls, your Daddy is in grave condition. The doctors have done everything they can. His heart is weak, and they are not sure he can pull through this." Tina Leslie didn't even ask; she came busting in the recovery room. Like the squall bag she has always been, she broke down into tears when she saw me. She grabbed my hand and made me open my eyes. "I know you can hear me, Daddy! Squeeze my hand! Squeeze my hand! I am unresponsive. That girl, with all the equipment, tubes, and monitors controlling my body, climbed on that bed! She straddled over me, holding both my shoulders, as she began to yell at me. "Daddy, you listen to me here. You have fought all your life. You taught all of us to fight. You cannot give up now. How selfish can you be? You have to come to my college graduation, dammit! You have not seen Terri, or me get married! You have a grandbaby girl who adores you! You have not met your future grandchildren! You perk up here. You got a lot of living left in you, and we need you, Daddy." She was crying uncontrollably, and tears were dropping on my hospital gown. I lie there with my eyes barely open. I reasoned with myself, fighting my sick and dying body. The heart monitors were still showing a weakened and irregular heartbeat. Then, I gave her the signal, the Colt revolver! Pheeeww, pheeeww, I barely got a whisper out. She looked over smiling from ear to ear as she shot me back. Knowing I needed my rest, she kissed me goodbye and left the room. I knew she was right; they were all right. I was reminded of all my brothers back in prison camp who just willed themselves to death. I could see how horribly close I came to doing the same. My family had always been there for me, and nothing was going to stop that now. Seeing all my girls reminded me of the great blessings I have, and I found the way to muster up enough to fight some more.

> *"And let us not grow weary of doing good, for in due season we will reap, if we do not give up."*
> *Galatians 6:9*

They Have No Answer

Around 1990, I had one more health scare. I was having trouble using the restroom again and went into the hospital with another blockage. The doctors determined that I had a 'kink', like a garden hose, somewhere in my intestines. My tough guts twisted up clenching off any passage. I not only have a weakened colon, but I also have a loopy one as well. This *'colonic volvulus'*, causes an obstruction which can be deadly. They put me in the hospital right away and were prepared to do surgery again if needed. They all felt certain that would be the case. It is fairly rare for intestines to just 'unkink' themselves, especially ones in as bad a shape as mine. I prayed that would not happen. I had a tube inserted down to my stomach through my nose. The tube would keep a steady suction keeping all fluids, even my spit off of my stomach to let my 'guts' rest for a few days. After a few days, my 'kink' untwisted itself and straightened itself out. I avoided abdominal surgery number four! The doctors knew my medical history, they have read every word. They also know the condition of my abdomen. They sign my discharge papers, admitting they have no answers for how I escaped the knife.

The Final Cut

In 1994, I had my fourth and so far, thank the good Lord, my final surgery. Once again, it was my gut. During my first surgery, the doctors removed so much tissue from my belly that all the organs and tissue that were left began a downward migration to the pit of my pelvis. Everything that was remaining began compacting together in a very small cavity. Gravity had taken its toll. All of my guts were gathered and mashed on top of each other. They could not move or do their jobs correctly. Once again, I am on the steel table. Nine feet of my colon is removed and resectioned. The doctors kept me on that table for over nine hours for one reason alone. They were doing any and everything they could do, to avoid me becoming a colostomy patient as well. They sectioned and cleaned and cut away the remaining webbed mess of forty months of tortured and battered flesh. It had formed intricate spider webs and tunnels of diseased and leathery flesh. It took a team of four highly-trained surgeons to complete the task. They had to be careful not to hurt my urine pouch and ostomy, put all of my guts back into functioning position, and avoid a colostomy. It was an extremely complicated surgery. I asked God to guide their scalpels well. My doctors respected my journey and knew how hard my life had become living with the urostomy bag. They knew I couldn't hold up long with urine draining into one abdominal bag and feces draining into another. A colostomy was a common surgical treatment for a case like mine, and it was a high possibility I would end up with one. It would have been much easier for the doctors to just to go ahead and do the colostomy. I have thanked God many times over the years for sparing me that colostomy, and for my surgeons' skill and determination.

On that day, the doctors installed a mesh hammock in my belly. They "done put my guts in a sling!" They lifted all of my innards up and out of the pelvis, placed them on a mesh hammock, and stapled the hammock to my right and left pelvic bones. The hammock keeps my abdomen contents from compacting down into my pelvis again. I have a few problems now but have not required any further surgeries since 1994. God is indeed good!

I have never had a recurrence of cancer in my abdomen. I continue to have skin cancer treatments and will do so until the end of my life. The doctors have all said I will have active skin cancer somewhere on my body until the day I die. As terrible in so many ways as my bladder amputation was, emotionally, mentally, physically, and psychologically, I know the right decision was made for me to remove the bladder. I have celebrated forty-five birthdays since my original surgery. I am so thankful for the incredible team of doctors I have had. I have had many cancer-free years because of them.

> *"Giving thanks always and for everything to God*
> *the Father in the name of our Lord Jesus Christ."*
> *Ephesians 5:20*

I Will Carry Her in My Heart to Heaven

The girls and I lost Lee Beth on March 10, 1995, after a brave battle with breast cancer. Soon after, she suffered a massive stroke that eventually took her from us. We laid her to rest right there with our baby girl, Katie Beth. My chapter with her closed, but not forever. I will see her again someday. It is the only thing I can hold on to with this incredible pain in my heart.

> *"It is a trustworthy statement: For if we died with Him, we will also live with Him." 2 Timothy 2:11*

I continue to love that woman with every ounce of my being. I have never taken off my wedding band, as it is my solemn oath and the circle of love I have for her. I have never met a stronger human being. She was the bravest soldier of us all, and not a day goes by that I do not think of her.

Chapter Fifteen

" All a Big Circle Houston, all a Big Circle"

Fifty plus years have passed since I finally got to see the hula girls and islands Miss Carvet showed me on that movie poster, in the one-room schoolhouse in Glen Rose, Texas. A lot of life and death has been woven in-between the pages of my story. All the highs and lows, like the tides of the ocean, washed over us all. I often fell back on the wisdom of my father, looking for the great circles before me. His words still ring with me today. How quietly and slowly everything is just a circle in life. Some of us blindly and stupidly stumble around this circle trying to avoid pain at every bend. We question and curse the God of the universe. We run from the very master who carved our place in this world. God does not create evil acts or intentionally bring harm to men. As a loving father, he provides a place of refuge through the storms. *"And we know, all things work together for good for them that love God, to them who are the called according to His purpose." Romans 8:28.* The pain and suffering in my life shaped my life, made me stronger, kept me in my faith, and allowed me to keep walking that ole circle until now. Now that I have lived almost a hundred years, I can see how the pieces of what you might think are breaking you, are just a puzzle, your puzzle, the one only you were divinely meant to put together someday. Sometimes the pieces do not fit together right away, or you think one is missing. Know that your Heavenly Father knows when your puzzle is complete. You may sometime wish to have the pain passed from you. Even Jesus asked His Father to do so. *"And going a little farther he fell on his face and prayed, saying, "My Father, if it be possible, let this cup pass from me; nevertheless, not as I will, but as you will." Matthew 26:39.* In time, your circle will all come together. Some circles are completed quickly. Those are the ones we question the most. "Why so young Lord?" You will see that God had plans for you all along, even from your suffering and loss. Your suffering may help others to take their next step. None of us realize how equipped we are to help someone with just a word or a touch. I have seen many miracles in my own life that have no explanation in a physical world. They have gone beyond what many feel were possible, and can only be defined as extraordinary. There is a spiritual world that is unseen by man. It is divinely designed to stay this way. It is the very basis of faith. I am grateful for my father's wisdom and my Mama's prayers. I will attempt to finish my story with how many of the things I endured did circle back in my life, including the miracles. All were illustrating the wisdom of my earthly father and the divine presence and promises of my Heavenly Father.

> *"What do people gain from all their hard work under the sun? Generations come, and generations go, but the earth lasts forever. The sun rises, and the sun sets, and then it rushes back to the place where it will rise again." Ecclesiastes 1: 3-5*

'The Spirit of Thomas Jefferson'

Jefferson High School circled back in my life in two ways. It gave me plenty of opportunities to see football games at Alamo Stadium. I am back in the very stone arena where I once was a mason here with the CCCs. The very first game had not been played there when I left for the war. Now countless games and events have been showcased in this place. Jefferson High School was the first football team to play there against Corpus Christi in a double-header. I can't imagine how those boys from Jefferson High School must have felt as they were running out on that majestic field for the first time, surrounded by the beautiful white, glistening stone, and lit up by those towering lights. I am proud to have been a part of the history of this city, and this school. Secondly, Thomas Jefferson High School students and staff were behind us in the war efforts. During 1944, while I was interred, the students at this school bought enough war bonds to fund some jeeps, and an airplane for the Air Force aptly named 'The Spirit of Thomas Jefferson'.

Joe

Joe saved my life, and I saved his. We had a bond that was forged in captivity and secret. He lived next door to us until 1980 when he had to move away. No one in my family ever knew he was the person I mouth-fed in prison camp. We kept that secret between us.

Train Them Up In The Way They Should Go

I was blessed with three virtuous women. My girls grew into strong, intelligent, and independent women. I gave my blessings to three men who I thought were worthy of my girls. Although, I did give them all a hard time before I said yes! I especially gave it to Buger's husband, Terry Wade! I put that boy through the wringer! My girls all married wonderful men who I consider to be the sons I never had. They each married good men, solid, salt of the earth men. They are great mothers to my three granddaughters and grandmothers to all eleven of my great-grandchildren and my great-great-grandson. They are all still married today with a total of over a hundred years of marriage between them. I am proud of my girls. They are all in the helping professions and have been such a blessing to me. My life is complete. After taking care of my girls, now they are taking care of me. My little-skinned rabbit, Terri Lyn, who I coddled and protected, is now my primary caretaker. Each of my girls and their husbands have been here for me, caring for my health and well-being. They are all fiercely protective of me and have ensured that I have a quality of life filled with family.

My Return to the Philippines

In 1986, I went on an Ex-POW trip back to the Philippines. My heart never left the island and the local village people who lived there. I had to go back and see what remained after all of the destruction. I was always torn knowing their primitive, simple farm ways may be forever changed. My memories and nightmares always took me to bombed-out corridors, leveled buildings, and the once beautiful countryside, in complete ruin. Bodies were strewn in the streets, people were starving, as they were dying along the pathways. We all walked away from there with shame on our face, and guilt in our hearts. To bring me back to wholeness, I had to know the Filipinos were alright. Going back gave me peace. I saw the villages rebuilt, the roads repaired, and the locals chewing their beloved betel nuts! Universities were in the place of prison camps, and monuments to the brave people who took this country back were positioned in strategic battle areas. I was never the same after closing that circle; I was a man with peace. My last nightmare of the Philippines at war was the evening I returned home.

> *"Now may the Lord of peace himself give you peace*
> *at all times in every way. The Lord be with you all."*
> *Thessalonians 3:16*

The Promise Fulfilled

In 2016, my girls set up a trip for me to go back home to my beloved Glen Rose. I love that little town. It holds so many good memories for me. I was born in the cedar brakes there, I almost died there, I grew up there, I became a man there, and I fell in love there. My story began there, and I wanted to go home to pay respects to my parents. Thank you Mayor Sam Moody for your hospitality and naming it Houston E. Lowe day while we were there. I met a life-long friend in you, and I love you dearly. Thank you for your service, soldier.

My Mama is buried in Granbury, a little piece down the road, and Daddy was buried in Hopewell Cemetery, in Glen Rose. I wanted to go home and see their final resting place one more time. I remembered the promise I made to myself almost eighty years earlier. My Daddy was not going to have a pauper's gravestone any longer. We ordered up a beautiful red granite stone with an engraved picture of a farmer with a hand plow, and Waitus and Charlie, flanking each other in front. We laid that stone in place and left him with a signature black full-crown Stetson hat, and some bluebonnets. "Rest in peace Daddy. Rest in peace."

Education

Toni Lee and Terri Lyn both went to school and received their licenses as registered nurses. Because of my service and captivity as a POW, Tina Leslie was able to go to college on a GI Bill scholarship. She got her bachelor's degree and became a teacher. Later in her life, she completed her master's and doctoral degrees and became a school district administrator. So now, I call her 'Dr. Buger'! My education did not stop my girls from completing their circles, and their circles were instrumental in me receiving my diploma.

My High School Graduation

I did circle back to Glen Rose High School, where I received my high school diploma on May 6, 2017, just shy of seventy-five years late! Toni Lee contacted the local Superintendent, Wayne Rotan, inquiring about the opportunity to have an old WWII veteran, who had to leave town to go to war, to graduate with the upcoming 2017 class. He was gracious and kind as he shook my hand. I walked that ole stage alongside about one-hundred other graduates. I am proud to carry my high school diploma, and to complete this circle as an official Glen Rose, Tiger!

The U.S.S. Dickman

Thank you, Dr. Ed Mergele, Navy Yeoman, U.S.S. Joseph T. Dickman. You are another miracle in my life. We found you seventy-two years later on March 15, 2017, you, the very man who processed me in and welcomed me aboard the U.S.S. Joseph T. Dickman for my return home. Thank you for your service, your outstanding articles, and for taking care of me while I was aboard. Finding you living only twenty-five miles away from me and giving us the opportunity to see each other again, brought another circle in my life to a close.

Dr. Mark Dine

In 2017, my daughter Tina, sought out the genius pediatrician, Dr. Mark Dine. She wanted to explore what had happened in his later life. She knew he had gone on to do great things, and she was right! She found his office in Cincinnati, Ohio. He served as a pediatric doctor until he was ninety-years old! He built a lifetime of caring for little ones, and he saved many babies. I am grateful he was placed in my path, he saved my little-skinned rabbit. I am thankful we were able to make contact with his office and his children, to tell them how much he had done for us. "Thank you, Dr. Dine. Rest in peace."

Living With Life-Long Illness

Through all the suffering from the many illnesses I have endured, it all had a purpose. I know it was a miracle that I survived all the jungle diseases I contracted and recovered from, without any medication. Those very diseases that I overcame developed within me the immune system of a bull elephant! Now, I am thankful for those diseases and the suffering. It shaped my health today and contributed to my long life. In my later life, I have lived through a full hip replacement, two bouts with pneumonia, a traumatic brain injury and brain-bleed from a nasty fall, and I contracted the MRSA virus, which kills hundreds of people all over the planet. I learned to thank Him, even for my suffering.

"Give thanks in all circumstances; for this is the will of God in Christ Jesus for you." 1 Thessalonians 5:18

Miracles Are Around Us

As I trudged through this life path of mine, sometimes on my knees, it took me a long time to accept the fact that I was surrounded by miracles. I hesitated to ever call these incidences miracles. People think you are crazy if you claim something is a miracle. I must have just been extremely 'lucky', or what some folks say, 'have good karma', for this all to work out in my favor. After all, it has been over two-thousand years since earthly miracles of mass healings and Jesus was seen walking on water. But over time, I saw those explanations were just a bunch of hooey! I cannot explain why my circle is covered in miracles. I know it is hard for us to understand that miracles do exist today. Some of us still believe a black cat can bring you bad luck, and breaking a mirror can make it last for seven years. If that is plausible, why on earth is it so hard to believe that the God of the Universe can orchestrate situations on our behalf? Just a few words that are used to define a 'miracle' are: surprising, marvel, wonder, phenomenon, and mystery. Merriam Webster's Dictionary defines a miracle as: *"an extraordinary event manifesting divine intervention in human affairs"*. I do not take being involved in miracles lightly. These events are usually quite extraordinary and highly improbable. I think when we get to Heaven someday, and God opens up our book, all the 'coincidences and near misses' in our lives, are going to be very clear to us. Our heavenly father had a divine hand in it all. We must not question what we cannot see in the limited physical world we live in. I thank my Heavenly Father for my circle of miracles, as I know I am here today because His mighty hand has intervened on my behalf more than once.

> *"He is the one you praise; he is your God, who performed for you those great and awesome wonders you saw with your own eyes." Deuteronomy 10:21*

Chapter Sixteen

Words from a Survivor

I just celebrated my ninety-eighth birthday with my three girls by my side. They are the very best reflection of their mother. I miss her to this day. She suffered through some of my darkest days. If you are not a military family with someone who has seen combat, you will never know the personal toll and sacrifices made by these families. Uncontrollable rage, fits of anger, deadly silence, heavy drinking, and unkind words you can never take back, often engulf their lives. Families feel like they are suspended in a tidal wave that keeps crashing upon them, rolling them over the razor-sharp reefs. Small emotional cuts work into life-long emotional wounds. Nursing a soldier back to mental health is a daunting and painful journey filled with countless dark days and lonesome nights. My easily startled nature, jumpiness, and jitteriness, put her in a continual high-alert, defensive posture. I had a hard time controlling my emotions, and I was irritable much of the time. My nightmares could consume me. She would be awakened from the deadest of sleep with me grabbing the slats on the headboard screaming. I woke up sweating profusely trying to hide my eyes from the charred bodies and the smell of rancid death. I avoided many social situations and alienated many good friends. I just couldn't connect to people the same way, and I didn't trust anyone. I was intensely jealous of other men, and I always worried that she might just have enough of the war remnants of her husband and leave me. I wanted to protect my family and be in our safe little cocoon. That led to my depression and hers. I am grateful we were able to work through it, and we shared many joyful days in our forty-nine years together.

If you have a combat veteran in your life, be patient and get some help. The U.S. Department for Veterans Affairs has support and has developed *the National Center for PTSD* to assist. Get you a Medical Alert Service Dog. Find you a non-profit organization like TADSAW (Train a Dog, Save a Warrior, tadsaw.org). They work with veterans and their families and place rescued shelter dogs together with veterans with Military Induced Anxiety Depression Syndrome (MIADS). With all the joys that come with being rescued, all survivors suffer from some degree of survivor guilt. I have for seventy-plus years. Why did so many lose the fight, lose the will to live another day, or lose their minds? So many young women and men in the prime of their lives taken. Why did God spare me and not so many others? How did my body overcome so much disease and so many fell with the first signs of starvation? I lost many good friends in prison camp, and I heard too many last words spoken to loved ones. I felt like no one could relate to me except my brothers and sisters in the American Ex-POW Association. There is no support that can reach the deepest ravines of your pain without sharing captivity as our deadly mistress. I am grateful for this organization and the support they have brought to so many. There are not many American POW's left in America. If you know of one, go thank them. If God has blessed you, contribute to them. Hopefully, the day will come when America can close this chapter and never need an organization to support prisoners of war.

Healing in Helpings

After taking the lives of many and seeing lives taken or wither away, you have to find a place of solace. Somehow you have to reckon with the amount of death you have been a part of or it will take you into a deep hole. I found it in the kitchen. Cooking became my joy and my peace. I served as the head of the consolidated mess hall at Lackland Air Force Base for over twenty-five years when I was not on duty in Hawaii, or Thule, Greenland. I felt at home there. I could give back what was taken from me. I didn't serve food to people; I served people through food. It was my mission. I could nourish soldiers, doctors, nurses, and military families who were sending their boys overseas. I helped bring a little bit of home to homesick warriors. I provided meals that built the muscle and mass of the American foot soldier by putting them in the best condition I could before they were deployed. I helped heal the broken and the sick. I made a gloomy Thanksgiving away from home, a Thanksgiving feast better than home. I brought smiles through chocolate cake and a perfect golden crust. Making nutritious, appetizing, and delicious food fed their stomachs along with my soul. Along the way, I found myself again. I was slowly being restored. These people were my responsibility to nourish. When they walked in my sparkling clean dining room, I always wanted the aroma of fresh coffee brewing and fresh cookies in the oven. My mess hall was their home, and I was gonna make sure it felt as much like it as possible.

Never underestimate the power of a great meal. When you are surviving on nothing, a meal may be the closest thing to God. Meals are meant for sharing. Families are bonded over good meals. Presidents and kings bring people together through a feast. There is a reason for that. Get to the table with your family. Put your damn phones down! Never underestimate the power of conversation over a well-turned pot roast. If you do not cook, buy a meal for someone who needs it. Cooking food is a great service to mankind. Good food's first ingredient is love. If you have a cook in your life, a real cook, someone who loves to serve you through food, thank them. They have given you more than nourishment. This is how I gave back and how I found myself again in the process.

Honor your Mama and Daddy

If I ever get stopped by little kids in public, I always tell them to mind their Mama and Daddy. It is such a simple concept. Many parents want to become their child's friend. Because parenting is missing more and more, it is affecting all of society, especially our teachers. My kids may not have had everything. They rarely got to go out to eat, and vacation was going to Glen Rose to see Ruth,

my sister. But, they are good women who are kind, intelligent, educated and love others before themselves. I might not have been real popular with them sometimes, and their Mama, well you just better not be disrespectful or unkind; or you would shore see her belt on your bottom! We are commanded to raise these kids up to be trustworthy, respectful, kind, and hard working.

> *"All Scripture is breathed out by God and profit-*
> *able for teaching, for reproof, for correction, and*
> *for training in righteousness, that the man of God*
> *may be competent, equipped for every good work."*
> 2 Timothy 3: 16-17

No matter where you are with your parents, you will never understand the depth of their love for you. They did the best they could raising you. Somehow in the universe, God picked them to raise you. How could you possibly argue with that? Live one day without them, and it is too late for you to decide to tell them you love them. One thing I learned from the Japanese, they honor their elders. They have great respect for their wisdom and the deep roots they laid down building the family name. Multiple generations of families live together, as they lay tribute to the descendants who came before them. God gave us one simple commandment to follow, but it is also the only commandment that has a promise directly tied to it. *"Honor your father and your mother, so that you may live long in the land the LORD your God is giving you." Exodus 20:12* I guess, the one thing I did right in God's eyes, is I honored my mother and father; and I taught my girls to do the same.

Unparalleled Care

I have always been a physically fit and strong man. I was blessed with the capacity to work hard, and my body has been the tool that has made that possible. However, there are lasting life-long, effects of internment. To say my life has been barraged with illness due to my exposure and treatment during my captivity is an understatement. Like many of the internees I shared this experience with, I have carried life-long medical effects. Those of us who were imprisoned in Japan near Hiroshima or Nagasaki at the end of the war, are known as 'Atomic Soldiers'. That glow in the distant Japanese sky over Hiroshima was the implosion of 'Little Boy', the plutonium implosion device, dropped by the Enola Gay. We were all bathed with nuclear fallout, blown by the Pacific Ocean trade winds, across our camps. The resulting end was years of devastating cancers and bodies wrought with basal and squamous cell carcinomas. I do not know of any records or statistics that tracked any of the soldiers or POWS who were exposed; but I am certain many fell to diseases later on, as a result.

If it were not for the military, the greatest trained and prepared forces in the world, and their doctors, I would have been dead a long time ago. First, there is not a chance we could have afforded the treatments I have received over these many years. Secondly, these are the most caring, dedicated, knowledgeable, and mission-based doctors on the planet. They love bringing comfort and healing to the wounded warriors who have served. I have been told hundreds of times what an honor they believe it is just to work on me. They too are in the military serving our country. I am just another Joe here. I assure you one thing; they can make a lot more money as a civilian doctor.

I have had recurring basal cell carcinoma across my head, neck, and arms. It is a condition I have lived with since 1960. Due to my bladder removal, I have lived for forty-five years with an exterior bladder prosthesis. I have been an ileostomy patient treated by military doctors the entire time. I have had one-fourth of my left ear surgically removed, one-third of my right ear surgically removed, hundreds of small squamous cell carcinomas either chemically burned, or surgically removed from all over my neck, chest, and arms, and a four-inch gaping hole cut to my skull, where squamous cancer cells were removed. I am telling you this for one reason alone, honoring the brilliant, military physicians who have treated me over the years, and the dedicated care they have provided me. They are some of the finest doctors in the world, and they have dedicated their lives to the care of soldiers. My broken and diseased body moved from the U.S.S. Dickman to Letterman Hospital, to

Carswell Hospital, to Lackland AFB, Wilford Hall, Brook Army Medical Center, to Tripler Army Hospital, and finally returning to Lackland AFB, and the newly formed Brooke Army Medical Center. That circle found one common thread. A ring of life-saving, dedicated physicians, surgeons, and level-one trauma specialists, who committed their lives to the care and well-being of airmen and soldiers like me. For you, I am grateful. I have seen all three girls graduate, complete their educations, marry, and live full lives; and I thank you for that.

National Responsibility

I do regret the harm that comes with the price tag when men go to war. The horrors inflicted by all nations are unspeakable. Shame for what we had to do to survive will always haunt those of us who were captives. All nations are guilty as charged and we will someday have an accounting in front of Almighty God for it. We cannot release Barabbas in our place. We contributed to the efforts to bring peace to our nations and stood for country. Only God can reside over all mankind.

> *"For the kingdom is the Lord's: and He is the governor among all nations." Psalm 22:28*

I do not hold any hatred in my heart. I would not turn a page in my life differently, and I would do it again to protect this great nation. Holding hatred and bitterness toward anyone is a deadly pill you shove down your throat, as it slowly kills you. I choose to forgive my captors. They too were doing for country what they were instructed to do.

> *"Therefore judge nothing before the time, until the Lord come, who both will bring to light the hidden things of darkness, and will make manifest the counsels of the hearts: and then shall every man have praise of God." 1 Corinthians 4:5*

I know many mercies were bestowed upon me that I am still unaware. For the incidences of kindness and beauty I was granted while a prisoner, I thank the Japanese people. They are some of the most loving, loyal, and family-first people I have had the honor to meet. Kanoko, for your family who was scarred by the bomb in Hiroshima, your grandmother running down the street covered in the ash and soot, with only her iron pot to cover her head; you did not come into our family by accident. I am grateful you were a foreign-exchange student with my daughter Tina, and that we have made a life-long bond with your family. Poppie will always love you.

> *"Get rid of all bitterness, rage and anger, brawling and slander, along with every form of malice. Be kind and compassionate to one another, forgiving each other, just as in Christ God forgave you."*
> *Ephesians 4:31-32*

Blood Stained Old Glory

I love this country and the beautiful red, white, and blue flag flying proudly above is one of my most cherished symbols. If it takes every bit of strength I have, I will stand every time she flies. I will honor this grand nation and those who are leading us. As a nation, we have overcome so much for our people. In my lifetime, I have seen women earn the right to vote, black citizens afforded their God-given rights, phone lines with blue glass insulators turn to cell phones, and a man walk on the moon. I have also seen the lives of millions of babies taken in their mother's womb, swept away like the ashes of a fire, and prayer removed from schools. I still believe this is the greatest country in the world. We have been so richly blessed. I fought for our freedom and your right to burn or spit on the flag or kneel when she is raised if you so choose. But on behalf of my veteran brothers and sisters, I ask that you remember the enormous cost of that right. Men and women wrote you a blank check that they willingly paid in full with crushed limbs and spirits, lost eyesight, burns, battered bodies, and finally with the ultimate sacrifice, their lives. Countless family lines were severed so you could rebel against the nation that bore you. We are all accountable to our children, grandchildren, and great-grandchildren, to accept the responsibility for what we bore upon each other, and to do everything possible to avoid it ever happening again.

> *"I have said these things to you, that in me you may have peace. In the world you will have tribulation. But take heart; I have overcome the world."*
> John 16:33

My Bride

Lee Beth, my sweetheart, thank you for 'soldiering up' like no man could have ever done, and helping me raise three wonderful girls who fiercely love us and have an iron-clad bond with our families. My wife, my love, and forever my gallant protector, you stood by my side when I was not worthy. I will honor you all the days of my life. I will see you soon sweetheart. Not a day goes by that I do not miss you. Hold on to Katie Beth, my little-crippled fawn. I will see you soon.

The Mighty Hand of God

I look back on the experiences that I had knowing with full confidence that God had a purpose in all of it for me. *"For I know the plans I have for you, declares the Lord, plans for welfare and not for evil, to give you a future and a hope."* Jeremiah 29:11 It was my cross to bear along with so many others. It was my story, and He and only He carried me through it. *"Be strong and courageous. Do not be afraid or terrified because of them, for the LORD your God goes with you; he will never leave you nor forsake you."* Deuteronomy 31:6 What came out of this suffering? I learned I could count on Him and His infinite wisdom. *"Trust in the Lord forever, for the Lord God is an everlasting rock."* Isaiah 26:4. I learned I could use my wits to help me get by. I learned that my country smarts were worth more than any degree I could have earned. *"For the wisdom of the world is folly to God. "For it is written, He catches the wise in their craftiness." 1 Corinthians 3:19.*

I have the utmost respect for cooks and a homecooked meal. I have learned not to be so critical all the time, and how to be grateful for what you have. I may have a gruff exterior sometimes, but God has given me a tender heart. I plan on asking Him someday, why me? Why did he pick me to survive? If you feel you are in your darkest place, and no one knows where you are or how you feel, be comforted. The Lord Jesus sees and hears you. Let my story be witness to that. You have never been alone, abandoned, or orphaned. Your Heavenly Father takes watch over you. It is one of the great mysteries of the universe.

> *"The LORD your God is with you, the Mighty Warrior who saves. He will take great delight in you; in his love he will no longer rebuke you, but will rejoice over you with singing." Zephaniah 3:17*

I am an imperfect man in an imperfect world. I have failed God in so many ways. I am imperfect, but I am forgiven. I have disappointed my Father in my thoughts, words, and deeds. If God can still love me, after all I have done, know with certainty; He loves you. I know with certainty that I will see Him in Heaven someday. Jesus told us all so Himself: *"In My Father's house are many rooms. If it were not so, would I have told you that I am going there to prepare a place for you? And if I go and prepare a place for you, I will come back and welcome you into My presence, so that you also may be where I am." John 142-3.* I am grateful that a poor little farm kid with a sixth-grade education can understand the simple message of the gospel. A humble man was sent by his father, God, to earth and became the Savior of the world; and He wants YOU to be His. He wants to pluck you out of the hands of harm and make you a child of the King. Nothing you have ever done, NOTHING, can separate you from your Heavenly Father. It is simple. It is a child-like prayer, of child-like trust and innocence. If you have never accepted the Lord Jesus into your heart, do so now. Talk to the Father. He is right there with Jesus and the Holy Spirit at His side.

> *"And the Word became flesh and dwelt among us, and we have seen his glory, glory as of the only Son from the Father, full of grace and truth." John 1:14*

If you are ready to stop being afraid, if you want real peace, repeat this prayer. Similar ones have been recited millions of times all over the planet:

> *"Dear Jesus, I am lost. I am afraid, and I am tired. I have made many mistakes that the Bible tells me are sins in my life. I see that I am a sinner, just as everyone else is. I know you are the God of the Universe, and you tell us to call on you for salvation. I repent of my sins and ask your Son, Jesus, to come into my heart to live forever. I accept Jesus as my Lord and Savior and want to someday live in eternity with you in Heaven. Amen."*

> *"For the wages of sin is death, but the free gift of God is eternal life in Christ Jesus our Lord." Romans 6:23*

Now, new Christian, welcome to the Kingdom! Go find you a Bible-believing church, and join a church family that will help support you in your walk with Jesus. You will never regret the commitment you made today. God bless you, and God bless America.

> *"Because he has set his love upon Me, therefore I will deliver him; I will set him on high, because he has known My name. He shall call upon Me, and I will answer him; I will be with him in trouble; I will deliver him and honor him. With long life I will satisfy him, And show him My salvation." Psalm 91:14-16*

305

"But those who hope in the LORD will renew their strength. They will soar on wings like eagles; they will run and not grow weary, they will walk and not be faint." Isaiah 40:31

Houston E. Lowe, Toni, Terri, and Tina, Meeting Senator Bob Dole, WWII Memorial, Washington D.C., Honor Flight, San Antonio De Valero, October 2015, Courtesy personal collection, Houston E. Lowe

Houston E. Lowe, WWII Memorial, Texas, Washington D.C.,
Honor Flight, San Antonio De Valero, October 2015,
Courtesy personal collection, Houston E. Lowe

References

Andrus, Pearl. *Juana: A Spanish Girl in Central Texas*. Burnet: Eakin Press, 1982.

Author Unnamed, *Birth of a Base*, Life Magazine, Vol. 33, No 12, New York, Time Inc, September 22, 1952

Bailey, Ronald H., and the Editors of Time-Life Books. *Prisoners of War*, *World War II*. Alexandria: Time Life Books, 1981.

Barnett, James P.; Burns, Anna C. T*he work of the Civilian Conservation Corps: pioneering conservation in Louisiana*. Gen. Tech. Rep. SRS-154. Asheville, NC: U.S. Department of Agriculture Forest Service, Southern Research Station. 101 p., 2012.

Belote, James, H. *Typhoon of Steel*. New York: Harper and Row, 1970.

Berhow, Mark A.; Terrance C. McGovern. *American Defenses of Corregidor and Manila Bay 1898–1945 (Fortress)*. Oxford: Osprey Publishing, 2003.

Block, Alan, Hecht, Donn, *Walkin' after Midnight*, (California, Four Star Records, 1954). Retrieved from http://www.thomaslyrics.com

Butow, Robert, Joseph Charles. *Tojo and the Coming of the War*. Redwood City: Stanford University Press, 1961.

Brown, Charles. *Bars from Bilibid Prison*. San Antonio: The Naylor Company, 1947.

Carlson, Carl. R.. *Return Ticket: My Diary as a POW Airman in WWII*. San Antonio: The Watercress Press, 2001.

Connaughton, Richard. *MacArthur and Defeat in the Philippines*. New York: The Overlook Press, 2001.

Daws, Gavin. *Prisoners of the Japanese: POWs of World War II in the Pacific*. New York: Morrow, 1994.

Dickson, Paul. *War Slang: American Fighting Words and Phrases from the Civil War to the Gulf War*. New York: Pocket Books, 1994.

EX POW Bulletin, *Japanese Order Posted in POW Camps, 1944, August 1995, page 34*

Felton, Mark. *Never Surrender: Dramatic Escapes from Japanese Prison Camps*. Barnsley: Pen & Sword Military, 2013

Friedman, George, Lebard, Meredith. *The Coming War with Japan*. New York: St. Martin's Press, 1991.

Hall, Brent, *The Real Billy the Kid AKA: Brushy Bill Roberts*, e-book, 9781105459689, 2013.

Holmes, Linda Goetz. *Unjust Enrichment: How Japan's Companies Built Postwar Fortunes Using American POWs*. Mechanicsburg: Stackpole Books, 2001.

Jasinski, Laurie E. *Dinosaur Highway: A History of Dinosaur Valley State Park* . Fort Worth: Texas Christian University Press, 2008.

Kandler, Richard. *The Prisoner List*. Mansworth Publishing, 2010.

Karnow, Stanley, «Hideki Tojo/Hideko Tojo». *In Our Image: America›s Empire in the Philippines*. New York: Random House, 1989.

Kennett, Lee. *G.I.: The American Soldier in World War II*. Norman: University of Oklahoma Press, 1997.

Leinninger, Bruce and Andrea, and Gross, Ken. *Soul Survivor: The Reincarnation of a World War II Fighter Pilot*. New York: Grand Central Publishing, 2009

Lippincott, C. L. *Ecological consequences of Imperata cylindrica (cogon grass): Invasion in Florida Sandhill*. Dissertation. Botany Department, University of Florida, Gainesville, Florida. 1997.

Lowe, Houston, E. American Ex-POW, WWII, Interview with Tina Farrell, Ed.D. Personal Interviews, San Antonio, Texas, May 2015 – February 2018

MacArthur, Brian. *Surviving the Sword: Prisoners of the Japanese in the Far East, 1942-45*. New York: William Morrow Paperbacks, 1996

McElvaine, Robert S. *The Great Depression: America, 1929-1941*. New York: Times Books, 1993.

Merriam Webster's Dictionary, s.v. "Miracle", accessed: November 28, 2017, from https://www.merriam-webster.com/dictionary/miracle

Mergele, Edward, Ph.D, Interview with Tina Farrell, Ed.D., Personal Phone Interview, Friendswood, Texas, April 21, 2016

Mercer, Johnny, Kern, Jerome, *Dearly Beloved*, (Los Angeles, Capitol Records, 1942) Retrieved from http://www.thomaslyrics.com

311

Mitchell, Greg. *Atomic Cover -Up: Two U. S. Soldiers, Hiroshima & Nagasaki, and the Greatest Movie Never Made.*, New York: Sinclair Books, 2011.

Nunn, W. C. *Somervell: Story of a Texas County.* Fort Worth: Texas Christian University Press, 1975.

Pearson, Judith. *Belly of the Beast: A Pow's Inspiring True Story of Faith, Courage, and Survival Aboard the Infamous WWII Japanese Hell Ship Oryoku Maru.* New York: Penguin Books, 2001.

Schaller, Michael. *Douglas MacArthur: The Far Eastern General.* New York: Oxford University Press, 1989.

Sides, Hampton. *Ghost Soldiers: The Forgotten Epic Story of World War II's Most Dramatic Mission.* New York: Doubleday, 2001.

Sledge, E. B. *With the Old Breed at Peleliu and Okinawa.* Annapolis: Naval Institute Press, 1996.

Smith, Craig B. *Counting the Days: POWs, Internees, and Stragglers of World War II in the Pacific* (2012), *E book- 978-1-58834-356-7*

Smith, Kenneth, *Sawmill, The Story of Cutting the Last Great Virgin Forest East of the Rockies.* Fayetteville: The University of Arkansas Press, 1986.

Speaks, Oley, and Kipling, Rudyard, *The Road to Mandalay*, (Ohio, The John Church Company, 1907). Retrieved from https://www.steynonline.com/6870/on-the-road-to-mandalay

Tanaka, Yuki. *Hidden Horrors: Japanese War Crimes In World War II.* New York: Avalon Publishing, 1998.

Taylor, Vince. *Cabanatuan: Japanese Death Camp.* Waco: Texian Press, 1987.

The Holy Bible, New International Version. Grand Rapids: Zondervan Publishing House, 1984.

The Holy Bible, The King James Study Bible Version. Nashville: Thomas Nelson, 1988.

Toland, John. *The Rising Sun: The Decline and Fall of the Japanese Empire, 1936–1945.* New York: Random House, 1970.

Warren, Cliff, American Ex-POW WWII, Interview with Tina Farrell, Ed.D., Personal Phone Interview, Friendswood, Texas, March 13, 2016

Yenne, Bill. *The Imperial Japanese Army: The Invincible Years 1941–42.* Oxford: Osprey Publishing, 2014.

Yoshimi, Yoshiaki. *Comfort Women: Sexual Slavery in the Japanese Military During World War II.* New York: Columbia University Press, 2000.

Websites

http://mentalfloss.com/article/71124/
american-dentist-who-drilled-secret-message-tojos-dentures

http://www.fsmitha.com/h2/ch22b4.htm

http://wonderfulrife.blogspot.com/2015/05/tojos-suicide-attempt-and-coded-teeth.html

https://twotwoeight.wordpress.com/2011/08/30/
appearance-pulse-grimace-activity-respiration/

https://armyhistory.org/the-other-foe-the-u-s-armys-fight-against-malaria-in-the-pacific-theater-1942-45/

http://www.militaryhistoryonline.com/wwii/articles/
AmphibiousAssaults.aspx

https://www.awesomestories.com/images/user/f8aefd5148.jpg From
the Vault: 'Beautiful' Alamo Stadium dedicated 70 years ago

http://www.west-point.org/family/japanese-pow/ShipsNum.htm

https://www.thoughtco.com/world-war-ii-battle-of-corregidor-2361467
(Random House, 2005), 458p.

http://www.hawaiinewsnow.com/story/24048116/
jfk-remembered-a-look-back-at-the-presidents-hawaii-visit

https://www.roadsideamerica.com/story/42546–Bonnie and Clyde, Red
River Plunge

https://virus.stanford.edu/uda/

http://www.micc.army.mil/pdf/Long_Barracks_Fact_Sheet.pdf

http://www.maulesl.info- what is a hinny.html

https://tshaonline.org/handbook/online/articles/dlauy history of the brackenridge park

http://www.thenation.com/blog/162864/last-great-untold-story-world-war-ii%E2%80%94and-lingering-effects-today

US Army Center of Military History: Siege of Corregidor
http://www.living-prayers.com/children/prayer_for_pregnant_women.html#ixzz4317Bm7JA

Handbook of Texas Online, William R. Hunt, "Hico, TX,"
http://www.tshaonline.org/handbook/online/articles/hjh08.
http://philippine-defenders.lib.wv.us/html/bilibid_prison.html

https://www.forces-war-records.co.uk/
prisoners-of-war-of-the-japanese-1939-1945

G.I.: The American Soldier in World War II *https://books.google.com/books?isbn=1476793131*

Eagle Against the Sun: The American War with Japan *https://books.google.com/books?isbn=1476727422*

World War II — prisoners of war POWs Japan–Post-war Years *histclo.com/essay/war/ww2/pow/pow-jap.html*

https://armyhistory.org/the-other-foe-the-u-s-armys-fight-against-malaria-in-the-pacific-theater-1942-45/

https://en.wikipedia.org/wiki/Battle_of_Okinawa

https://en.wikipedia.org/wiki/Great_Famine_(Ireland)

https://ww2vetsstory.wordpress.com/2011/11/16/
chapter-3-hell-ships-bound-for-japan/

http://www.theprisonerlist.com/order-to-kill-all-pows.html

http://www.dailymail.co.uk/columnists/article-482589/Beheaded-whim-worked-death-Japans-repugnant-treatment-Allied-PoWs.html#ixzz4PBLUvfoS

https://www.biblestudytools.com

https://www.bible.knowing-jesus.com

https://www.biblegateway.com

https://www.ancestry.com.au/genealogy/records/
edna-gaskill_101442782

https://www.history.com/topics/1918-flu-pandemic

http://www.mansell.com/pow_resources/camplists/sendai/hanawa/
murph_1.html

http://www.factfiend.com/children-philippines-train-spiders-fight/

http://luckythreeranch.com/lucky-three-ranch-training/mule-facts/

http://www.hawaiinewsnow.com/story/24048116/
jfk-remembered-a-look-back-at-the-presidents-hawaii-visit

http://www.navsource.org/archives/10/03/03013.htm

http://www.mansell.com/pow-index.html

http://www.mansell.com/pow_resources/camplists/philippines/pows_
in_pi_report.html#ODonnell

https://www.csmonitor.com/1995/0817/17051.html- Tojos dentures

http://militaryhistory.about.com/od/worldwarii/p/World-War-Ii-Battle-
Of-Corregidor.htm

"The May Act," *San Antonio Light*, December 4, 1941, editorial page.

http://www.lonelyplanet.com/philippines/weather#ixzz42znwYIbM

http://www.us-japandialogueonpows.org/Nelson%20Hanawa%20
trip.htm

http://www.combinedfleet.com/Noto_t.htm

http://archives.hcea.net/?p=creators/creator&id=399

http://www.lingerandlook.com/Names/Detectives.php Boston Blackie

Handbook of Texas Online, John Manguso, "Fort Sam Houston,"
accessed January 22, 2017, http://www.tshaonline.org/handbook/
online/articles/qbf43. http://www.lindavdahl.com/index.html

Handbook of Texas Online, Ada Ferrer, "Glen Rose, TX," accessed June 09, 2017, http://www.tshaonline.org/handbook/online/articles/hjg03.

http://www.airplanesofthepast.com/b36-at-carswell-afb.htm

http://www.eaec.org/bibleanswers/playingcards.htm

http://www.mansell.com/powresources/camplists/philippines/pows_in_piOPMG_report.html#MarchThroughManila

http://www.loc.gov/teachers/classroommaterials/presentationsandactivities/presentations/timeline/depwwii/newdeal/

https://www.marxists.org/history/etol/newspape/ni/vol05/no08/pytlak.htm

http://www.ccclegacy.org/CCC_Brief_History.html

http://www.tadsaw.org

http://philippine-defenders.lib.wv.us/html/bilibid_prison.html

"Civilian Conservation Corps (CCC)" (n.d.). In *Encyclopedia Britannica online*. Retrieved from https://www.britannica.com/topic/Civilian-Conservation-Corps

So I returned, and considered all the oppressions that are done under the sun: and behold the tears of such as were oppressed, and they had no comforter; and on the side of their oppressors there was power; but they had no comforter.
-- Ecclesiastes 4:1